SUDAN

INTERNATIONAL PEACE ACADEMY
OCCASIONAL PAPER SERIES

SUDAN

The Elusive Quest for Peace

Ruth Iyob
Gilbert M. Khadiagala

LYNNE
RIENNER
PUBLISHERS

BOULDER
LONDON

Published in the United States of America in 2006 by
Lynne Rienner Publishers, Inc.
1800 30th Street, Boulder, Colorado 80301
www.rienner.com

and in the United Kingdom by
Lynne Rienner Publishers, Inc.
3 Henrietta Street, Covent Garden, London WC2E 8LU

Library of Congress Cataloging-in-Publication Data
Iyob, Ruth, 1957–
  Sudan : the elusive quest for peace / Ruth Iyob and Gilbert M. Khadiagala.
    p. cm. — (International Peace Academy occasional paper)
  Includes bibliographical references and index.
  ISBN-13: 978-1-58826-350-6 (pbk. : alk. paper)
  ISBN-10: 1-58826-350-9 (pbk. : alk. paper)
  1. Sudan—History—Civil War, 1983– 2. Sudan—History—Civil War,
1983—Peace. I. Khadiagala, Gilbert M. II. Title.
DT157.672.I94 2006
962.404—dc22

                                                2006019110

British Cataloguing in Publication Data
A Cataloguing in Publication record for this book
is available from the British Library.

Printed and bound in the United States of America

    The paper used in this publication meets the requirements
        of the American National Standard for Permanence of
        Paper for Printed Library Materials Z39.48-1992.

  5 4 3 2 1

Contents

Foreword

Terje Rød-Larsen,
President, International Peace Academy

The publication of this volume on the "elusive quest for peace" in the long-lasting civil war in Sudan affords enormous pride to the International Peace Academy. A product of the IPA's Africa Program, the book is written by two leading scholars of politics and conflict in East Africa and the Horn. Ruth Iyob of the University of Missouri and Gilbert Khadiagala of Johns Hopkins University's School of Advanced International Studies (SAIS) have produced a remarkable volume that will offer valuable insights for policymakers and academics alike.

It is a particular pleasure for me to introduce this book as both authors have been long-standing friends and partners of the IPA. Ruth Iyob is a former director of our Africa Program, and it was during her highly productive stay at the IPA that this volume was conceived. Gilbert Khadiagala, in addition to having consulted on many IPA policy projects, is editor of our recent volume *Security Dynamics in Africa's Great Lakes Region.*

Sudan adds to a long list of IPA publications on conflict dynamics and peacemaking and peacebuilding efforts on the African continent, looking at a wide variety of actors ranging from civil society and national governments to subregional organizations, the African Union, and the United Nations.

This book is also eminently timely as it appears at a critical moment of growing international involvement in Sudan. In southern Sudan, the UN is deploying one of its largest peacekeeping missions tasked to support the implementation of the Comprehensive Peace Agreement signed in early 2005 by the government of Sudan and the Sudan People's Liberation Army. In the meantime, peace negotiations on the Darfur crisis seem to have achieved important breakthroughs in the spring of 2006, but it remains questionable whether they can be translated into real peace in the region. Against this background, heated discussions are under way on plans to have a UN force replace the African Union's mission in Sudan, which has been unable to stop the mass killing in this conflict-ridden region.

In the following chapters, the authors compellingly analyze the opportunities and limits of current conflict resolution efforts in Sudan. They do so by placing them in the historical context of the modern Sudanese polity, as well as considering the role of geography in the construction of modern identities. Looking both at the north-south conflict and the more recent Darfur crisis, the authors help us move well beyond the oversimplified and misleading dichotomies that are usually offered to explain Sudan and its wars, variously described as "Muslim vs. Christian," "Arab vs. African," "east vs. west," or "black vs. nonblack." By contrast, the authors provide us with a deeper understanding of the complex interplays of political, historical, cultural, and geographical factors and what they imply for current peace initiatives.

As such, this study provides an immensely valuable resource for policymakers working on the quest for sustainable peace in southern Sudan and Darfur. This volume also carries a message of hope, discerning among the different communities a strong yearning for peace and identifying multiple openings and building blocks for reconciliation.

As with all of our work at the IPA, this volume could not have been possible without the generous support of our donors. We thank particularly the governments of the Netherlands, Canada, Denmark, Finland, Germany, Sweden, and the United Kingdom, as well as the Rockefeller and Ford Foundations for supporting not only this present volume, but also the IPA's Africa Program over a number of years, enabling us to maintain several generations of research programs on Africa's peace and security.

Acknowledgments

It has been our privilege to be associated with the International Peace Academy (IPA) project on Sudan. The IPA commissioned this study as part of its efforts to foster understanding of contemporary trends in peacebuilding and conflict resolution in Africa. The primary purpose of the study was to highlight the role of regional and international actors in prodding Sudanese parties toward peace under the rubric of the Intergovernmental Authority on Development (IGAD). As we delved more deeply into the myriad reasons why peace has continued to elude Sudan for half a century, it became clear that we needed to situate our study in a synoptic historical perspective to lend some structure to the rich flavor of Sudanese politics. Throughout this enterprise, we have covered only a small part of this richness and complexity. Moreover, as the Darfur conflict reveals, peace in Sudan remains a work in progress and an ongoing story.

This book has undergone revision and rewriting to ensure that its publication was not overtaken by new agreements, including those that were broken as soon as they were penned. Nevertheless, promises of peace—although derailed by acts of violence and destruction by all protagonists on the ground—reemerge when concerted regional and international efforts lead to dialogue, which then requires us to reassess our knowledge of Africa's giant nation. In the pages that follow, we have sought to provide a historical background and analytical frameworks that will yield some insights into the reasons, rooted in both the distant and recent past, why peace in Sudan continues to be elusive.

The government of the Netherlands, which funded this project, deserves our heartfelt thanks for understanding the need for the various extensions that we requested and were graciously granted. We are grateful to our colleagues at the IPA and Lynne Rienner Publishers, who continued to believe in us and accommodated our constant updates of past versions of the manuscript. Along the way, we have benefited from the encouragement of a number of people: John Hirsch, acting director of IPA's Africa program; IPA publications officers Clara Lee and Reyko Huang, who have been generous with their time; and program officers Kapinga Ngandu and Mashood Issaka.

We are indebted to all who took time from their hectic schedules to answer our questions about prospects for peace and to those who shared their hopes for reconciliation and their fears that the preservation of the status quo may have too high a cost for future generations. Space does not allow us to list all of them by name, but we hope they will accept our sincere thanks for providing us with multifaceted perspectives. Any errors or weaknesses in the analyses remain our full responsibility.

—*Ruth Iyob and Gilbert M. Khadiagala*

Sudan

EGYPT

Lake Nasser

disputed territory

Red Sea

Port Sudan

CHAD

Dongola

Ed Damer

Kassala

Khartoum

ERITREA

D A R F U R

Al Fasher

Wad Medani

Gedaref

El Geneina

El Obeid

Rabak

Sennar

Nyala

Ed Damazin

Al Fula

Kadugli

White Nile

Blue Nile

Nile River

Bentiu

Malakal

ETHIOPIA

Aweil

Warab

Wau

Rumbek

Bor

CENTRAL AFRICAN REPUBLIC

Yambio

Juba

Kapoeta

DEMOCRATIC REPUBLIC OF CONGO

UGANDA

KENYA

1

Sudan's Quest for Peace:
Exploring the Complexities

Sudan is a land where peace always seems to hover over the horizon while numerous destructive wars scar its inhabitants. Paradoxically, the prospect of peace appears to fuel more violence as rival leaders and their opponents clash over its realization. Peace agreements—whether between the government and armed combatants or between those aggrieved enough to take up arms—are as numerous as the wars fought. Broken promises always seem to lead to the rearming of former signatories or allies of reformist causes. Sudanese history is littered with the abnegation of promises made by hegemonic elites to grant equitable citizenship instead of a life of inferiority, insecurity, and indignity.

Since 1955, Sudanese leaders have been constantly engaged in suppressing uprisings in their western, eastern, and southern peripheries. They have also waged ideological wars pitting sectarian leaders against advocates of secularism and communists. In this tumultuous period spanning half a century, it is remarkable to note that the Sudanese have never stopped talking about peace while conducting multiple wars. Why, then, has peace eluded Sudan? The most recent accord for a "comprehensive" peace was signed in 2005. Although the state of war between the government and its opponents in southern Sudan had ended, the country became engulfed in violent wars in the west and east. It has become even more urgent at this juncture to examine the gap between the official discourse of peace and the unofficial pursuit of war. In this arena of Sudan, it appears to the gladiators that seekers of peace turn to violence so that they too can have their voices heard. We must look beyond the signing of proclamations to the hidden sociohistorical and political factors that militate against the achievement of peace as a reality rather than as a distant mirage.

We began our inquiry by addressing the importance of the weight of history on the present conflicts, and the efforts to resolve the multiple wars that have plagued the nation since it gained its independence in 1956. By addressing the

13

various legacies of conquest, migration, commerce, membership in the Islamic *umma,* and the kinship and cultural ties that bind the disparate peoples of the Sudanic polity, we seek to shed light on the complex history of the different peoples that make up contemporary Sudan. In light of the international media's reportage of the various conflicts in Sudan in bipolar terms—north-south, Muslim-Christian, Arab-African, black-nonblack, etc.—we found it useful to take a longer perspective of history than has usually been made available to policymakers and conflict resolution analysts.

Chapter 2 introduces readers to the making of the modern Sudanese polity, a polity that straddles Africa and the Middle East. This chapter addresses not only the millennial encounters of the indigenous populations inhabiting the areas of the Red Sea, the Nile Valley, and the Lake Chad Basin, but also the construction of modern identities stemming from these encounters. We argue that neither the popular dyads (African-Arab, white-black, Muslim-Christian, modern-traditional, north-south) nor the deterministic explanations (oil, ethnicity, religion, land hunger, drought, Western imperial cupidity) to which the country's conflicts are reduced lead to an understanding of the complex interplay of all these factors.

Chapter 3 addresses the role of geography in the construction of modern identities and the conflicts that arose between the various communities competing for resources and hegemonic control. A presentation of the "geographies" of Sudan, including the territorial, ideological, civilizational, and cultural arenas within which the different communities of Sudan waged many struggles, is followed by analyses of boundary/frontier making, patterns of human settlement, migration, economic activity, and the political and spatial dimensions of rule by conquest and conversion—all of which impinge on the contemporary conflicts. This approach offers perspectives on how geography has been reconstructed in concrete as well as abstract forms, as demonstrated by the redrawing of provincial boundaries and the politicization of a theological geography demarcating the domain of war whose inhabitants are relegated to a subordinate position versus those who are decreed "true" believers.

Chapters 4 and 5 focus on the regionalization and internationalization of the conflict in southern Sudan through analysis of the political contests and alliances between northern and southern political actors as well as between southern figures and international and regional institutions, thereby providing opportunities for external intervention and mediation. External presence and mediation shaped the north-south conflict in ways that redefined the objectives of the southern rebels and the government of Sudan (GOS) and the mediation processes that ensued. Both chapters analyze the various peace agreements, betrayed promises, and missed opportunities as well as challenges that preceded the signing of the Comprehensive Peace Agreement in 2005.

Chapter 6 focuses on the conflict in Darfur, a region where centuries-old social, economic, and political networks attest to the acculturation of Afro-Arab-Islamic values and institutions. Darfur, also a geopolitical frontier within the larger Sudanese state, has a long history of autonomous rule and expansion through conquest of adjacent and distant populations. We argue that the pragmatic policies of the last Kayra sultan on the role of religion and government, commercial networks, and relations with regional and international allies may yield valuable lessons for twenty-first-century "Darfurians" seeking social justice and economic prosperity. Adjusting lenses to take into account historical and sociopolitical factors, this chapter highlights the intricate linkages between past and present that led to the articulation of the desiderata of equitable citizenship and the launching of militant and rebellious defiance against the central government.

Chapter 7 highlights, in historical contexts, the particular socioeconomic relationships and organizing ideologies that have made peace so elusive in Sudan. The multiethnic Sudanese polity has yet to confront the legacies of its recent and distant past, a result of the hegemonic dominance of the Khartoum-centered elite over the southern, western, and eastern peripheries. The post-1956 governments have failed to rectify the nefarious structural inequalities perpetuated by previous exploitative and discriminatory regimes, despite their many public declarations of equality for all Sudanese. The multiple conflicts that have scarred the political and physical landscape of this giant nation have, without exception, been triggered by the demands for equal citizenship and social justice. Unless the socioeconomic injustices that have been perpetuated by the old predatory politics of Sudan are expunged and all Sudanese are guaranteed citizenship rights, the prospects for an equitable peace remain dim. We argue that for Pax Sudanica to blossom, Khartoum's power brokers must stop treating peace agreements as temporary pacts to be abrogated at will. The cycle of violence can be broken only when peace is no longer a prisoner of past paradigms.

The transformation of the African and Arab political landscape in the first decade of the new millennium may give us reason to expect that the long-awaited Pax Sudanica will be honored by the power brokers in Khartoum and their militant critics in the south, east, and west. But the peoples of Sudan have long learned not to expect real progress to emerge out of agreements reached by politicians and armed men—be they top military brass or veteran guerrillas. Two lessons have been learned in the half-century of war between Khartoum and southern nationalists since 1955. The sectarian "northern" elites who claim to be the *awlad al-balad* (children of the land) do not wait for the ink to dry on the agreements signed with much fanfare before resuming their hegemonic ways. Khartoum's opponents, who demand the right to participate in the national arena as equals, enter into dialogue with their hegemonic rivals only to internally fragment along ethnic or religious lines.

Sudan has nevertheless been fortunate enough to have antisectarian elements among its diverse inhabitants: individuals who reject the unequal social premise that privileged the Afro-Arab-Islamized Sudanese over all others. The fusion of cultures and peoples of Sudan also provides for numerous interactions that lead to recognition of plurality and the need for a shared vision for the entire nation. Therefore, peace agreements that are comprehensive in name but partial in their applicability, such as the one signed between the Sudan People's Liberation Movement/Army (SPLM/A) and the GOS, are not sufficient to address the deep-rooted grievances of Sudan's diverse communities. This is not to diminish the significance of the Comprehensive Peace Agreement (CPA) of 2005 in ending the state of war in southern Sudan, but to point out that peace continues to elude contemporary Sudan. We argue that peace agreements should be conceptualized and crafted to enable every element of the multinational Sudanese polity to come to terms with both the grievances of the past and the promises of the future.

The vexatious elusiveness of peace that continues in Sudan lies in the complexity of political, economic, and sociocultural encounters of its multinational peoples, resulting in atrocities being meted out to communities targeted for "war" on the basis of ideological tenets and vulnerable communities being cordoned off into hamlets of terrorized people deprived not only of their dignity and property but also of their rights as free human beings. In the process of identifying the realities of domination and resistance that led to numerous wars, one also encounters sociocultural blending of victors and vanquished leading to an admixture of populations sharing past legacies and thus, one would hope, prospects for future coexistence. The mobility of the many peoples of Sudan—the coerced and consensual alike—also leads us to question the veracity of the ethnic and geographic boundaries now assumed by contending parties. A closer look at the ties that bind the communities may also provide clues to why peace conferences and tribal reconciliation efforts have been more successful at healing wounds of war than have bureaucratic peace agreements.

The moral geography of medieval ideological constructs such as *dar al-Islam* (domain of Islam), *dar al-harb* (domain of war), *dar al-ahd* (domain of the covenant) and *dar al-sulh* (domain of truce) has been distorted to justify wars of conquest, pillage, and territorial expansion as *jihads* (holy wars). Nowhere is this more evident than in the wars that created *dar fertit* (lands of enslavable communities) from the seventh century onward and that were repeated throughout the land, creating *'abdiyyas* (slave estates chained to master communities). Where the resistance of indigenous peoples proved strong, one can find examples of Nilotic *quilombos*, composite communities that fled to the mountains and hills to avoid becoming the chattel of the more powerful of the land. The Nuba of central Kordofan, the Fertit of the Bahr al-Ghazal–Darfur borderlands, and the Ingessana illustrate the indomitable spirit of human beings defending their right to be free. These Sudanic communities also are living proof that populations with different languages and institutions can operate as a collective and create a polis to ensure their survival and security as equals. Hybridity in Sudan, then, means more than *métissage* or *mestizaje,* incorporating as it does a deeper, richer, and more nuanced conceptualization of complex ways of self-identification in the sociocultural, economic, and political arenas.[1] In other words, it is time that those seeking to understand Sudan go beyond the outdated descriptions of the medieval geographers who left us their writings of the *bilad as-Sudan*—writings that have become blinders disabling us from appreciating the making of a multinational state in Africa's misunderstood giant.

Drawing a new political, social, and economic contract to enable more equitable governance may be attained by revoking the tradition of *dar al-ahd* as the template for pact making between nonequals, as it placed conquered inhabitants under the suzerainty of a hegemonic elite claiming both a temporal and divine mandate to rule over others.

Put simply, the one obstacle to a just and lasting peace is the unwillingness of hegemonic rulers (and their constituents) to acknowledge the plurality of Sudan's peoples and their rights of empowerment as equals in the land.

Note

1. See Jean-Loup Amselle, *Mestizo Logics: Anthropology of Identity in Africa and Elsewhere* (Stanford: Stanford University Press, 1998).

2

The Making of
the Sudanese Polity

There is no simple, clear-cut program by which the people, the groups, and the events they created in Sudan can be identified. The binary terms conventionally used in the media (African-Arab, white-black, Muslim-Christian, modern-traditional, and north-south), and the simplistic explanations that are too often proposed do not serve us well. Such arguments do not lead to understanding, since what is beneath the visible surface is far more complex—and infinitely more revealing—than all the superficial "wisdom" now taken as truth. We therefore offer an examination of historical myths, shifting identities, metaphors of mazes, and paradoxes constructed from ambiguous social understandings, confused beginnings, and uncertain endings—all part of the extraordinary complexity that was, and still is, Sudan.

The Peopling of Sudan and
the Making of Sudanese Identities

Sudan is a land of paradoxes where the multiple pasts of a conquest state joust for acknowledgment against a hegemonic perspective that privileges one of the many constituent parts of the contemporary polity. The complexity that is often attributed to the Sudanese state and its multiethnic and multireligious society can be traced to the dilemma faced by modern Sudanese as they seek to fit their sprawling state and its subjugated nations into a single unitary modern state. Numerous "organizing ideologies"[1] have been instituted by both indigenous and alien ruling elites to sculpt or pummel this unwieldy multinational state into a cohesive modern political entity.

The first of these organizing ideologies—one that has defined a key element of Sudan's multinational identity—revolves around the interpretation of the long process of *Arabization*. This phenomenon began with the

Arab conquest of Egypt in A.H. 26 (C.E. 647) and the subsequent southward and westward migrations of nomadic Arab tribes to the areas known as *bilad as-Sudan* (land of the blacks).[2] The earliest Arab invasion of Dongola in Nubia did not lead to an easy victory over the Nubian rulers who, according to early-ninth-century documents, were able to renegotiate the victors' demand for *baqt*—an annual tribute of slaves—into barter-trade agreements. Medieval and modern documentation of the millennial encounter provides insights into how the encounter of Sudanic peoples with the migratory, and later invasive, peoples from the Arabian Peninsula was institutionalized to spearhead Islam as the transnational organizing ideology.

Although Arabization preceded *Islamization,* the latter became the justification for the establishment of the hegemony of *Arabism* over that of either *Islamism* or the unifying concept of *Sudanism.*[3] Arabism can be defined as the ideology of ethnocultural superiority that manifested itself in Sudan following the rule by the Ottomans in 1821, while Islamism provided the theological and economic justification for the continued subjugation of unbelievers. Sudanism is a territorially centered nationalist formulation that rejects both the racialization of Arabism and the sectarianism of Islamism. This flexible formulation of a multinational Sudanic state—with equality and dignity for all its citizens regardless of ethnicity or religion—carries the promise of a peaceful resolution in the twenty-first century.

The Afro-Arabs of Sudan, inheritors of a peripheral Arab civilization and its organizing transnational ideology of Islam, constructed a paradoxical identity that selectively combined some legacies of the invading/trading Arab, Ottoman, Islamic patriarchal ancestors with those of the resisting, pact-making, Non-Arab/African/ Islamic/Christian/matrilineal progenitors. The paradoxes are found in the selective appropriation of Sudanic/black/ African identities, which link them to the indigenous population, and the negation of blackness, which came to be associated with subaltern status, thereby privileging not the *Arab* but the *Africanized* or *Sudanized* Arab without acknowledging the process by which the fusion had taken place. The composite product of these encounters is a cosmopolitan and contradictory Afro-Arab polity, self-proclaimed as *awlad al-balad* (children of the land)—a progeny of settlers and natives rooted in the land of the blacks (*bilad as-Sudan*). This hybrid entity, a product of millennial admixture of competing norms and diverse genetic pools, rejects the image of the superiority of the Bedouin-Arab nomads popularized by medieval Muslim scholars like Ibn Khaldun.[4]

The *awlad al-balad* claimed birth from the ancestors of the land and effectively deprived the indigenous inhabitants of their birthright claims.[5] This acknowledgment and privilege is in stark contrast to the *fallata,* descendants of West African *faqihs* (holy men), who were referred to as *muwalid* (born in the country) and feared as religious rivals who straddled an "anomalous social position" due to their similarity to the other "blacks."[6]

In contrast to the *fallata,* the *falaliyh,* or descendants of Turco-Egyptian Mameluks, were accorded *muwalid* status in 1916, followed by their formal inclusion into the Sudanese polity without any acknowledgment of their equally hybrid status as settlers.[7] Although these settler communities were Arabized and Islamized, ethnocultural markers that separated the new hybridized generations as "Arabs" and "blacks" accompanied their integration into the Sudanese polity. This sociocultural differentiation resurfaced in the twenty-first century as battles fought between "Arabs" and "Africans," camouflaging the complex realities of Sudan's Afro-Arab polity.

The official discourse of Arabized Sudanese is to claim genealogies linking themselves to Arab holy men, while the unofficial sotto voce societal discourse remains contemptuous of "Arab nomads," who are available for hire. This interesting paradox is also found in the official discourse of neighboring Abyssinian populations claiming a hybrid Afro-Semitic heritage.[8] The complexity of this fused identity and the imperial supporting framework that provided the processes of both Arabization and Islamization with the technologically superior firearms and ideological justifications for the subordination of the non-Arabized Sudanic peoples such as the Beja, Nuba, Ingessana, Fur, and Nilotes are at the heart of the dilemma faced by this enormous nation. As the second millennium dawned, modern Sudanese are faced with two options: (1) a surgical separation of the land into a North Sudan, espousing a discredited racialist ideology of Arabism, and an underdeveloped South Sudan, accentuating its African identity and distancing itself from its Arabized kin; and (2) the establishment of a flexible Sudanic state based on an acknowledgment of the multiple pasts of its peoples and a common future guided by consensus on the sharing of power and land wealth.

The Sudanese of the twenty-first century are being asked to face the truth about the ties that bind them to each other and to seek reconciliation in order to equitably share decisions regarding the allocation and distribution of resources in ways that would benefit *all* citizens. This entails a disavowal of all socioeconomic discriminatory practices and the privileging of any ideology justifying coercive unity. To ignore the demands of the peoples whose histories have been erased by the official scribes of Arabization and Islamization and to condone the razing of homelands, the burning of fields, the desecration of wells, and acts of inhumanity against women and children is to invite more violence. If peace is not to elude twenty-first century Sudan, the country's legacy of inequities must be addressed and a more equitable and dignified future charted out.

Bilad as-Sudan: The Land of the "Blacks" and Its "People(s)"

The many and varied historical processes by which the different "peoples"[9] of Sudan have been incorporated into the modern Sudanese state include commerce, migration, raids, counterraids, conquest, resistance, coexistence, and subjugation. In a period spanning almost a millennium, C.E. 651–1504, Nubians, Bejas, Nilotics (Dinka, Nuer, Shilluk, and their kin), and Equatorians (Azande and related peoples inhabiting the Nile-Congo frontier) interacted with each other and with Arab traders, migrants, and invaders. Four "tides of Arab immigration" have been identified[10] that once again opened up this ancient land that had traded with the Mediterranean world of the Greeks and Romans. Outsiders viewed this vast territory as one ruled by darker peoples whom they differentiated from themselves by their skin color, which led to the use of interchangeable terms such as the hellenized *Ethiopian* (burnt skin) *Kush,* and the *Sudan,* a medieval Arabic term. Numerous communities and kingdoms, each presenting the Arab invaders with particular socioeconomic and political circumstances that shaped their relations with the indigenous populations and rulers, therefore peopled the vast territory.[11]

The arrival of the Arabs did not necessarily result in the subjugation of the indigenous populations. In some instances, the Arab tribes were vanquished and had to pay tribute to their hosts until they were integrated as a clan or subclan into the host society. The matrilineal lineage of these societies enabled many Arabs to become integrated into the host societies. Such seamless incorporations were reversed by the institutionalization of the process of Arabization and Islamization—by the arrival of Islamic holy men who introduced patriarchal institutions that gradually supplanted the matrilineal kinship networks on which indigenous institutions and identities were based. Although documentation is scant, there remain rich oral histories of the Nubians and Beja that narrate the frequency of intermarriages with Arab strangers. This produced a synthesis, the core of which was to form the antecedents of the contemporary Sudanese distinguished by the fusion of both indigenous/African and nonindigenous/Arab communities, which gave rise to the creolized population that we now recognize as Afro-Arab, northern Sudanese, Africanized Arab, or Arabized African. Whichever category one chooses, it is clear that the Arab invasion led to the establishment of permanent settlements that transformed not only the sociocultural fabric of the indigenous societies but also altered the political balance that may have existed previously.

The first wave of Arab conquest took place during the seventh and eighth centuries and resulted in a series of wars and resistance leading to the reestablishment of trade between Nubia and Egypt.[12] The second wave of immigration occurred during the eighth and ninth centuries from across the Red Sea into the lands of the Beja, followed by the exodus of Arab tribal warriors—who under the Abbasid Caliph Mu'tasim (833–842) were replaced by Mameluks—into Nubia.[13] The gold mines of the Red Sea Hills were rediscovered by Arab adventurers who made themselves masters of

the areas they renamed *bilad al-Ma'adin* (land of the mines). They intermarried with the Beja communities, cooperated with the emissaries of the
distant Caliphs when necessary, and at other times evaded their reach. In
the early years of the eleventh century, the Arabized Bejas, who controlled
the gold mines, gave rise to new communities that would later become what
P. M. Holt has aptly termed the "marcher-lords" on the frontiers of Islam.
This process of fusion of Beja institutions with Arab invasions gave momentum to the process of Arabization that had began two centuries earlier.

The Mameluks, who replaced the Ayubbids in the second half of the
thirteenth century, sustained the third wave of Arab invasions. These war-
rior-sultans, not satisfied with tribute from their vanquished populations,
also demanded their conversion to Islam. In C.E. 1276, the Mameluks,
accompanied by allied Arab militias, invaded Nubia, were victorious at
Dongola, and transformed the Christian rulers of Nubia and al-Muqurra into
vassal-kings.[14] Through the renewal of the *baqt,* the Nubian populations
were turned into *dhimmis* (protected status) with more stringent obligations
of payments that had lapsed under the Ayyubid dynasty. The steady infiltra-
tion of Arabs and their intermarrying with indigenous populations resulted
in quasi-tribal groupings of Arabized Africans. This gradual process, which
began in the seventh century, did not dislodge Christianity but initiated a
superficial Islamization that was institutionalized only with the rise of the
Funj kingdom in the late fourteenth and early fifteenth centuries. The fourth
wave brought large numbers of Arab settlers, Islamic jurists (*faqih*), and
missionaries (Sufis) from the Hijaz and the wider Islamic regions of western and central Africa, commonly referred to as the Maghrib.

Paradoxically, it was the rise in 1504 of the Funj kingdom—a non-Arab
and non-Muslim dynasty—that, although it had initially checked Arab encroachment in the central and eastern regions, led to the effective Islamization of indigenous Sudanic societies.[15] From 1504 to 1762, the Funj kings
exercised hegemony over both indigenous and Arabized communities, such
as the Abdallab, whose chief became the first *manjil* (viceroy) to enforce
the suzerainty of its *makks* (indigenous rulers), the Sultana Zarqa (black
sultanate), founded by Amara Dunqas. The Funj *makks* throughout their rule
did not adopt the Arabic term *sultan,* although later correspondence referred
to their kingdom as Sultana Zarqa, or black sultanate. They ruled over a vast
region stretching westward from the confluence of the White and Blue Niles
to Kordofan. In the east and north, their domain included the areas from the
First Cataract to the Abyssinian plains. The most sustained resistance came
from established confederacies like the Shaqiiyya and Ja'aliyyin, which
refused to acknowledge the chiefs of the Funj and their Abdallab deputies.[16]
The Funj's hold over the western frontier areas of Dar Fur were also more
tenuous and flared into tensions over the exercise of control of the caravan
routes to the west, north, and east. Numerous conflicts erupted over

resources, which led unruly subjects on the periphery to forge alliances against the Funj rulers.

Arabization was facilitated by the preponderance of the matrilineal structure of indigenous societies, which enabled the incoming groups to intermarry and inherit positions of power and decisionmaking in the host societies.[17] Islamization, which to varying degrees had accompanied the racial/ethnic fusion of Africans and Arabs since the seventh century, was facilitated by the existence of indigenous social norms and structures that (1) welcomed the Muslim scholars and missionaries as "wise strangers" and (2) accepted the mysticism of the Sufi as a *baraka* (blessing), a gift from the gods that would enable the holder to be a medium between people and divinities and enable divinities to respond to demands from ordinary mortals. Islam had been introduced by the various Muslim traders as well as by learned men who had begun to convert the various adherents of traditional religions in the fourteen and fifteen centuries. But it was not until the consolidation of Funj power in the sixteenth century that effective Islamization began to take place.

Before the rise of the Funj dynasty, many missionaries succeeded in converting followers to Islam. One of the earliest proselytizers was Hamad Abu Dunana, who is credited with the introduction of the Shadhiliyya order early in the fifteenth century. Abdallah Jamma, a son-in-law of Abu Dunana, is remembered as the Arab leader who vanquished the Christian kingdom of Soba and held power over the Arabized Nubian sedentary communities known as Ja'aliyyin, whose ruling class was known as the Abdallab. In the same period, a Yemenite settler, Ghulmollah ibn Ayd, began proselytizing in Dongola, and his sons later established quranic schools in Kordofan. In the sixteenth century, reformists replaced these early missionaries by attracting thousands of students who later returned to their homes and established religious orders and schools whose impact was felt throughout the land. A number of these reformers were descended from earlier Arab waves of immigrants or visitors invited by the Funj kings. Arabization produced new generations who went on to study abroad in Cairo, Hijaz, or the Maghrib and returned to their home communities to spread their teachings.

In the sixteenth century, scholars of both the Egyptian Maliki and Shafi schools of law visited Arbaji and Sennar and established the Qadriyyah order. The *tariqahs* (literally, path/paths) of the Sufi groups were also transplanted to Sudan by different scholars from Baghdad and the Maghrib, increasing the number of adherents in the Funj territories. Both the "founding members" of the Sufi lodges and the sociocultural ethos of the societies that nurtured the new religion and indigenized its rituals shaped Sudanese Islam. The process of Islamization produced a new political construct—the *umma*—which in theory provided the impetus for the reorganization of the ways in which societies had been structured. A new transethnic and transterritorial identity emerged that countered the geographically and ethnically based kinship systems that guided the rules and norms of economic and political exchanges.

Arabization produced hybrid communities that identified more with the Arab culture and social structures and relegated their African/indigenous identities to a secondary tier. Islam, with its division between "enslavable" infidels and those who belong to the *umma,* provided ideological justifications that condoned the inhumane practice of slavery, the legacy of which was to become the wedge separating the Sudanese multinational polity into two groups—those who were stigmatized and disenfranchised by a servile past, and those whose privileged position was threatened by the demands for equality of the disenfranchised. The Baggara nomads of southern Kordofan and Darfur[18] who arrived as cattle-herding settlers provide an example of the urgent need of contemporary Sudanese to acknowledge the inequities of their past and seek reconciliation in the present in order to live in peace.[19] Seeking to reconfigure the organizing ideologies of the last millennium—which have disenfranchised the majority of the peoples inhabiting the borders of modern Sudan—without attention to the impact of the past on the present, is to perpetuate the political and humanitarian crises that have plagued postcolonial Sudan and its divided inhabitants.

Funj rule over these large tracts of territory brought together diverse communities in a loosely organized framework that established the basis for the emergence of an Islamized Afro-Arab polity. Theirs was not a centralized rule but conquest followed by the imposition of rule by viceroys and later by the heads of "holy families." They reigned over a seamless empire, inhabited by numerous self-contained indigenous communities, that they gradually wielded into a commercial and political network and that brought the recalcitrant Bejas in confrontation with Arab adventurers who, through coercion and intermarriage, took over the positions of social and political authority and transformed the irascible Blemmys of antiquity into mining communities of emerald and gold.[20] During the heyday of the Funj rulers, the Arab-Nubian encounter that began in the seventh century mushroomed into quasi-tribal formations of mixed populations known as the Juhayna and Ja'aliyyin, who spearheaded the campaigns of Arabization and the Islamization of territories of the plains of Kordofan and southward beyond the *sudd.*[21] Whereas some of these communities in the northeast and eastern regions fused together to create the composite character that has become recognizable as the Afro-Arabized-Africans, or simply northern Sudanese, certain communities preserved distinctive indigenous traits and institutions that were later highlighted to mobilize their aggrieved communities in the struggle for the right to self-determination.

Some of these communities, like the Nubians in the environs of the Atbara River and the Bejas of the Red Sea Hills, were more effectively Arabized and Islamized in comparison to the inhabitants of the Nuba Mountains, the Blue Nile Hills, and borderland regions such as the Abyei. Nevertheless, neither membership in the Islamic *umma* nor acceptance of their affiliation with Arab civilization have created the conditions that would guarantee peaceful coexistence of the communities of the ancient land with the strangers from across the Sahara and the Red Sea. The transnational promise of Arabism and Islamism finds itself confronted with the nationalist demands of peoples seeking an equitable political framework that transcends a millennial past of conquest, bondage, and economic alienation.

The cleavage between Arab and African remains wide, as demonstrated by the array of indigenous cultures preserved by the *montagnards,*[22] who inhabit the *jebel* (hills or mountains) and by the *frontiers.*[23] Some sought asylum in the Nuba Mountains and Ingessana Hills and continued to defy the coercive assimilation by the proponents of Arabization and Islamization. These communities came to be known by the geographic names that provided them asylum, such as the Nuba and the Ingessana. Those who were both culturally uprooted and territorially displaced came to be known as Fertit. The Nuba of Kordofan, like the inhabitants of the Blue Nile Hills and the Abyei, who straddle the regions of Bahr al-Ghazal and Upper Nile, confront the harsh legacies of the process of Arabization and Islamization that began in the second half of the first millennium and that have yet to be resolved in the first decade of the twenty-first century.

More attention needs to be paid to the potential of these fragmented communities to wage war as well as to maintain peace. Both the armed insurgents and the government forces need to widen the scope of the binary lenses they use and consider the roles of communities that have either defied or succumbed to the campaigns launched by both Arab and non-Arab "warlord masters" and who by the eighteenth century were reduced to slaves and in the twentieth century occupied a serf-like status.[24] The destructive conflicts between armed southern groups in the 1990s demonstrated the negative impact on the peace process when smaller communities perceived that their interests were being subordinated to the larger, better-known groups.

While the "Nuba"[25] have gained international attention due to the Western media, the disenfranchisement of the other lesser-known, smaller communities remains outside the calculus of both regional peacemakers and their international counterparts. Peace, if it is to be sustained, must not only provide for the larger and well-known communities but also nurture the aspirations for social justice and equity of those Sudanese whose histories have been rendered illegible and illegitimate by elite groups seeking to consolidate their hegemony over Africa's giant nation. The numerous and sustained intercommunal encounters and exchanges of the past, which resulted in the fusion of cultures, ethnicities, and identities, need to be considered in creating twenty-first century Sudan.

The quest for a just peace in southern Sudan, the struggle for self-determination in the borderlands straddling the North-South divide, and the violent crises in Darfur all constitute part of the construction of a modern Sudanese polity that is capable of and willing to envision a state-society framework that acknowledges the multiplicity of identities and guarantees the rights of its diverse citizenry to an equitable citizenship.

Keys to Understanding the Sudanese: Complex Historical Legacies

Contemporary Sudan is mired in multiple conflicts whose origins can be traced to the distant precolonial past and the eccentric colonial heritage of Anglo-Egyptian overrule. Its ancient, precolonial past includes an imperial heritage linking it to the pharaonic civilizations of the Nile, to the Christian kingdoms of ancient Nubia and Merowe, and to the Islamic Nilotic sultanates that emerged in the region's central riverain areas and western savannah lands. The historical relations between the rapacious central riverain sultanates and the territories beyond the *sudd* bequeathed a legacy of political disenfranchisement and socioeconomic inequalities contributing to the interlocking regional conflicts that characterize today's Sudan. In sum, it is no exaggeration to argue that the raging conflicts are all manifestations of the continuing quest of Sudan's multiethnic inhabitants for a more equitable membership in a Sudanese polity that recognizes the worth of each and all within it—in short, citizenship.

The making of contemporary "Sudan" and the "Sudanese" needs to be understood in terms other than a binary reduction of a perennial conflict between idealized caricatures of "Arab/Non-African/nonblack" and "African/Non-Arab/black" protagonists engaged in a zero-sum game of hegemonic competition. Rather, it should be seen as an ongoing process that must acknowledge its ancient roots as well as its transformation during thirteen centuries of interaction with distant and proximate chieftaincies, kingdoms, and sultanates, all of which brought to power the conquest states (Sennar, Waddai, Dar Fur) that ruled their hybridized and indigenous subjects until they were incorporated into the Ottoman realm in the nineteenth century.

The first millennium (C.E. 650–1650) was a period of sociopolitical and economic transformations due to waves of Arab and African settlers, whose arrival, at times peaceable and at other times brutally violent, changed the lives of the indigenous inhabitants of the banks of the Nile Valley and its eastern Sudan hinterlands. Put another way, the process of state formation of the Sudan was directly affected by power struggles in the Nubian/Egyptian north and in the West African caliphates, all of which resulted in a series of Arab and African Muslim migrations to the Nile Valley. The encounters of the indigenous Sudanese with the first waves of Arab migration from the north and, later, by African Muslims from the west, resulted in the selective adaptation of forms of Muslim governance and in the opening up of new markets for gold, slaves, salt, and ivory. It also facilitated the construction of a Janus-faced polity that only acknowledges the imported "Arab" identity or the "African" sociopolitical construct that emerged as an antidote to the hegemony of the former. The "Sudanic" identity, which embraces both the indigenous claims of those who inhabited Sudan as well as those of the self-styled "children of the land," provides the forum for an equitable and just interaction for all its constituents. Here then is one piece—or perhaps two or three pieces—of Sudan's patchwork quilt of identities, and an ill-fitting one at best. There are similarly equivocal religious pieces as well.

Religious Complexities

The nation's quest to find a balance between its indigenous form of Sunni Islam, as practiced by its Sufi mystics and shaikhs, and the more centralized orthodoxies advocated by the legatees of West African jihads,[26] Ottoman *pashas,* and Anglo-Egyptian governors of the nineteenth century also serves to highlight the different interpretations of Islamic identity in contemporary Sudan.[27]

In any case, the brief and bloody interlude of the Mahdiyya (1881–1889)—a syncretic, millenarian movement that fused protonationalist aspirations with the resentments of the northern merchant classes (*jellaba*) against the Turkiyya and the equally strong resentment of the peoples of the south against the very same *jellaba* and Egyptian rule[28]—provided a glimpse into the eruption of the "politics of resentment, " all couched in terms of the religious messianism, claims of territorial ownership, and political volatility that characterize the resource wars that triggered such movements. While the British, under Lord Kitchener, defeated the Mahdist army on the hills of Karari in September 1898, the themes that animated the Mahdiyya lived on into the twentieth century, nurtured by the lineal descendants of the self-declared Mahdi, Muhammad Ahmad (including Sadiq al-Mahdi, a former prime minister who is still active on the Sudanese national scene), and the erstwhile supporters of the Ansar[29] Party which, naturally, takes its inspiration from the Mahdiyya itself. A major inspiration for this overtly religious uprising was also the economic interests of the elite slave merchants who had established their *kubaniyas,* trading companies comparable to those of the British and the Dutch East India Companies that preceded empire building.[30]

Although it is a much easier task to undertake an inquiry into the outward manifestations of such conflicts (i.e., religious puritanism, identity/ethnic wars, and alien invasions), it is the conflicts over resources—agricultural land, water, pasturage, and, recently, oil—that underpin the attenuated rivalries that followed, leaving behind new hostilities that were, in turn, woven together to become the poles of identity/ethnicity around which the contesting groups rallied. Thus, it becomes ever more important to keep looking for these strands of the partially uncovered narratives of intercommunal hostility, including, for example, those having to do with so-called intruders—that is, new settlers who forced their way into grazing or farming areas; with cattle and slave raids; and, finally, with the wars of conversion (often officially sponsored) that have yet to give the Muslims of Sudan respite from social discrimination, economic disenfranchisement, and political marginalization. It is in these interstices of the contemporary Sudanese polity that those who seek a permanent peace must be ever vigilant to identify the opportunities for making that peace a reality.

The Maze of Identities and the Paradox of Choices

In a demonstration of the malleability (and paradoxical quality) of ethnic identities, we find on the one hand that in contemporary Sudan, the most vociferous defenders of an "Arab" identity are those whose antecedents can be traced to indigenous communities overtaken by Arab invaders, or to those who intermarried with West African settlers. The "African" identity, on the other hand, appears to be prominent among elites of marginalized communities who have preserved their "indigenous" or "Sudanic" heritage. For these self-proclaimed Africans of the Sudan—like the Nuba in Kordofan, the Fur and Masalit in Darfur, and the majority of those who inhabit the southern provinces—the adoption of this African identity is equated with an affirmation of "blackness" and a negation of the "slave or servile" status associated with darker skin pigmentation.[31]

Identity—ethnic, religious, political—as a trigger of conflict has dominated the contemporary discourse on the conflicts in Sudan. The repetition of the mantra of this approach has led to an oversimplification of intercommunal relations and the ascendancy of one or another single anthropological, economic, or ideological factor.[32] This, in turn, has led to reductionist analyses that resort to binary representations of the complex array of actors in a supposed face-off between Arab and African, Northerner and Southerner, Muslim and Christian, Communist and Islamist, Islamist and secularist.[33] More recently, with the rise of the National Islamic Front (NIF) and its various political and armed branches, the modern Islamists have had to confront the gap between the ideal of the *umma* as an inclusive society embracing all races and regions and the competition for resources that engender intra-Muslim violence.[34] In addition to the vexing question of how to "innovate" without straying too far from the Islamic orthodoxy that had engaged Muslim scholars in debates about *itjihad* and modernization throughout the twentieth century, the rise of radical Islam and its use of apostasy to punish Muslim dissidents requires a better understanding of the adaptation of Islam in an increasingly cosmopolitan Sudan.[35]

Legal scholars such as Hassan Turabi and followers waxed eloquent about the need for a revolutionary Islam with claims to political liberalism.[36] While these theoretical intricacies command the attention of the ruling elite and intellectuals, the harsh realities on the ground are demonstrated by lesser-known shaikhs whose fatwas justify the extermination of Sudanese Muslims and non-Muslims who stand in the way of rule by militant theocrats and the declaration of jihad.[37] An important point to note is that some of the gaps in our knowledge of Sudan as a conquest state and the impact of the incorporation of non-Arab and non-Islamic peoples into the sprawling state were effected in alliance with indigenous rulers and communities as well as rulers from distant sultanates. The unfolding saga of Darfur demonstrates the importance of the alliances and counteralliances forged between non-Arab rulers such as the Daju, Tunjur, and Fur kingdoms and the existence of feudal institutions that have left an imprint on contemporary state-society relations. Apocalyptic images such as the rifle-toting Janjaweed can better be understood in their historical context of accommodation and coercion relationships, which are composed of numerous interrelated processes of "political expansion and exploitation . . . [and] other processes [which] may be termed ethnic change, that is, the progressive displacement or assimilation of the existing peoples by incoming Fur or Arab. Both processes were reinforced by Islam's power to redefine social and political frontiers."[38]

Failure to understand the complex and intertwined histories of the different peoples and the impact of the "explosion" of Islam in the seventh century and its subsequent transmutation into a religion claimed by some of the natives as well as the mercantilist and evangelical settlers leads to ill-fitting solutions for the conflicts that threaten to rent the society apart.

The other consequences of this situation are that while the internal discourse of Sudan provides periodic reinterpretations of these paradoxically (yet flexible) identities, the external discourse freezes those identities in ahistorical narratives. Some of the current analyses of Sudanese politics distort the picture, claiming that the "blacks" were always black, the "Arabs" were always Arab, and Muslims and Christians were forever imbedded in their respective sects. The internal discourse resorts to constructed genealogies to explain distant affiliation—for example, with the Abbasids or Fatimids—or to claim linkage to the Banu Hillal invasions into the Maghreb, and thereby provide unlikely yet socially sanctioned legitimacy to what are in fact fairly recently constructed identities for Arabized and Islamized Sudanese. Moreover, these "genealogical" constructs have actually become the unintentional vehicles of transmission for unverifiable identities collected by colonial anthropologists–cum–civil servants. Not all, but a large part of, colonial administration policies reflect the influence of these internal discourses and "descriptions" that legitimate particular strands of identity already heavily tinged with subjectivity.[39] What is interesting is that the constructed genealogies, legitimated by "outsiders," were frozen in place not by those who claim them on the ground, but by the outside world.[40] Another paradox is that the outside world has belatedly come to terms with the fact not only that it had a hand in the creation of fabricated identities, but that these very constructs are now proudly acclaimed as authentic by the members of such "invented" tribes and traditions.[41]

The internal discourse was externalized during the European-Sudanese encounters through missionaries, explorers, anthropologists, and colonial officials. Also, it should be remembered that the term *African* was used by the colonizers to refer to the "natives" and was appropriated by the Western-educated anticolonial nationalists as a unifying identity for colonial subjects seeking self-rule. In the context of Sudan, such assertions must be understood in light of the fact that its indigenous societies were transformed first by Arabization and Islamization, foundations on which were overlaid the structures and nomenclatures of the Anglo-Egyptian period. Thus, the anticolonial nationalists of the 1920s reappropriated the term *Arab* rather than *African* or *Sudanese*.[42] It was only later, in the postindependence era, that the latter terms came into common usage in the struggle of disenfranchised Sudanese facing the hegemonic rule of their Arabized compatriots.

The Africanization of the struggle of disenfranchised Sudanese seeking political space took place in the second half of the twentieth century, when educated Nilotes and Nubians adopted the term *African* to describe themselves. Contemporary external discourse, emanating from the ideological outposts of the SPLM/A and international humanitarian organizations, portrays the conflict as an epic battle between Arab/Muslims and African/Christians. The Sudan Liberation Movement/Army (SLM/A), formerly known as the Darfur Liberation Front, also evolved into a guerrilla army and adopted an "African" identity similar to that of the SPLM/A, reproducing a polarized discourse pitting "Arabs" against "Africans." This binary image of ethnically distinct antagonists proved difficult to reconcile in Darfur due to the historical hegemony of the Fur sultanate, which arose from a

Fur-Arab blended dynasty that also pursued a policy of assimilation of both indigenous and settler nomadic communities in Sudan's western region.[43] The sultanate's demise in 1916 and its forced incorporation into Anglo-Egyptian Sudan led to residual resistance imbued with a more militant Islamism associated with the past glories of the independent polity. Since independence, large numbers of westerners from Darfur constituted the rank-and-file soldiers in the civil war in the south.

The environmental degradation of the pasturelands of Northern Darfur and Kordofan also led to yet another polarization between cattle and camel nomads and sedentary farmers, on whom were imposed the organizing ideologies of the Islamists in Khartoum and displaced Arabs from war-torn areas affected by the Libyan-Chad wars of the 1980s. The economic marginalization of disaffected groups led to the mobilization of guerrilla armies by southerners and westerners who expressed an African identity in response to the primacy of the Arabized ruling elites. Sectarian rulers such as Sadiq al-Mahdi armed "Arab" militias (*murahaleen*), which were later formally institutionalized as *mujahidin* by the National Islamic Front, which seized power in 1989. The 1990s were a decade when the Sudanese state was confronted with the emergence of guerrilla groups in the west, east, and center while the south held onto a stalemate.

This simplistic portrayal remains dominant in the dialogue on Sudan despite the fact that, with the exception of the ruling elites, Arabized/Africanized Muslim and non-Muslim Sudanese have been disenfranchised by the various regimes exercising power from Khartoum. It is also true that the ruling elites of Khartoum have, at different times, included members of marginalized communities, such as the Fallata, Nuba, Nuer, and Dinka. That the Arab-African dichotomy makes little sense is already clear from the historical documentation of demographic shifts and the sociocultural exchanges that have taken place between the many peoples of the Sudan spanning a millennium. Put another way, blackness, like the proverbial beauty, is in the eye of the beholder. Power, the capacity of individuals and/or communities to ensure their physical security, autonomy, and social cohesiveness, determines whether blackness is a symbol of disempowerment or preordained servility, or is a social construct to bridge the gap between the ideals of the *umma* and the interests of dynasties and mercantilist elites.[44]

The rise of a theocratic state and its accompanying ideology in 1989 provides additional historical data to support the fact that the state-sponsored as well as societal violence has not spared Muslims. Rather, religious tenets have been utilized and manipulated to justify the killings of Muslims by Muslims, as is exemplified by the campaigns of ethnic cleansing in the Nuba Mountains in the 1980s and of Darfur in the 2000s. The conflict in the south, which has pitted both Christians and Muslims against their rulers in Khartoum, points to the need to differentiate between political myth and reality. Failure to see beyond the facile Muslim-Christian dichotomy prevents the analysis of localized foci of violence and counterviolence. This also leads to a refusal to acknowledge the role of local customs, traditions, and ancestral rituals, which have led at times to peace agreements between rival groups and at other times to a spiraling violence between communities.[45] Once again, it remains a paradox that the indigenous Sudanic element, with its syncretistic sociological and polytheist theological framework, remains excluded from the narratives of the nation. It is this rigid nomenclature that has found its way to the pages of the international media and has perpetuated the binary perspective that, in effect, discourages the internal dialogue that could usefully engage the many Sudanese factions, groups, and outlooks. Sadly, as the casualties of war increased during the twenty-year period 1983–2003, so did the strident bipolar language of Sudanese nationalists of the south, the north, the west, and the east.

In January 2005, fifty years after the mutiny of southern soldiers garrisoned in Torit and thirty years after the establishment of the SPLM/A, John de Mabior Garang, SPLM/A's leader, signed a historic peace agreement with the government of Sudan based on acknowledgment of the interrelated root causes of the conflicts in the south, east, and west. With the signing of the long-awaited Comprehensive Peace Agreement (CPA) in the first years of the twenty-first century, the outlines of a new organizing ideology of Sudanization emerged as a feasible alternative to that of the Arabization and Islamization that had accompanied the rise and fall of sultanates, caliphates, and the hegemonic rule by Arabized and Islamized elites since the seventh century. Garang's call for Sudan to "nucleate as a nation with its own specific identity, not as a satellite of other nations" found resonance in the new millennium as the fictional solidarity of Arabism and Islamism collapsed amid images of murahaleen and mujahidin inflicting violence on their coreligionists in the Nuba Mountains, the Ingessana Hills, the Red Sea Hills, and the savannah lands of Darfur.[46] In July 2005, a mere six months after his ascension to the post of vice-president in accordance with the terms of the CPA, Garang died in a helicopter crash. Amid calls of unity and appeals to live up to the legacy of its visionary and militant leader, Garang's deputy, Salva Kiir, was inaugurated as the new guardian of the interests of the south. Garang's legacy is a secular ideology of Sudanization, with its composite vision of the "New Sudan" where all Sudanese would participate as equals. This organizing ideology was buttressed by Garang's strategic alliances with disaffected Sudanese of the west, east and center, which had coalesced in opposition to a regime unwilling to relinquish its hegemony and institute an equitable framework of governance for its multiple communities.

It was not until the eruption of the Darfur conflict—which had been bubbling since the 1980s—that the weakness of the binary frames of analysis was exposed internally and externally. In the killing fields of Darfur, as in those of the south, Muslims and non-Muslims perished at the hand of their conationals and coreligionists. Modern technology's electronically transmitted color photographs and videos of the now infamous Janjaweed— represented as the dark-skinned defenders of Arab superiority—effectively camouflaged the complex history of the many communities—Arabs, West Africans, Nilotics, displaced southerners—that make up the former sultanate of Darfur, which was forcibly integrated by British forces into Khartoum's domain as late as 1916.[47] The question of who is fighting whom— Arab/Muslim versus black/African—continued to dominate international media and succeeded in deflecting the more urgent question of why Sudanese are fighting each other. In this instance, there has also been the local reproduction of the stereotypical image of the "Arab" seeking to annihilate the "African" as the two Darfurian rebel groups—the SLM/A and the Justice and Equality Movement (JEM)—turned their guns on each other. The destructive violence in Darfur spiraled out of control in 2004 overshadowing the socioeconomic political dynamics at play since 1916.[48]

Darfur, site of numerous pre-Islamic kingdoms such as the Daju and Tunjur dynasties as well as the powerful Keira sultanate, represents a microcosm of the socioeconomic and political challenges that confronted the postcolonial Sudanese state. In fact, whereas the Arabization of the northeast and the central riverain areas had taken place in the distant past, the Arab conquest of Darfur was completed by the eighteenth century. Moreover, the southward expansion of the Fur and their alliance with the Arab settlers established hybrid dynasties that extended their domain into the areas straddling northern Bahr al-Ghazal and southern Kordofan.[49] The crisis in Darfur is rooted in the institutionalization of inequalities between indigenous and settler societies that began with the expansion of the Fur kingdom from their ancestral home in the Marrah Mountains in the 1500s and continued with their conversion to Islam under the Keira dynasty in the early 1700s and with the failure of subsequent campaigns of Arabization and Islamization— campaigns that erupted into intracommunal conflicts in the late 1980s, culminating in the crimes against humanity in the early 2000s.[50]

The crisis in Darfur, which had been relatively sidelined by regional and international mediators engaged in the quest for closure of the longstanding war between the government and the rebels in the south, was "internationalized" due to a combination of factors. First were the flamboyant acts of defiance by armed rebels against government forces that resulted in the government's brutal acts of retaliation against guerrillas and militias who openly plundered, burned, and raped.[51] Second was the timing of the announcement, in March 2004, by a UN official resident in Sudan, that the government of Sudan and its militias were engaged in a campaign of "ethnic cleansing" in Darfur amid worldwide commemoration of the tenth anniversary of the 1994 Rwandan genocide.[52] Last, but not least, were the legal precedents that had emerged following investigations of the failures of regional and international institutions to prevent catastrophic acts of genocide in the twentieth century (see Chapter 6 for a detailed discussion of Darfur).

The combination of the above factors created the political conditions that internationalized the crises in Darfur and enabled the two liberation movements, the SLM/A and the JEM, to attract world attention to their plight, which had been overshadowed by the prospects of the resolution of the war in the south through a bilateral peace agreement between the government and the SPLM/A. The images of the Janjaweed, apocalyptic horsemen hurling fires of destruction on civilians and cattle alike, transmitted to all corners of the world, enabled the twenty-first century global audience to witness a replay of the millennial scourge visited upon the Sudanese peoples. Despite the accuracy of the digital images of the warring parties and their hapless victims, Western media continued to portray the government forces and militias as "Arab/Muslim" and the civilian victims as "black/African," despite the pictorial images that showed that attackers and victims looked uncomfortably similar to each other. This makes it even more necessary to seek further explanations that take into consideration the historical context of Sudan in its entirety.

Our present knowledge of Sudan and the formation of the Sudanese state remains very vague and sketchy despite the attention that its conflicts have attracted. The predominant focus of extant works has been mainly historical: the study of ruling classes and dynasties paralleled by anthropological studies highlighting the particularities of what Douglas Johnson has aptly called "emblematic" peoples like the Nuba, Nuer, and Dinka—a scholarly tactic that effectively hides from our memory the thousands of other communities inhabiting this giant land.[53] The cumulative knowledge of colonial-era anthropologists undergirded the numerous "country studies" that informed political scientists of the postcolonial period. The historians of Sudan, who occupied the middle ground between these "academic" poles, led to the production of micro- and macronarratives that, with few exceptions, highlighted the politicization of identity as a trigger for the multiple conflicts of modern Sudan.[54]

What might the outlines of such an inquiry look like? An approach that takes the peopling of the land as its point of departure could point the way. During the first millennium, the different rulers and power brokers that sprang up in the communities of the Nile Valley interacted with the waves of alien invaders from northern and western Africa as well as from Arabia. Some accommodated the newcomers and gave birth to the composite

"Sudanese" with whom we have become familiar and whom we identify as those who inhabit the "north." Other communities, such as the Nuba and the Nilotes, maligned by their northern and western adversaries as primitive pagans or barbarians doomed to extinction or servile status, fought against those who would convert them to Islam and then enslave them. Unable to withstand the constant onslaught of the slave-raiding armies, the survivors retreated to more defensible mountainous or swampy areas and thus have preserved their cultures and identities. There were also those who, defeated by the newcomers, were either exterminated on the spot or chained and sold off to distant markets.[55] Many more were inducted into the armies of their new masters in lands as distant as mogul-ruled India and French-occupied Mexico, where their skills as leaders, fearsome warriors, and military strategists were celebrated.[56] Sudanese slaves contributed to the glories of foreign empires as well as to the guarding and strengthening of the fortified slave-holding settlements—known as *zaribas*—led by notorious slave raiders. Some fought on the side of the Anglo-Egyptian forces against the Mahdi, while others sought salvation as the *amirs* of the Mahdiyya.

The insertion of this vast terrain into the Ottoman realm at the beginning of the nineteenth century (mainly through the efforts of Mohammed Ali's Turkish-Egyptian troops, called Turkiyya by the Sudanese) precipitated the conflicts between natives and settlers and also provided institutional support[57] for the large-scale trade in slaves and ivory that pitted northern merchants against the inhabitants of the lands beyond the *sudd,* as well as those in the bordering African kingdoms and communities that had begun to face European armies seeking to secure footholds for their colonial empires—such as the ill-fated Ethiopian emperor Tewodros (Theodore) against the British in 1868.[58]

Modern Sudan has yet to find a comfortable fit in the institutional garb of modern statehood. The diverse peoples of contemporary Sudan have yet to reach consensus on the legacies of their shared past and craft a form of government that can operate within the rules of an international state system that condemns such past practices of conquest states as slavery, theocratic rule, and racialized citizenship. Be it by design, inadvertence, or accident, precolonial conceptions of identity and community were carried over to the colonial and postcolonial periods. Given that in Sudan, which had contained literally hundreds of indigenous communities—each with its own authority structure—as well as the competing kingdoms and sultanates that sought to subjugate the smaller groups, it is not surprising that there is no agreement on how the state is to be "imagined" in the contemporary period.[59]

As the country achieved its independence, it bore the burden of memories of the broken promises made by rulers of the distant and recent past. Those promises—of peace, prosperity, and just rule—underline the failure to create the conditions for equitable coexistence that has thus far marked the struggle in Sudan. It is the failure of Sudan, as Garang put it poetically, to find its "soul."[60] In practical terms, the history that binds the peoples of Sudan as well as the history that pulls them apart need to be examined. Truth has been a casualty in the studies of history, with the different sides highlighting only those elements that would justify their current demands: northerners demand their indigenous heritage but insist on calling themselves *awlad al-balad,* children of the country, without explaining how the children of the soil—the indigenous ones—were deprived of their land; southerners insist on a homogenous identity that hardly stands the test of inquiry, mainly because of the contentious relations that have marred intercommunal relations in the past and that mirror the internecine rivalries of the guerrilla armies of the twentieth century.[61] Sudan's westerners—divided by tribal affiliations, occupational status, and native-settler frictions—seek to assert their newfound identity as "Africans" and "blacks" without acknowledging that their regional armies decimated their fellow African/black southerners throughout the nineteenth and twentieth centuries.[62] Marginalized northerners, who seek to keep the moral high ground by espousing a political union of all aggrieved citizens, do not acknowledge the horrors faced by their Nuba and Beja compatriots.[63] Analogous to the long quest for the many parts of the Nile and the conflicts that have emerged over how its bounty is to be shared, and among whom, the truth needs to be drawn from multiple sources if a viable solution to the multiple conflicts is to be found. If the right of self-determination for sovereign states and peoples is not be turned into a farce, Sudanese must themselves begin framing their conflict in ways that reflect historical, socioeconomic, and political realities. This will enable them to find ways to craft agreements on how to either live together peacefully or find mutually beneficial ways to live separately.[64]

The narrative of the Sudan is more than a "tale . . . full of sound and fury, signifying nothing." Deciphering the meanings of its history provides opportunities for reconciling its differences and crafting an equitable and lasting peace for its peoples. The modern Sudanese state and its ruling elites have yet to distance themselves—credibly—from past practices of coercive rule and institutionalized servility of racialized communities. Those at the helm of the state have yet to convince their own constituencies that they need to demonstrate that the "premise of inequality,"[65] which for thirteen centuries legitimated expropriation of land, enslavement, coercive religious conversion, looting and rape, is no longer acceptable in the twenty-first century.

Sudanese of different regions, religions, creeds, and ideological affiliations constantly reiterate their willingness to hold dialogues on the future of their state and agree that outsiders should not be allowed to dictate to them. Yet, as the various failed peace talks and signed agreements have shown, it is going to take more than talk. It will require the political will to abide by the promises of equality and dignity for all citizens. This willingness to hold dialogues is always contingent on the trustworthiness of both the peacemakers and the guarantors of the peace. It is also heavily tinged with bitterness of too many betrayals. Not addressing the historical factors and the economic and social inequalities that have been borne by Sudanese subalterns has been at the core of the failures to find peace. Peace will continue to be elusive if the importance of the past to the present continues to be ignored.

Notes

1. Barry Buzan, definition of "organizing ideologies"; see Buzan, *People, States and Fear: An Agenda for International Security Studies in the Post–Cold War Era*, 2nd ed. (Boulder, CO: Lynne Rienner Publishers, 1991), p. 70.

2. The Banu Hilal were nomadic Arabs who were induced to invade Ifriqiya by the weakened Egyptian Fatimids, who were besieged by the resistance of the Zirid-Berber Sahaja groups. The use by ruling regimes of nomadic Arab militias (who claimed ancestry to the Hilalian invaders) in the conquest of new lands and peoples was to become a feature of the numerous conflicts that are characteristic of contemporary Sudan. For details, see Mervyn Hiskett, *The Course of Islam in Africa* (Edinburgh: Edinburgh University Press, 1994), p. 5.

3. Both Arabization and Islamization can be understood as the process of incorporation, integration, and/or assimilation of the sociocultural norms, values, and institutions associated with Arab societies and adherents of Islamic religious doctrines. In contrast to these gradual processes, Arabism and Sudanism can be defined as antithetical ideological constructs, with the former claiming the ascendancy of a transnational diasporic identity and the latter believing in the right to equal claims of all the "nations" and/or "peoples" who constitute Sudan. Islamism, a sociopolitical institution, as well as an ideological construct that demands the establishment of *sharia* laws, represents the block to the opportunity for reconciliation represented by Sudanism as an inclusive nationalist framework based on a separation of faith and state to accommodate the diverse polity of Sudan.

4. Ibn Khaldun, *The Muqaddimah: An Introduction to History* (Princeton: Princeton University Press, 1969). Translated from the Arabic by Franz Rosenthal.

5. This cultural category denoting descent or lineage has acquired new political meanings in the twentieth and twenty-first centuries that have overshadowed the impact and import of this category in its earliest stages. While southern Sudanese have highlighted their kinship as Sudanese to the hegemonic *awlad al-balad* and addressed the issue of *uruba* (Arabism), western Sudanese have politicized and narrowed the definition of the term to refer to the three riverain communities of Shayqiya, Ja'aliyyin, and Danagla. By 2005, the term had acquired currency as an analytical category by Western analysts. For details, see Sharif Harir, "Recycling the Past in the Sudan: An Overview of Political Decay," in Sharif Harir and Terje Tvedt (eds.), *Shortcut to Decay: The Case of the Sudan* (Uppsala: Scandinavian Institute for African Studies, 1994), p. 21; Gérard Prunier, *Darfur: The Ambiguous Genocide* (London: Hurst, 2005), pp. xiii, 7.

6. Mark Duffield, "The Fallata: Ideology and the National Economy in the Sudan," in Norma O'Neill and Jay O'Brien (eds.), *Economy and Class in Sudan* (Aldershot, UK: Avebury, 1988), p. 124.

7. For a discussion on the transformation of the settler *falaliyh* into an integral part of the modern Sudanese polity, see El Haj Bilal Omer, *The Danagla Traders of Northern Sudan: Rural Capitalism and Agricultural Development* (London: Ithaca Press, 1985), pp. 14, 20, 22.

8. *Sotto voce* refers to informal terms of references encoded with symbols reflecting racial, ethnic, and religious slurs, often disallowed in the official discourse of modern sovereign states, but which serve to pinpoint the social basis for ideologies perpetuating asymmetrical relations. For a critical inquiry into the transformative relations of settlers and natives, see Mahmood Mamdani, "When Does a Settler Become Native? Reflections on the Colonial Roots of Citizenship in Equatorial and South Africa," University of Cape Town, Inaugural Lecture, *New Series* 208, May 12, 1998, pp. 1–16. For a discussion of the relations between local vernaculars and official discourse, see Ruth Iyob, "The Foreign Policies of the Horn: The Clash Between the Old and the New," in Gilvwer Khadiagala and Terrence Lyons (eds.), *African Foreign Policies: Power and Process* (Boulder, CO: Lynne Rienner Publishers, 2001), pp. 109–112.

9. Douglas Johnson makes the case for avoiding the anthropological term *tribe* except in cases where the populations willingly assert their tribal identification and membership. In the case of Sudan, he highlights the importance of the flexibility of the term as used by the British and argues that "one cannot, therefore, speak of *the* Dinka tribe or *the* Nuer tribe: rather of the Dinka people and the Nuer people, each of whom are organized into a number of different tribes at any one time, some of which may be socially and politically closer to tribes of neighboring peoples than to more distant tribes of the same people. In this sense, too, it is not correct to speak of tribes as universal in the southern Sudan. The Shilluk and Azande were organized into kingdoms, subdivided into chieftaincies, all of which contained persons of diverse origins. It was the organizing principle of the kingdom that made the king's subjects into a people." Douglas Johnson, *The Root Causes of Sudan's Civil War* (Bloomington: Indiana University Press, 2003), p. xv.

10. Harold A. MacMichael, *A History of the Arabs in Sudan: Some of the People Who Preceded Them and the Tribes Inhabiting Darfur* (New York: Barnes & Noble, 1967), pp. 10–11.

11. The Funj in the east, the Fur in the west, and, to an extent, the Azande in the extreme south represent examples of well-organized militant societies where the earliest wave of Arab groups entered into a patron-client relationship with the indigenous rulers. This relationship was cemented by kinship ties, while traders and religious leaders introduced Islam, adding to the many existing layers of deities and forms of worship. Among the more decentralized societies, whether the encounter with the Arabs was accommodative or coercive depended on the existence or absence of traditional norms of assimilating newcomers into the societies.

12. The *baqt,* or the annual tribute of slaves described in medieval Arabic sources, is a diplomatic term in usage during Hellenistic times as *pakton,* later Latinized as *pactum* to refer to "a compact of mutual obligations and its connected payments." According to scholars of this period, "the survival of the Hellenistic term suggests that . . . [the C.E. seventh-century Arab invasion] did not originate this annual transaction but re-established, perhaps after interruption, a trade of long standing." See P. M. Holt and M. W. Daly, *A History of the Sudan: From the Coming of Islam to the Present Day* (London: Longman Group, 1988), p. 16.

13. P. M. Holt, "The Islamization of Nilotic Sudan," in Brett Michael (ed.), *Northern Africa: Islam and Modernization* (London: Frank Cass, 1973), p. 14.

14. The term *Mameluk* refers to white slaves of Turkish origin. Black slaves, known simply as *Sudan* and *Berbers,* constituted the core of the standing armies of the Fatimid dynasty.

15. Although historians have yet to reach a consensus, it is claimed that the militant Shilluk established the Funj dynasty.

16. Holt and Daly, *A History of the Sudan.*

17. Yusuf Fadl Hasan, "External Influences and the Progress of Islamization in Eastern Sudan Between the Fifteenth and Sixteenth Centuries," in Yusuf Fadl Hasan (ed.), *Sudan in Africa: Studies Presented to the First International Conference Sponsored by the Sudan Research Unit, 7–12 February 1968* (Khartoum: Khartoum University Press, 1971), p. 77.

18. Ian Cunnison, *Baggara Arabs: Power and Lineage in a Sudanese Nomad Tribe* (Oxford: Clarendon Press, 1966).

19. Prunier identifies the Baggara as "arabized Africans . . . [who] . . . are prime examples of Western Sudan's ethnic ambiguities." See Prunier, *Darfur,* p. xviii.

20. For a discussion of the histories of these ancient peoples, see Carolyn Fluehr-Lobban and Kharyssa Rhodes (eds.), *Race and Identity in the Nile Valley: Ancient and Modern Perspectives* (Trenton, NJ: Red Sea Press, 2004), pp. 77–79.

21. The term *sudd* comes from the Arabic *sadd* meaning "barrier," indicating the natural obstacles presented by the marshy swamps of the lands beyond the River Kiir (later known as the Bahr al Arab).

22. The legatees of the neighboring sultanate of Wadai and of Bornu in contemporary Chad face the same dilemma. For an excellent analysis of how the violence of the past shapes present-day conflicts, see Mario J. Azevedo, *Roots of Violence: A History of War in Chad* (The Hague: Gordon & Breach, 1988).

23. R. O'Fahey provides some insights into the emergence of this composite term *fartit* as "one of a number of generic and pejorative names used by the savannah Muslims to describe the stateless, non-Muslim and therefore enslavable peoples of the wetter lands below them." See O'Fahey, "Fur and Fartit: The History of a Frontier," in John Mack and Peter Robertshaw (eds.), *Culture History in the Southern Sudan: Archaeology, Linguistics and Ethno-History* (Nairobi: British Institute in Eastern Africa, 1982), p. 77.

24. Ibid.

25. Although the term *Nuba* has become associated with the non-Arabized populations of the hills of southern Kordofan, the various communities that live on this cluster of hills have only recently adopted the name Nuba and use it interchangeably with African. For details on the making of the Nuba, see S. F. Nadel (ed.), *The Nuba: An Anthropological Study of the Hill Tribes in Kordofan* (London: Oxford University Press, 1947).

26. For an extremely valuable comparative regional analysis see Thomas Hodgkins, "Mahdism, Messianism and Marxism in the African Setting," in Yusuf Fadl Hasan (ed.), *Sudan in Africa* (Khartoum: University of Khartoum Press, 1971), pp. 115–120.

27. This can be understood as the continuation of the politics of "river imperialism" that had attracted ancient Egyptians, Greeks, Romans, medieval Arabs, Ottomans, and nineteenth-century Europeans to the land where the White and Blue Niles meet. For details on how the "politics of water" shaped the "resource wars' of Sudan, see Terje Tvedt, *The River Nile in the Age of the British: Political Ecol-*

ogy and the Quest for Economic Power (London: I. B. Taurus, 2004).

28. Robert O. Collins, *The Southern Sudan, 1883–1898: A Struggle for Control* (New Haven: Yale University Press, 1962), pp. 22–51.

29. *Ansar* (helpers) was the honorific given those in Madina who welcomed the Prophet upon his "migration" from Mecca. It is also used to distinguish from the *muhajirun,* the immigrants from Mecca. Thus, the Sudanese *ansar* not only endowed themselves with a religiously powerful honorific, but also cast themselves as a religious force in their own right.

30. Despite the numerous parallels between these "armed companies" present throughout the medieval *bilad as-Sudan,* Western scholars and policymakers have tended to ignore the non-Western counterparts of the mercantilist companies that paved the way for European colonization.

31. There are numerous terms to describe the different shades of "blackness" in (northern) Sudan. They are (1) *asfar* (yellow) denoting *ahmar* (white); (2) *asmar* (shades of light-to-dark brown) encompassing *dahabi* (golden), *gamhi* (the color of ripe seeds), and *khamri* (the color of red wine); (3) *akhdar* (literally green but denoting the color of dark soil) used to refer to a dark northerner; (4) *azrag* (blue) used interchangeably with (5) *aswad* (black), the color used to describe *abids* (slaves) and southern Sudanese. See Al-Baqr al-Affif Mukhtar, "The Crisis of Identity in Northern Sudan: The Dilemma of a Black People with a White Culture," in Fluehr-Lobban and Rhodes, *Race and Identity in the Nile Valley,* p. 216.

32. Colonial-era ethnographers, historians, hydrologists, explorers, and geographers have produced numerous volumes focusing on ethnic identities, narratives of the conquerors, and statistical data on the impact of the Nile on the hinterlands. Arabic language sources provide the histories and genealogies of the Afro-Arab population while dismissing the pre-Islamic kingdoms and populations.

33. Ahmad A. Sikainga, *Slaves into Workers* (Austin: University of Texas Press, 1996); Richard L. Hill and Peter C. Hogg, *A Black Corps d'Elite: An Egyptian Sudanese Conscript Battalion with the French Army in Mexico, 1863–1867, and Its Survivors in Subsequent African History* (East Lansing: Michigan State University Press, 1995).

34. It should also be noted that the same holds for the concept of Christendom with its global claims to sharing the teachings of Christ.

35. One of the most illuminating studies on the gap between the "Islam" of the ruling elite(s) and that of the postmodern Sudanese "volk" is T. Abdou Maliqalim Simone, *In Whose Image: Political Islam and Urban Practices in Sudan* (Chicago: University of Chicago Press, 1994), pp. 168–177, 192–201.

36. Abdelwahab El-Affendi, *Turabi's Revolution: Islam and Power in Sudan* (London: Grey Seal Books, 1991).

37. Alex de Waal and A. H. Abdel Salam, "Islamism, State Power and *Jihad* in Sudan," in Alex de Waal (ed.), *Islamism and Its Enemies in the Horn of Africa* (Bloomington: Indiana University Press, 2004), pp. 100–106; A. Mohamed Salih, "The Bible, the Qur'an and the Conflict in South Sudan," in Niels Kastfelt (ed.), *Scriptural Politics: The Bible and the Koran as Political Models in the Middle East and Africa* (Trenton, NJ: Africa World Press, 2004), pp. 103–112.

38. O'Fahey, "The History of a Frontier," p. 77.

39. Ian Cunnison and Wendy James are two of the few anthropologists who unambiguously pointed out the long-term implications of accepting genealogies as "fact." See Yusuf Fadl Hasan, *Sudan in Africa,* pp. 186–195, 197–211.

40. For the period of European rule, see Terence Ranger, "The Invention of Tradition," in Eric Hobsbawm and Terence Ranger (eds.), *The Invention of Tradition in Colonial Africa* (Cambridge: Cambridge University Press, 1983); Douglas H. John-

son (ed.), *The Upper Nile Province Handbook: A Report on Peoples and Government in the Southern Sudan, 1931,* compiled by C. A. Willis (Oxford: Oxford University Press, for the British Academy, 1995).

41. Fatima Babiker Mahmoud, in her 1984 analysis of the political economy of Sudan, pointed out the nexus between tribal identities and the "economic mode of life in the definition of a tribe." The eruption of conflicts in the country that have been dubbed "tribal" by both Sudanese nationals and foreign observers begs the question of how economic transformations have also altered the contemporary notion of tribalism in Sudan. For details, see Fatima Babiker Mamoud, *The Sudanese Bourgeoisie: Vanguard of Development?* (Khartoum: Khartoum University Press, 1984), p. 13. For a comparative analysis of colonial constructs of identities and their legacies in the contemporary status of former African subjects, see Mahmood Mamdani, *Citizen and Subject: Contemporary Africa and the Legacy of Late Colonialism* (Princeton: Princeton University Press, 1996), pp. 62–108.

42. Adb al-Latif, of mixed Dinka and Nuba slave parentage, emerged as an anticolonial nationalist embodying the complexity of Sudanese identity. For a nuanced reading of the 1924 uprising and the role of Abd al-Latif and contemporaries, see Heather J. Sharkey, *Living with Colonialism: Nationalism and Culture in the Anglo-Egyptian Sudan* (Berkeley and Los Angeles: University of California Press, 2003), pp. 78–80.

43. Sharif Harir provides an excellent study shedding light on the socioeconomic and political linkages between the numerous communities that make up contemporary Darfur. For details on his discussion of the use of interethnic political marriages, military force, and the patron-client relations of the Fur sultanate with other the ethnic groups such as the Zaghawa and others, see "'Arab Belt' vs. 'African Belt': Ethno-Political Conflict in Dar Fur and the Regional Cultural Factors," in Harir and Tvedt, *Shortcut to Decay,* pp. 152–153.

44. For an excellent analysis of the different meanings of "blackness" and its relationship to servility, see John Hunwick and Eve Troutt Powell, *The African Diaspora in the Mediterranean Lands of Islam* (Princeton, NJ: Markus Wiener Publishers, 2002), pp. xviii–xxi, 35–50.

45. See Douglas Johnson, *Nuer Prophets: A History of Prophesy from the Upper Nile in the Nineteenth and Twentieth Centuries* (Oxford: Clarendon Press, 1994) on the role of "prophets" in the Nuba Mountains.

46. For details, see John Garang, *The Call for Democracy in Sudan* (London: Kegan Paul International, 1992), p. 139. See also M. W. Daly and Ahmad Alawad Sikainga (eds.), *Civil War in the Sudan* (London: British Academy Press, 1993).

47. See Sikainga, *Slaves into Workers,* pp. 4–12. On the subject of the Dar Fur dynasties, see R. S. O'Fahey and M. I. Abu Salim, *Land in Dar Fur: Charters and Related Documents from the Dar Fur Sultanate* (Cambridge: Cambridge University Press, 1983). See also J. Spaulding and Lidwien Kapteijns (eds.), *An Islamic Alliance: Ali Dinar and the Sanusiyya, 1906–1916* (Evanston, IL: Northwestern University Press, 1994).

48. The complex conjuncture of political and economic marginalization of Darfur since 1916, the environmental degradation of pasturelands, the emergence of clandestine resistance movements, and the militarization of ethnoregional grievances from 1963 to 2003 faded into oblivion as the debate centered on whether the horrific violence could be called "genocide" or not. For details, see Prunier, *Darfur,* pp. 148–158.

49. See O'Fahey and Abu Salilm, *Land in Dar Fur,* for a general introduction to the region.

50. For a detailed discussion on the nature of crimes committed against civilians and on guerrilla armies, see United Nations, *Report of the International Commission of Inquiry on Darfur to the United Nations Secretary-General* (Geneva: UN, January 25, 2005).

51. Amnesty International UK, "Darfur: Rape as a Weapon of War: Sexual Violence and Its Consequences," July 2004, available at www.amnestyusa.org/countries/sudan/document.do?dz23FE42969B6C168A80256EC900529EDO.

52. Dr. Mukesh Kapila, a medical doctor by training and the UN humanitarian coordinator resident in Khartoum, gave a radio interview to the BBC in Nairobi that highlighted the contradictions between the declarations on genocide from the UN headquarters in New York and the lack of concrete actions on the ground to prevent the loss of lives and destruction of property. See BBC, "Mass Rape Atrocity in Sudan," March 19, 2004.

53. The history of the Dinka, like that of the Nuer and the Shilluk, was brought to the attention of the Western world and came to constitute required reading for post-1945 students of anthropology in institutions of higher learning. The plight of the Dinka, by virtue of their numerical superiority and dispersal both throughout Sudan and globally, has also been widely disseminated through missionaries and the work of Francis Deng, in his versatile capacities as both an academic and an international civil servant. The absence of such an articulate interlocutor for some of the smaller communities has led to a subsuming of the variegated histories of the hundreds of fragmented communities into the framework of these "emblematic" peoples who have come to symbolize "southern Sudan."

54. Among the first generation of venerated historians of Sudanese history are Robert O. Collins, *Land Beyond the Rivers: The Southern Sudan, 1898–1918* (New Haven: Yale University Press, 1971); Holt and Daly, *A History of the Sudan;* and M. W. Daly, *Imperial Sudan: The Anglo-Egyptian Condominium, 1934–1956* (Cambridge, Cambridge University Press, 1991).

55. Roland Segal, *Islam's Black Slaves: The History of Africa's Other Black Diaspora* (London: Atlantic Books, 2001).

56. For details, see Hill and Hogg, *A Black Corps d'Elite.* For a general introduction to both pre-Islamic and Islamic military slavery, see Daniel Pipes, *Slave Soldiers and Islam: The Genesis of a Military System* (New Haven: Yale University Press, 1981). For a sustained comparative inquiry between the evolution of an Islamic polity and the institutionalization of patron-client relations between the slave soldiers and their masters, see Patricia Crone, *Slaves on Horses: The Evolution of the Islamic Polity* (Cambridge: Cambridge University Press, 1980).

57. Romolo Gessi Pasha, *Seven Years in the Sudan—Being a Record of Explorations, Adventures, and Campaigns Against the Arab Slave Hunters,* collected and edited by his son, Felix Gessi (London: Sampson Low, Marston, 1892).

58. Augustus B. Wylde, *'83 to '87 in the Soudan: With Account of Sir William Hewett's Mission to King John of Abyssinia,* vol. 1 (New York: Negro University Press, 1969).

59. Benedict Anderson, *Imagined Communities: Reflections on the Origin and Spread of Nationalism* (London: Verso, 1991).

60. John Garang, *John Garang Speaks,* edited and introduced by Mansour Khalid (London: Kegan Paul International, 1987), p. 128.

61. Sharon Hutchinson, *Nuer Dilemmas: Coping with Money, War, and the State* (Berkeley: University of California Press, 1996). See also Deborah Scroggins, *Emma's War* (New York: Pantheon Books, 2002).

62. Ahmad Alawad Sikainga, "Military Slavery and the Emergence of a Southern Sudanese Diaspora in the Northern Sudan, 1884–1954," in Jay Spaulding and

Stephanie Beswick (eds.), *White Nile, Black Blood: War, Leadership, and Ethnicity from Khartoum to Kampala* (Asmara, Eritrea: Red Sea Press, 2000), p. 25.

63. Garang, *John Garang Speaks,* p. 130.

64. International Crisis Group, *The Khartoum-SPLM Agreement: Sudan's Uncertain Peace,* Africa Report No. 96 (Washington, DC: ICG, July 25, 2005).

65. Jacques Maquet's excellent analysis of the institutionalization of inequality in the former Belgian colonies provides important lessons. See Maquet, *The Premise of Inequality in Ruanda: A Study of Political Relations in a Central African Kingdom* (London: Oxford University Press, 1961).

3

The Geography of Conflict

Geography and war are the products of human activity; war creates geographies of borders, states, empires, and so on, and in turn these geographic entities are the terrain over which peace is maintained or new wars justified. Rather than being as permanent and sedate as a mountain range, the geography of war is as fluid and volatile as a lava flow.[1]

The sudden spread of claims to certain identities in a particular region . . . reflects the development of the social and political situation in that region, rather than the physical ousting of one set of tribes by another.[2]

Ecological borders are, in many cases, also ethnic and cultural borders. . . . Violence is irrational but not incomprehensible. . . . We may not be able to fully understand the rationality of social violence at the level of individuals, but we have a better chance in discerning some of its design and part of its scheme as the collective behavior of a large number of people.[3]

The classical geographers, true to their craft and the literal meaning of their profession, described the earth in its physical dimensions and features. Because it is the base upon which other geographies are built, we begin this chapter by establishing the physical geography of Sudan, which we then link to the country's boundaries, both natural and artificial. We devote the rest of the chapter to the more complex human geography: this includes boundary/frontier making, but also the geographies of human settlement, migration, economic activity, and politics—encompassing (among other matters) authoritative decisions about the use of natural resources, the spatial dimensions of rule and conquest, and, finally, the geography of conflict, which touches all of the geographies but is unique in its power to help explain why some conflicts, such as those that afflict Sudan, configure as they do.

Sudan emerged as a sovereign state in the mid–twentieth century with a multinational territory cobbled together by various rulers and sultans. The spatial ontology[4] of modern Sudan has been shaped not only by its long history of encounters with distant and near regions, but also by the geographic metaphors applied to its territory and its inhabitants. Thus, *bilad as-Sudan* (land of the blacks), the traditional Arabic designation for the non-Arab lands of Africa, was both a geographic and ethnic terminology bequeathed by medieval Arab geographers. The Arab invasions and the transformation of Islam into the political ideology of the ruling Sudanic dynasties also introduced an ideological geography, which divided the *umma* (domain of the believers of Islam) into *dar al-Islam* (abode of peace) and *dar al-harb* (domain of war, domain of the unbelievers). The *umma* itself is an abstract representation of a transnational community within which members of the Islamic faith are embraced as equals.

The geography of conflict in the Sudan is inscribed in the gaps between the idea of the *umma* and the ideology of its proponents pursuing hegemonic policies of Arabization and Islamization as justifications for the territorial expropriation of their conationals (denigrated as "nominal Muslims," *kafirs* [unbelievers] and *abids* [slaves]) and the maintenance of a political system premised on the logic of conquest. Delineating the numerous communities and processes that have at times clashed violently and at other times accommodated each other's needs provides a useful framework for an understanding of twenty-first century Sudan. This geopolitical approach also offers a historical perspective on the emergence of the spatial/geographic identities that characterize Sudan's dissident groups. The conflicts in Sudan have been rooted in both the expropriation of vast tracts of territories by a dominating group as well as by the superimposition of a theological geography that continues to demarcate boundaries between self-defined members of the polity and those consigned to the domain of war, destined to become objects of violence, pillage, and servitude.

Connections, Resources, and Conflicts

The geography of Sudan provides useful insights into identifying recurrent patterns of conflict over resources. Its geographic location, especially its proximity to North Africa and the Red Sea, facilitated the migration of Arab nomads into the Nile Valley and the expansion of their settlements from the Nubian areas in the northeast to the scattered homelands of the Nilotic peoples in south-central Sudan. The vast plains of the country are punctuated on three sides by mountains: to the west the Jebel Marrah, to the east the Red Sea Hills, and on the southern frontier the Didinga Hills and the Dongotona and Imatong Mountains. The Nuba Mountains and Ingessana Hills interrupt the monotonous pattern of the plain in the south-central part of the country and provide haven for the numerous communities that sought shelter from the unremitting demands of tribute by stronger confederacies.

Like the Boma Plateau, which demarcates the border with the Ethiopian highlands, these geographic features have provided natural shelter for a variety of indigenous political communities. Contact with each other and with immigrants from the west and south led to intra-Sudanic hybridization of cultures and the emergence—in the second half of the twentieth century—of a multiracial, multiethnic Sudanese nationalism that challenged the hegemony of the Arabized/Islamized riverain communities of the *awlad al-balad* (children of the land). Such natural enclaves led to the creation of new communities such as those of the Nuba Mountains and Ingessana Hills and the construction of modern ideologies of Sudanism that presented the vision of the New Sudan advanced by the late John de Mabior Garang as a homegrown antidote to Sudanese dependence on imported nationalisms.[5] Garang asserted that all Sudanese were "children of the land," whose claims to equal citizenship and equal access to the wealth of the land require constitutional safeguards in a pluralist Sudan. With his untimely death—a mere seven months after the signing of the Comprehensive Peace Agreement of January 2005 and his accession to the post of vice-president of the nation for three weeks—the prospects diminished that the New Sudan ideology would supplant the enduring hold of Arabization and Islamization, the twin ideological forces that had guaranteed the hegemony of the *awlad al-balad* throughout the first millennium.[6]

It remains to be seen whether the geography of conflict inscribed into modern Sudan that enabled the Arabized Africans in the central riverain areas to displace indigenous communities (who also call themselves "peoples of the homeland") or, worse, place them in servitude, can be negotiated by the armed protagonists of the twenty-first century.[7] It should be noted that such territorial and ideological conflicts are not unique to modern Sudan but continue to flare within many of the Afro-Arab societies, from Mauritania to Mogadishu, shaped by the Arabo-Islamic "civilizing mission."[8] Although the nexus between the construction of new sociopolitical identities (especially the construction of Arabo-Islamic genealogies) and the disenfranchisement and displacement of indigenous ruling systems have been well documented by colonial-era scholars, these confluences have rarely been accorded due attention by policymakers engaged in conflict resolution processes in Sudan, in particular, or the Horn, in general.[9]

Systematic inquiry into the plight of indigenous communities subjected to pillage, enslavement, and conquest by both Sudanese and Abyssinian hegemonic groups yields precious insights (currently limited to a narrow circle of enlightened anthropologists) into understanding the rise and ebb of identity-related, resource-driven conflicts.[10] Failure to address the linkage between geographic displacements and the shifting of sociopolitical identities has contributed to a misunderstanding of the role of historical memories of the long and violent process of displacement and of assimilation into the hybrid political systems that are the embodiment of the ecogeographical region—the Horn of Africa—within which Sudan is embedded.[11]

Mapping the Terrain:
How History and Geography Drew Lines in the Sudan

The long north-south war was triggered by orders from decisionmakers in Khartoum to transfer southern troops to the north. The violence those orders unleashed has been tragically reenacted time and again in ethnically driven bloodletting, itself revealing deep-seated grievances between those who have the protection of the power center in Khartoum and those who are opposed to its hegemony. The territorial conquest and pacification of the south and west were preceded by waves of pioneers who established frontier settlements and alliances—or feuds—with indigenous communities. Western Sudan, with its competing sultanates, was the last to be incorporated into Khartoum's orbit in the early 1900s. This was accomplished through the might of the British Empire, which was determined to limit French influence in northeastern Africa.[12] The defeat of Sultan Ali Dinar of Darfur, and the consolidation of the Anglo-Egyptian Condominium, enabled the areas that were under the Keira dynasty to be settled by pastoral communities seeking more grazing land and water for their cattle and camels. The Baggara Arabs of Kordofan and Darfur, through the submission of their chiefs to Anglo-Egyptian rulers in Khartoum, legitimized their claims over smaller indigenous communities, such as the Berti and Masalit, which were reduced to serf-like status under their Fur and Arab overlords. Except for geographic enclaves—such as the Jebel Marrah, the Nuba Mountains, and the Ingessana Hills—it was the hybridized Sudanese (the Afro-Arabs) who, by adopting the ideology of Arabism, denied their African heritage and altered the demographic and geographic boundaries that had held during the eighteenth and nineteenth centuries. The indigenous communities, which had accepted Islam but had not necessarily been embraced into the modern Islamic republic, began to forge a bond based on their racialized exclusion as "non-Arabs/slaves/Africans." Like the Maroon communities of Brazil and the Caribbean, they managed to nurture their Sudanic heritage in isolation but developed a sense of solidarity with their conationals beyond the *sudd,* who had already risen in rebellion against the hegemony of the riverain *awlad al-balad.*

The Nile, hailed as the source of life, has also been a source of conflict. Before the advent of technological innovations such as steamships and firearms, it had also shielded its people and lands from the gaze of outsiders—Egyptian pharaohs, Greek travelers, Roman centurions, and European empire builders—who sought to unlock its gates.[13] Before the advent of steamships armed with dredgers manned by Ottoman envoys and accompanied by northern Sudanese merchants armed with superior weaponry, the river had constituted a natural barrier that necessitated seasonal migrations—and the forging of mutually beneficial relationships between the various communities that inhabited the land beyond the *sudd*. The desertification of the land north of the second cataract propelled waves of Arab populations into Sudan, where some were accommodated, assimilated, or subjugated, while others attained positions of power. These migrations not only altered the sociobiological fabric of Nilotic society but also transformed its political and economic structures. Thus, the Nile may also be examined as both a bridge between the many peoples of this land and the basis for the formulation of an equitable sharing of the resources of the *bilad as-Sudan*. This perspective may also be equally useful in resolving the unaddressed grievances by the various riparian states whose exclusion from shares of Nile waters has continued to exacerbate tensions in the region.

Sudanese identity is qualified by regional, geographic, or ethnic prefixes. For example, some northern Sudanese communities self-identify as "Arab Muslims" while others might call themselves "non-Arab Muslims," such as the people of the Nuba Mountains and Blue Nile Hills who preserve some of their indigenous customs. There are also West African populations, descendants of the Fulani pilgrims and Hausa traders (locally referred to as "Fallata"), scattered throughout the land and spilling over to the Ethiopian borderlands. In addition, there are various collated communities that as a result of centuries of conquest raids and assimilation now have hyphenated kinship identities, such as the Dinka-Nuer; the Anuak-Nuer of the Upper Nile region or the Dinka-Arab; Arab-Dinka region of the Bahr al-Ghazal and Kordofan and Darfur.

The south, too, has been a region where its inhabitants have been mainly presented to the world as the victims of predatory northern Arab-Muslims. This view neglects the numerous feuds and wars fought between the many southern communities that have confronted each other and engaged in resource wars, leaving behind them a legacy of grievances, memories of slave and cattle raids, and territory lost to stronger groups. This messy reality does not conform to the dominant image of southern Sudanese as a monolithic group of people, often portrayed as noble savages embraced by a Christendom mandated to protect them from its counterpart, the Islamic *umma*. Interesting facts such as the existence of southern Muslims and the role of other non-Arab Muslims in the war between the north and the south were left unmentioned until the jihads of the 1980s and the internecine wars among southern rebels in the 1990s demonstrated that the "politics of God" were a veneer for the scramble for territory and resources.

The Nuer expansion to the east and south was halted only with the arrival of the Anglo-Egyptian overrule, leaving behind hybrid genealogies weaving Dinka and Nuer lines of ancestry. Although these lateral lines of kinship at times provided solidarity between the two Nilotic groups, they also created the basis for intercommunal conflicts that enabled the hegemonic Arabized ruling elites to drive a wedge between "southerners" seeking to establish a territorial state defined by the geographic boundaries separating the north from the south. The alteration of pigmentation that occurred with the "Arab-indigenous" encounter resulted in the production of a phenotype that has come to be known as the "Afro-Arab," distinguished by a skin coloring that can vary from light to dark brown. This enables the outside observer to identify individuals who would commonly be recognized as "northern Sudanese," whereas the external indicators of the hybridization that occurred among the southern peoples are not as obvious.[14] The Nilotic invasions and subordination of other peoples of the south, as well as the Azande kingdom's domination of the peoples of the southern boundaries, have also resulted in the establishment of hyphenated identities, such as the Nuer-Dinka. These new identities in the south may not be as visible as the Afro-Arab identity, but they have nevertheless altered the genealogies of previous generations. Thus, the hybrid identity of the Sudanese is not limited to the encounter with the Arabs but can also be traced to the mixing of groups and the assimilation of vanquished individuals into the communities of the victor. The quest for geographic *lebensraum,* or "living space," by the many groups seeking new resources contributed to the many conflicts that arose in later years.

We see then that the geography of conflict with which we have become so familiar—the north-south divide—also has a southern counterpart that deserves more scrutiny than it has received so far. The competition for resources, water, pasturage, cattle, and people plays a critical role in the conflicts at different historical times. It is only logical that these factors should be taken into account, not only in the examination of the conflict, but also in the quest for solutions that could lead to a sustainable and equitable peace.

Cartography, Mercantilism, and the Politics of Identity

Unlike most other modern African states, Sudan's sprawling domain did not fragment into smaller units but, with few exceptions,[15] emerged into modern statehood with its internally conquered territories virtually intact.[16] The fluid boundaries of the Sudanese conquest state, once financed by *zariba* economies (fortified settlements of slave merchants) and guarded by private militias, have also survived in different forms.[17] Some of the larger *zaraib,* which served as regional depots housing slaves and goods destined for distant markets across the Sahara and the Red Sea, have left a legacy of a "geographic" hierarchy that placed the "northerners" at the top of the socioeconomic and political pyramid of Sudanese society.

This privileged position was sustained by the importation of mounted horsemen armed with firearms who became the guardians of inequality. This innovation ushered in the rise to power of political dynasties that emerged from the encounter of settlers with the indigenous inhabitants of ancient Sudan. The *kubniyyas* (armed trading companies), which grew in tandem with the *jellaba*[18]—petty traders who served as the foot soldiers for the slaving magnates[19]—left in their wake a legacy of conflict between those deemed "enslavable" and inhabiting the *dar al-harb* and those who were accepted into the fold of the *umma*. Sudanese society was thus split into an ideological construct of a "north" and a "south," ignoring the various links between these halves as well as among the regions to the west and east of the Nile.

The cartography of Sudan—a hegemonic "north" with a "southern" subaltern—is a product of the politics of conquest, which accompanied the process of state formation based on an ideological division of the land into believers/masters and unbelievers/slaves. In the wake of the violent penetration of peaceable communities, the material cultures of non-Arab inhabitants and established modes of economic production were disrupted by technological innovations in transportation that altered traditional feuds over land, cattle, and slave raids that existed prior to the Arab invasions from the Maghrib and the Arabian Peninsula.[20] Mounted men on horses and camels forged new homesteads by conquest justified as expanding the frontiers of the *dar al-Islam* by men of commerce and religion. In addition to territorial wars of conquest, the patriarchal displacement of the indigenous matrilineal kinship networks through marriages between Arab settlers and the women of indigenous ruling elites enabled wealthy slave merchants and "wise men" from east and west to penetrate Sudanic societies, a development that added Islam (and Christianity) to their plethora of ancestral divinities.

Unfortunately, both the patriarchal and militant thrust of the Arabo-Islamic conquest struck at the core of the matrilineal and accommodative body politic of the pre-Islamic era. The *zariba* economy of the wealthy slave merchant Zubayr al-Rahma, which financed the conquest of the Bahr al-Ghazal, Equatoria, and Darfur, with the support of many indigenous communities, attests to the mercantilist aspects of the gradual conquest and subordination of Sudanic communities.[21] Some traditional communities collapsed with the onslaught of the men on horses and camels who altered the pace and objects of traditional wars. Others left their fields, wells, and grazing grounds and established new homesteads, initiating what was to become the beginning of more displacements and the multiple (dis)connections between birthplaces and new homelands. Although religion has been featured as the force fueling the conflicts that have arisen in various parts of Sudan since the seventh century, the roots of many conflicts lie in disputes over land, water, and mineral resources, which have been accompanied by radical cartographic and genetic remapping of the lands once traversed by the many peoples who followed the rhythm of the River Nile and its many tributaries.

But the Sudan is not simply a haphazard agglomeration of conquest states, nor is it simply the product of restless migration by its native inhabitants and marauding neighbors. Rather, the process by which the medieval *bilad as-Sudan* was transformed into the modern Jumhuriyat as-Sudan (Republic of Sudan) can be better understood as a geography of conflict, where the contours of the giant nation have been drawn and redrawn not only by both indigenous and exogenous elites who captured the power center, where the darker and lighter halves of the River Nile meet, but also by the many streams of peoples and cultures that constitute Sudan. The medieval geographers' conventional wisdom that the land between the Atlantic Ocean and the Red Sea constituted the *bilad as-Sudan* denoted a basic reality because the inhabitants were, in fact, linked by migration, conquest, local dominion, and sociocultural intermixing.

These territories and their inhabitants have undergone tumultuous upheavals and sociopolitical revivals, events obscured by the nationalisms of those seeking to fit the many histories and transformations of the identities of its peoples into a rigid organizing ideology that is antithetical to the duality/multiplicity of the Sudanese polity.[22] Sudan's polity reflects the many geographies that have come together—some willingly, others under coercion. Much like the River Nile with its many tributaries and countless streams, the Sudanese polity links its Sahelian-Saharan elements with its equatorial and Arabian sinews, and its multiracial and multilingual body politic streams outward from its eastern and western embankments and the length of the life-giving Nile.

Remapping Sudan: The Invention of Cartographic Identities

From Wadi Halfa to Omdurman, the *awlad al-balad* predominated and were recognized by European explorers, missionaries, and colonial administrators as "northern" Sudanese. The "eastern" region was one of the earliest areas to face the Arab invasions, which led to the demise of Nubia's Christian civilization. Stretching southward from the third cataract at Dongola to Sennar, the eastern region is arguably the earliest site of Sudan's resource wars. The ancient gold mines of the Red Sea Hills, as early as the ninth century, had resulted in the "formation of an Arab frontier-society in Beja territory—a development which had repercussions upon both al Muqurra and Egypt when an Arab adventurer, al-

Umari, made himself virtually the independent ruler of the 'Land of the Mines.'"[23] From Atbara to Suakin, to Port Sudan and beyond the Sudan-Eritrea borders lies the terrain of the tenacious Beja people, who have maintained a great deal of their own language and culture and who aspire to attain a modicum of coexistence as one of the oldest "peoples of the homelands" rather than as either an "African" or "Arab" people. The struggles for equity of the Beja Congress[24] and the efforts of the National Democratic Alliance to maintain an alliance of the numerous regional guerrilla armies indicate that the northeast is far from quiescent in its relations to the power centers at Khartoum.

From the Red Sea Hills and the Nubian heartland we find the starkest challenge to the binary representation of the Sudanese conflict as north vs. south and/or Arab vs. African. "Eastern" Sudan, with the longest history of resource exploitation, displacement, and disfranchisement, demands more attention as the site for the fusion of the indigenous Beja-Nilotic-Arab strands of the Sudanese entity. Its long history of resource exploitation—as a source of gold and slaves for the Egyptian and Mediterranean markets, and the partial "Arabization" that failed fully to assimilate the indigenous culture and ancient language—presents some fascinating possibilities for the quest for peace in the current conflict being waged by the eastern rebels. The conflict in eastern Sudan spills over to kinfolk across the seamless borders with Eritrea and Ethiopia, and across the islands littering the Red Sea. Whether it is the quaintly named Rashaida Lions, the Beja Congress, or the more conventional National Democratic Alliance, the interests of this region have been subordinated to those of the central riverain elites at Khartoum and the guardians of Egypt's interests (water, energy, geopolitics) on Nile waters.[25] The topographic diversity of this area as well as the heterogeneity of its inhabitants, who traverse between the foothills of the Red Sea and the embankments of the fifth and sixth cataracts, has been lost to analysts seduced by the concept of this area as the northeastern hinterland of the Egyptian hegemon.[26] The conflicts emanating from this region have been rooted in the struggle for gold in antiquity, for slaves and land in medieval times, and in the quest for political space amid the fragmentation of a Beja polity caught in the clutches of the first phases of a modernization and industrialization in which considerations of equity and dignity have been lost.[27]

The western expanse from the confluence of the Blue and White Niles to Lake Chad—encompassing the savannah lands of Kordofan and Darfur—connects the country to western Africa, while the Congo-Nile basin forms the boundaries with central and eastern Africa. Sudan's southwestern boundaries are portals to the vast hinterland of the medieval *bilad as-Sudan,* while the northern deserts and coastal areas provided entries to those seeking to unravel the mysteries of the Nile. In the south, where the swamplands mesh with the gallery forests, is where the meeting of the Nilotic peoples with those of the Congo basin typically occurs. These geoportals have placed the country at the confluence of the four major civilizations that have shaped the history of the continent: Pharaonic Egypt, Sudanic West Africa, Arabo-Islamic-Ottoman, and European.

These "civilizational" encounters were almost inevitably accompanied by conflict over Sudan's resources—water, pasturage, cattle, and land. The geography of Sudan has made it one of the continent's "marchlands": peoples pushing south from the Mediterranean shores, east from the central Sahel, west from the eastern Horn and the Red Sea, and north from the equator. Upon entering Sudan from all directions, they encountered established communities in the land of the two Niles that challenged the newcomers' attempts to control the region and natural resources. In the centuries that followed these periodic encounters with outsiders, ethnolinguistic and religious identities were gradually—but indelibly—transformed, giving rise to the current mosaic of hybrid communities of Arabized Africans and Africanized Arabs.

These geographic categories have remained more familiar to Western analysts than have the many peoples of Sudan who have yet to negotiate through the complex legacies of the past to forge a modern framework guaranteeing equitable relations of former rivals, allies, patrons, clients, masters, and slaves. The porous borders and the ease with which traders and religious schools and militias traversed the vast territory had not forced the Sudanese to develop long-term relationships based on mutually beneficial relations. With the freezing of the geoportals that had made Sudan the fusion of cultures and peoples from all parts of the world, the ancient trekking was halted, and some sought to consolidate their hegemony over others while some became accidental prisoners of geography.[28]

Whereas the process of the Arabization of Sudan continues to be a subject of interest to both Sudanic and Western scholars, the Islamization of Africa from Sahelian Africa has not been adequately addressed. That Islam—like Christianity—in Africa differs from the orthodoxy established in the Arabian Peninsula, and that it is manifested as a synthesis of indigenous belief systems that combine Islamic tenets, has been duly acknowledged. But what has been neglected is the process by which West African Muslims and anticolonial Islamic leaders have contributed to the making of modern Sudan and the state-society conflicts that have flared up in the twenty-first century.

Traversing the Land:
In Pursuit of Salvation, Submission, Wealth, and Water

Sudan served as a beacon to African Muslims waging their own wars against European (infidel) empire builders.[29] Fulani "holy men" had established settlements "scattered throughout Darfur and Kordofan with the Blue Nile representing the easterly limit of their main spread." They established centers for the Qadriyya religious brotherhood traveling throughout the land and leaving their cultural imprint, a legacy of yet another hybridized population.[30] These were joined by nineteenth-century Hausa traders, who flourished during the seasons of West African pilgrimages to Mecca land. The Hausa traders were regarded as "peddlers" (akin to the Sudanese *jellaba,* the Abyssinian Jeberti, and the Indian Banyan), who "traversed the savannah and forest belts trading slaves, kola nuts, cloth, leather, and other goods from their homeland.[31] Until the end of World War II, the British added to these multiple migrations and settlements by exporting Nigerian peasants to work in the newly established cotton plantations in the Ghezira.

What has emerged in twenty-first-century Sudan is a community of Sudanese descended from the Islamic kingdoms of West Africa who are competing for land, resources, and political representation against the *awlad al-balad,* who claim descent from Arabia and the indigenous Sudanic communities. The pilgrim-migrants of the nineteenth century, known as Takarir—who had established their membership in the *umma* by virtue of their adherence to the tenets of Islam and their literate *fakis,* and whose progeny in the twentieth and twenty-first centuries sought citizenship rights as *muwalid* (born into Sudan)—exposed the hypocrisy of Khartoum's ruling elites' invocation of Islam as a unifying factor for all Sudanese.[32]

The familial linkages between Sudanese and their kin across state boundaries deserve more attention from policymakers, who tend to ignore the role that kinship plays in either easing tensions between rivals or facilitating dialogue. Some Sudanese of West African descent have played important roles in peace talks sponsored by the African Union (AU) in the Nigerian capital, although they did not wield the degree of power enjoyed by their conationals claiming Arab descent. These unequal relations among Sudanese with membership in the ruling circles were reflected in statements by Dr. Ali al-Hag Muhammad that his presence was justified because "the GOS high-level delegation . . . were too busy in Khartoum."[33] An understanding of the intricate political relationships linking western Sudan—Darfur and Kordofan—hinges on an awareness of the rise and ebb of violence from the grassroots, where communities empowered and armed by the Khartoum government seek to secure water, land, and pasturage to ensure the survival of their particular communities at the expense of others. No one understood this better than Garang, whose vision of a New Sudan was based on an acknowledgment of the unifying potential of the modern concept of citizenship for the majority of disenfranchised Sudanese alienated by Khartoum's hegemonic elites:

> I greet each and everyone of you in all parts and workplaces of our great country, in the kitchens and schools.[34]

The SPLA/SPLM belongs to all those who work in the factories and earn so little . . . to those who wash carts . . . to those forgotten citizens who crowd under very difficult conditions . . . and in all the slums of our cities . . . to those in the North who have been callously displaced from your ancestral homes, to you the Hadendowa and the Ingessana who never know of schools in your villages, to you the Nuba and Baggaras of the Centre, to you the Fur, Zeghawa and Masalit of the West, to you all, the SPLA is yours.[35]

Suppose we solve the problem of the South, we will soon have to solve the problem of the Jebels [the Nuba Mountains] because the Nuba can also take arms; after that the problem of the Beja; and so forth. It is a national, not a Southern problem that we must address.[36]

It is often forgotten that the Sudan is not just North and South. The Sudan is also West, East and Centre, no matter what definitions you wish to attach to these labels. . . . All patriots must appreciate the reality that we are a new breed of Sudanese who will not accept being fossilized into sub-citizens in the "Regions."[37]

Understanding the SPLM/A's mobilization of these diverse groups of Sudan during the 1980s and 1990s around the concept of a new vision for the country—regardless of their geographic location, ethnic origin, or proximity to power centers in Khartoum—may enable policymakers to give due weight to the concept of a New Sudan rather than dismiss it as an impossible dream. The relationships that were fostered between political leaders and guerrillas in the 1980s and 1990s need to be viewed not only as short-term tactical alliances but also as long-term strategic ones that can bring about Sudan's transformation from a modern caliphate to a multinational state capable of governing the inhabitants of the west, south, north, and center as full-fledged citizens of the nation. The historical past of inequities and subaltern relations of indigenous as well as settler populations need to be addressed in the crafting of citizenship laws to ensure equal membership in the Sudanese polity of the twenty-first century.

The history of Kordofan and Darfur, which are linked to the kingdoms of Bornu, Wadai, and Bagirmi, has produced intricate genealogies linking Islamic figures of West Africa with those of the Red Sea. Even more striking than the fascinating construction of lineages are the quintessential representatives of the Afro-Arab encounter—the Baggara cattle and camel herders—who survived the demands of the tribute-seeking sultanates of Darfur, Bornu, Wadau to the west, and of Sennar to the east, and carved up "ancestral homelands" or *dar*(s) of their own.[38] What began as the search for wells and wetlands led to the establishment of gardens and oasis settlements, resulting in periodic conflicts and negotiated settlements between the newcomers and the indigenous pastoralists and cultivators who claimed the moisture-rich areas for cattle grazing. Western and southern Darfur and southern Kordofan, where the land and pasturage have long been contested, have been the battlegrounds for both ecological and political feuds. The second half of the twentieth century witnessed the catastrophic impact of drought conditions, which in combination with centuries of ill-governance, unleashed the fury of the inhabitants.

Whereas the economy and society of all the other regions of Sudan are dominated by the Nile, Kordofan and Darfur are the two areas that are dependent on rainfall, water wells, and oasis settlements rather than on the vagaries of floodwater. For example, the occasional failure of the seasonal rains in the north triggered conflicts in the Nuba Mountains, Ingessana Hills, and Abyei, due to out-of-season encroachment by the Baggara herdsmen into the areas of the indigenous cultivators and migrant agropastoralists from the southern borderlands. With the Islamization process, triggered by the Funj dynasty in the east, and the westward migrations of West African *al-muminin* (faithful) fleeing European incursions during the nineteenth century, most of the region's inhabitants were converted to Islam. Conversion to the religion of the conquering armies—be it Islam in Africa or Christianity in Latin America—did not guarantee the conquered communities relief from pillage and plunder.

The hardy nomads of Darfur and Kordofan, whose encounter with the diverse indigenous residents of the region was fitfully interrupted by slave raids and counterraids as well as feuds over wells and pastureland, were all lumped into a category of "western" Sudanese. Considering that these two historically distinct territories comprise an area of 850,000 square kilometers and link Sudan with the constant influx of settler-immigrants from West Africa and North Africa, this constructed identity served to veil the sociopolitical differences while highlighting a tense relationship based on the increasingly asymmetrical sharing of wells and grasslands.

The absence of perennial streams highlighted the importance of control or accommodation of different groups whose survival depended upon permanent wells for their human settlements as well as pasturage for their cattle. This region, in particular, highlights the contradictions between the organizing ideologies of the postcolonial Sudanese—based on Arabism and Islamism—and the racialized inequalities that undergirded the seemingly unifying geographic identities that would place subaltern communities such as the Dajo, Shatt, and Berti[39] with the loose tribal confederations of the Messiriya, Humur, Hawazma, and Rizeygat Baggara of Kordofan and Darfur. The majority of the smaller polities that were forced into servile labor by the centuries-long slave raiding, such as the Nuba, Berti, Dajo, Dinka, Zande, and many others, have yet to make the socioeconomic and political transition from the stigmatized legacy of being descended from slaves (*'abid*) to the status fitting a coreligionist, a citizen, and a brother (*atig*). This exclusion from membership from the polity as well as their relegation to positions of inferiority to their Arab compatriots led a number of twentieth-century descendants of these people to wage wars to regain their patrimony as well as pride and dignity as citizens.[40]

Wars of Patrimony, Borders, and Rivers

As old ties to ancestral patrimonies were severed, new ones were forged as the smaller groups sought protection within larger communities or refuge in difficult-to-access hillsides—such as the Ingessana of the Tabi Hills, the inhabitants of the Abyei, and the Nuba of Kordofan. The Ingessana, like the Nuba, represent one of the oldest indigenous communities ensconced in the craggy mountainous terrain watered by the tributaries of the Upper Blue Nile and the White Nile.[41] Their traditional kinship networks and alliances enabled them to defend their communities from slavers and forced conversions. Until the early twentieth century, they had preserved their internal social structures and consistently defied efforts by the armies of the *jellaba*, Egyptian expeditions seeking gold and slaves, Abyssinian slave raiders and "pacification" campaigns of Anglo-Egyptian forces. In the twenty-first century, their independence in the face of adversity and their alliance with the southern guerrillas led to their inclusion in the historic Comprehensive Peace Agreement, enabling them to exercise their right to choose to join the south or remain in the north.

Borderland peoples, such as those of Abyei, sought to compromise with the incoming groups of nomads, who competed for the same sources of water and pasturage. Displaced by the military might of the Arabized communities, they were violently dispossessed of their land, cattle, and belongings and forced to disperse throughout the nation, exemplifying the failure of equitable sharing between natives and settlers.[42] Left without viable options for coexistence, the Ngok Dinka of Abyei joined the southern guerrillas and emerged with a voice to choose their political community rather than remain prisoners of imposed boundaries. Other transplanted homesteaders, such as the Nuba, made their home on the "archipelago" of hills bordering the north-south divide. By mid–twentieth century, the Nuba people, who had been depopulated by the unrelenting slave raids of their encroaching Arabized neighbors, spearheaded a struggle affirming their indigenous rights and their membership in the pan-African community and celebrating their "blackness" with pride.[43] The Ingessana, Ngok Dinka, and Nuba—formerly dispossessed, dispersed, and resettled—exemplify how Sudan of the first millennium failed to recognize its constituent selves and create the needed space for mutually beneficial coexistence. The organizing ideologies of Arabization and Islamization created a wide chasm between the ideals of the *umma* and the practice of its members. The marcher lords of Islamized Sudan plunged the territory into varying degrees of conflict over geography, identity, and the resources needed to sustain the many peoples rooted in the ancient land, the incoming waves of settlers, and the resulting progeny who now crisscross the length and breadth of the land.

The so-called Scramble for Africa—of which the earliest protagonists were Egypt's many southern expeditions to control the resources of the Nile and its hinterlands—further aggravated the geography of conflict that has plagued Sudan since antiquity.[44] In the eighteenth and nineteenth centuries, with the arrival of newer invaders, the Turks and their European rivals, the cartography of the medieval *bilad as-Sudan* was transformed to accommodate new pressures in the lands where the Nile begins its northward voyage. To the east of the Nile and along the Red Sea coast, epic battles were fought by both Arab and non-Arab peoples to stave off the ever expanding reach of the British Empire. Multiracial Sudanese—volunteers, freedmen, and slave regiments hailing from east, center, west, north, and south—rallied around the banner of the Mahdiyya. Equally, the same types and numbers of Sudanese rallied around the Turkiyya. Their many stories and even more complex motives, failures, and successes have yet to be narrated in ways that would dispel the geographic myths that only northerners and westerners fought for the Mahdi.[45]

Southern troops also fought as vanguards of the Mahdi's *amirs,* as did the eastern Beja (the subjects of Rudyard Kipling's ode to the "fuzzy-wuzzies" who broke the "British Square").[46] The non-Arab peoples of the Nuba Mountains gave refuge to the Mahdi and his followers, but when its *makks* refused to join his movement, they were chained and marched to Omdurman in a distorted reenactment of the prophet Muhammad's *hegira.*[47] Unlike the original journey, which led to the victorious return of the prophet and his (voluntary) companions, the Mahdist coercive removal of dissenting indigenous peoples from their homelands and (at times) transforming them into chattel of the victors, the Nuban exodus marked the emergence of a self-conscious subaltern diaspora composed of returning prodigal sons and daughters of the jebel accompanied by other displaced Sudanese—their comrade-in-arms in their flight from the Mahdists—who joined their host communities in the Nuba Mountains.

A century later, the Nuba Mountains became the bastion of pan-Sudanic resistance[48] to the regimes of Sadiq al-Mahdi, Omar Bashir, Hassan Turabi, and their murahaleen militias who, like their nineteenth-century predecessors, fought for power and control of resources, which they justified as a "war for Islam" where the bounties of the land were reaped by the *awlad al-balad* while the non-Arabized Sudanese were displaced, disenfranchised, and relocated to the margins of the nation.[49] The Mahdist period, 1881–1898, consolidated and centralized the hegemonic position of the *awlad al-balad* and institutionalized the marginalization of the other members of the Sudanic polity. Feeding off the localized anger and grievances of Sudanese against Turko-Egyptian rule, the *ansar* left behind depopulated hamlets, where men were conscripted and women and children were packed off into bondage.

In September 1898, following the Battle of Karari, Lord Kitchener's Anglo-Egyptian army, backed by its anti-Mahdist Sudanese allies, defeated Khalifa Abdullahi and ousted him from his seat of power in Omdurman. As the Mahdist citadel crumbled, it disgorged forced converts, chained immigrants, recalcitrant sultans and *makks* of the Nuba and Blue Nile Hills, along with some former *amirs* and the Jihadiyya (slave troops) who had guarded the Omdurman garrison.[50] Sudan's millenarian reign of terror ended because of the lack of fit between the religious, protonationalist discourse of the Mahdist state and the ideals of the *umma,* which, in principle, embraced its constituents and invested them with the dignity of full membership. Instead, following the death of the Mahdi and the investiture of Khalifa Abduallahi as his main successor, the imperative of territorial conquest and the profits of the slave economy were the driving forces of the centralized state.[51] Wreaking havoc on both Arab and non-Arab communities as well as placing in bondage both Muslims and non-Muslims, the *ansar* created a deep well of resentment that gradually led to the forging of alliances between the disparate groups arrayed against the Mahdist state and its *zariba* magnates.

The post-Mahdist period witnessed a dramatic shift in the demographic settlement patterns of the jebel, which included Arab and non-Arab communities that had been displaced by the sixteen years of coercive state-building wars spearheaded by the *ansar* and their followers. The return of the diasporic Nuba to their homelands—accompanied by battle-hardened, detribalized ex-slaves—provided the conditions for the earliest gathering of non-Arabized Muslims hitherto excluded from the *umma* by the ruling strata of the *awlad al-balad.* The multiracial regiments of western Sudan who rallied against the Mahdiyya as well as the Turkiyya enabled the young sultan Ali Dinar of Dar Fur to carve out his mini-empire and preside over the heinous trade in slaves and ivory with Egypt and Libya, which brought him into confrontation with the encroaching armies of France and the hegemonic designs of Great Britain. The sultanate of Dar Fur's loss of autonomy and its inclusion in the conquest empire ruled from Khartoum provided the contours of the modern territorial state of Sudan—a vast region that remains mired in regional conflicts with distant roots in the second half of the first millennium.

The battles over the bounties of the Nile River that had pitted the southern region against the north and their Egyptian allies were early indicators of the ecological wars that presented as ethnic-religious wars. The slicing off the mineral-rich region of Hofrat en Nahas—historically a part of the south—and its status as part of the north begs the question of what the requirements are for belonging to that geographic region. Wealth—grassland, water, minerals, and oil—seems to be the concrete answer provided by the many divisions and redivisions of the map. While Hofrat en Nahas has a long-standing link with the south and Abyei straddles the north-south divide, the Blue Nile's most recent creation of Wahda State, carved out of the Upper Nile, can only be attributed to the discovery of oil.

The internal boundaries of Sudan have been redrawn frequently, but with little or no consensus from the country's inhabitants, who have been plagued by famine, drought, and death as they seek the right to a life of dignity and a share in the wealth of the land. Nowhere is this more evident than in the land beyond the *sudd*—which has come to be known as the "southern problem" for rulers from Khartoum and as the struggle for the right of self-determination for the Sudanese who have historically borne the brunt of Arabization and Islamization.

The "South" of Sudan: Yesterday's Dispossessed, Today's Inheritors?

Sudan attained independence in January 1956 with a total of nine provinces: six located in the north and three in the south, with an official population of 10,262,536.[52] By 1994, the internal boundaries had been redrawn producing twenty-six states. The southern provinces were further balkanized and redrawn to include as part of the north resource-rich areas in Upper Nile and the historic Hofrat en Nahas in Bahr al-Ghazal. In 2005, the signing of the Comprehensive Peace Agreement between the SPLM/A and the GOS heralded a new era where the rights of the dispossessed of the south to enjoy the fruits of their land were acknowledged.[53]

This was not the first time that agreements had been signed and discarded, but after more than a century of experiencing the most brutal appropriation of their waterways, peoples, and cattle by alien powers (since 1821), it appeared that the grievances of the Sudanese of the south had been duly acknowledged, leaving room for hope for a resolution of the wars that had bled the country since the eve of its independence. Nevertheless, memories of betrayed promises hung over the cautious optimism that underscored the conditions for the 2005 peace agreements, allayed by the conditions embedded in the CPA that, should members of the hegemonic elite in Khartoum renege on this latest accord, the south could exercise its right to secession.[54] The death of Garang in a helicopter crash in July 2005 occasioned rioting in Khartoum and Juba, casting a pall on the prospects for a smooth transition from war to peace.

The 1974 Addis Ababa Agreement provided a short-lived unified administrative structure for the autonomous south, which was then redivided back into three separate provinces in 1983. In 1994, following a decade of systematic campaigns of ethnic cleansing by the government army and its paramilitary militias, Sudan was divided into twenty-six states, some of which were reconfigured to coincide with parcels of land targeted for drilling.[55] Climactic changes, and displacements triggered by the guerrilla wars in the south, were exacerbated by the preliminary excavations for the construction of the Jonglei Canal, with the objective of augmenting the volume of water transported to Egypt to be shared by the signatories of the Nile Waters Agreement of 1959.[56]

As mapmakers drew many lines across the symbolic face of the nation, pastoralists and cultivators alike were evicted from their lands, and their political and legal predicaments increased with the rise of northern and southern militias, who—like their historic predecessors of the Jihadiyya (slave troops of the Mahdiyya)—heaped chaos and misery upon those unfortunate enough to stand in the way of the exploitation of hydrocarbon/hydrological resources.[57] As the northern militias, the murahaleen and the mujahidin, drove communities from their ancestral homes, their actions were paralleled by southern progovernment militias—all purportedly in the name of an ill-defined jihad or in the interest of preserving the "unity" of the nation.

The conflicts raging in Sudan embrace the needy, the greedy, and those who seek peace with dignity. In the ranks of the aggrieved are (1) the *naziheen* (the displaced) throughout the land—south, east, central, north, and west; (2) subaltern or detribalized "blacks"—stigmatized by a slave past and exploited as uncompensated laborers within the tribal hierarchy of the larger Arabized and non-Arabized communities of Kordofan and Darfur, condemned to a permanent condition of territorial and political homelessness; (3) transplanted indigenous communities that have preserved their culture and territorial claims to resources, such as the Beja, Nuba, Ingessana, Abyei, who have been grafted onto the larger northern tribal confederacies or southern clan systems; and (4) migrants to Sudan, categorized as "westerners," as well as refugees from the Eritrean lowlands whose families have settled in eastern towns and rural enclaves, seeking membership in the Sudanese polity rather than repatriation to the now independent nation of Eritrea. The various promulgations of "jihads" against coreligionists since the 1980s have fused resource wars propelled by land hunger and greed with wars of ethnic cleansing. The efforts to bring closure to the north-south war may be the first to pave the way for institutionalizing the rule of law in a pan-Sudanic polity, but it should be noted that a just peace cannot be recognized without a public acknowledgment of the injustices of the past and an equally public commitment to a future of reconciliation.[58]

The barriers to equal citizenship and an equitable peace are hidden in the interstices of the historical processes by which waves of settlers expropriated from indigenous inhabitants their liberty, their land, and the fruits of their labor. Among the many narratives of the numerous hybridized communities, such as the Messiriya-Humur Baggara of southwestern Kordofan and southeastern Darfur, we find a demonstration of the geography of war, which in turn necessitates a better understanding of the spatial ontology that has produced an entrenchment of hegemonic groups over numerous communities reduced to subaltern status. Ian Cunnison's account of oral "traditions" used to justify the expulsion of indigenous inhabitants and the establishment of the *dars* continues to be instructive in our quest for understanding the genesis of contemporary resource wars.

> The most commonly recounted tradition among the Humur is that they undertook the journey to evade the demands of the Sultan of Wadai. When they reached the land called Denga, whose centre was the place now known as the Muglad, they found a pagan people called Dajo and Shatt in possession and drove them out. The Humur quarreled successively with the other Arab tribes that had accompanied them, battled them all the away, and retained the place for themselves. It has since remained the headquarters (the dar) of the tribe.[59]

This construction of a territorial claim based on might but justified by the religious ideology of Islamization has led to what Celestin Monga has aptly and poetically termed the "politics of God," shedding some light on how, over time, fluid identities become imprisoned in rigid categories. In the early years of the twenty-first century, the world witnessed a more brutal reenactment of "driving those in possession of the desired land out" as the crises in Darfur escalated from resource-driven conflicts to crimes against humanity.[60] The plight of the Sudanese of this region, which has been reduced to easily digestible, not necessarily accurate, sound bytes by the Western media, continues to present ahistoricized reportage that diminishes the role of geography in the unfolding humanitarian crises. Without a well-grounded understanding of the ideologies and theologies of war and peace, the pattern from the distant past continues to be repeated as "settlers who have become natives" fight to the death to maintain their "established" rights to resources when faced by new settlers seeking access to diminishing resources. With the discovery of oil in areas such as Muglad—the ancestral homelands of the transplanted Dajo and Shatt—the stakes are even higher than in those distant days when defeated communities could find new homesteads.

The conventional geographic divide of Sudan as northern, southern, western, and eastern does not shed any light on the multiple identities that exist in the areas so designated. The "peopling" of the Sudan discussed in the previous chapter provides a bird's-eye view of how this vast land was transformed from a terra incognita protected by its deserts, hills, and swamps, to an arena of contestation between migrant settlers, indigenous communities, and those who would seek to subject those communities, to the alien rule of distant European empires. What has yet to be studied is the process of "Nilotization," triggered by the movements of the indigenous inhabitants of the Nile Valley and its vast hinterlands stretching from the eastern and western banks of the White and Blue Niles to the Lake Chad basin.

The fusion of a regional—that is, geographic—identity with an ethnically constructed identity, which generated conventional terms that became fashionable with authors of travelogues and with mapmakers, is at the root of the numerous confusions about the so-called north-south, Arab-African conflicts."[61] These are terms that not only confuse but also conceal a deeper, more complex and, in the end, more revealing reality: that of shifting identities resulting from a continuous history of restive migratory movement, resource wars, internal conflicts, and imperial subordination. The ancient population shifts recorded in archaeological reports, buttressed by the findings of concrete remains of nomadic civilizations in the desert areas, should serve as beacons to those seeking to understand the distant history of all the peoples that made up the Nile civilization. The transformation of the peoples of the contemporary western regions of Sudan—spanning the length of the country from the arid desert areas on the border with Egypt to the resource-rich areas in Hofrat en Nahas, Abyei, the Nuba Mountains, Bahr al-Ghazal and Equatoria—have yet to be undertaken with a view to understanding the ties that bind the peoples of Sudan.

The anthropological and historical studies of the most-studied Nilotic communities, such as the Shilluk, Dinka, Nuer, and Anuak, provide documentation of the various trajectories of migrations that crisscrossed the entire territory. The impact of the Nilotic centrifugal push in pursuit of water, pasturage, and arable land—spanning millennia—have yet to be analyzed in the context of the hybridization of the Sudanic peoples, who have all been homogenized as "southerners," "blacks," or, more recently, "Africans." Their traditional forms of socioeconomic governance captured the attention of colonial anthropologists, who focused on the inherent political advantages of centralized versus decentralized structures among the Nilotes. The end result was numerous volumes on "emblematic" southern peoples such as the Nuer, the Dinka, and, to a lesser extent, the Shilluk. What was ignored was their agency as triggers of geographic, demographic, and political transformation of the *bilad as-Sudan*. This dearth of empirical knowledge encompassing all aspects of the socioeconomic, historical, and political links between the Nilotic/Sudanic peoples and their diverse progenies has proved to be one of the major stumbling blocks in the quest for peace in the intrasouth, intranorth, and north-south conflicts that threaten to tear the country apart.

The Ties That Bind and Divide:
Settler Versus Native, Slave Economies, and
Hyphenated Identities in Comparative Perspective

Identifying historical parallels with other regions in the world may help us place the weight of the past on the contemporary dilemmas faced by the

Sudanese. Parallels can be drawn between Sudan and many other societies, including Brazil, South Africa, and the United States. Although at first glance their differences seem greater than their similarities, a closer look at their precolonial and colonial pasts, their "organizing ideologies," and the racial-economic divide that continues to polarize their multicultural communities reveals parallels in historic wars waged over resources—human and material—and the accompanying construction of new identities that transformed the settlers of past centuries into the "natives" of the new millennium.[62] In this long process, indigenous communities were disenfranchised, displaced, and denigrated and became subaltern communities to the settlers. In the new millennium, both regions have continued to experience the resurgence of political movements seeking to carve out political space(s) within which to exercise economic, social, and political "rights" as equal members of the postcolonial multination state. In both the old and new worlds, the dominant discourse had been mired in "master-slave" narratives,[63] "miscegenation,"[64] supremacist ideologies, the right of the disenfranchised to redress.[65] But scant attention has been paid to the transformation of the settlers of the first millennium into "citizens" with hegemonic rights over the disenfranchised and hybridized "natives."[66] It is crucial that those seeking to understand the conflicts in Sudan and the obstacles to peace must adjust their analytical lenses to include the sociopolitical grievances of past centuries with the contemporary demands for economic redress and political enfranchisement.

In contemporary Sudan, the wars in the north, south, and west appear to be racial, ethnoregional, and religious. A closer look at the identity of the numerous groups confronting one another nevertheless reveals that Sudanese, like other peoples, forge their alliances not solely on primordial ties of kinship and religion, but also on rational calculations of economic well-being and maximal utilization of available resources. In the south, despite the conventional belief that all "southerners" are united against the "Arab-Islamic" government of Khartoum, one finds that disparate southern communities are aligned with the government in opposition to guerrillas of the SPLM/A, which claims to represent "all the peoples of the South," and with the mandate to create a New Sudan that would maintain the territorial integrity of the country.

The factionalism of southern guerrillas and their engagement in committing atrocities against southern civilians demonstrates that unity is not skin-deep. Nor does slavery or the legacy of slavery alone lead to ethnic hatreds and rivalries. Distant memories of injustice and disenfranchisement are woven into nationalist or protonationalist ideologies and justify the use of violence over groups regarded as opponents. Both intrasouthern and intranorthern violence is fueled by a political past, fragmented along ethnic/clan lines or ideological rifts that have been adroitly utilized by the ruling elites of Sudan since independence. The contemporary state of disarray among southern communities, which has led to the alliance of some groups with the government in Khartoum while others drift in and out of the SPLM/A, needs to be understood as resource wars waged either by proxy or by competing armed groups in the south.

In the west, where long-term feuds over grazing rights and access to water wells exploded into a spiral of violence culminating in crimes against humanity, one finds that the fighting camps are not divided between "Arabs" and "black Africans" as portrayed by the international media. Rather, one finds that Darfurians, like their conationals in northern Sudan, consist of many shades of blackness, varying degrees of religious adherence to the Islamic tenets decreed by theocratic leaders in Khartoum, and varying claims to "Africanity" and "Arabness."[67] The presence of the Takarir or Muwalidin (descendants of Fulani pilgrims and Hausas traders and those "born to Sudan") forces us to question the assumption of solidarity based on identification with a particular race, ethnicity, region, or geography.[68] The Darfurian guerrillas of the Sudan Liberation Movement (SLM) and the Justice and Equality Movement (JEM) include members who identify themselves as Arabs, Afro-Arabs, and Africans all united in their opposition to the policies of the government in Khartoum and their associated militias. The encroaching desert, recurrent droughts exacerbated by mismanaged policies from Khartoum, and the competition for grazing and farming lands all indicate that the Darfurian crisis is rooted in the violent competition for resources.[69]

In the east, the National Democratic Alliance, which is allied with the SPLM/A, includes among its members the marginalized Beja, Nuba, and other groups that are not homogeneous in their ethnicity or home region. The hybrid population of Sudan can be viewed as a variant of the mestizo, creole, colored, or Africanized populations that face similar conflicts of geography and demography that have, through time, become construed as racial and/or religious wars; a perspective that camouflages the contestation of resources that is at the root of most contemporary conflicts.

The master-slave relations[70] that gave way to the colonizer-colonized syndrome and has endowed its inhabitants with a more nuanced "premise of inequality"[71] distinguished by the perpetuation of a privileged strata and a decentered subaltern populace are shared by Sudan, Brazil, the United States, and South Africa. The first two cases share a similar trajectory in the making of hegemonic elites. Sudanese and Brazilian elites, which emerged from settler communities, acknowledge a shared ancestry with the indigenous populations whom they later enslaved and transformed into a servile class. At the same time, both elites constructed race-based and religiously sanctioned ideologies—Arabization and Islamization in Sudan and *luso-tropicalismo* and Christianization in Brazil—to serve as the engines of the "civilizing mission" of the settlers over the natives.[72]

The northern Sudanese, much like the Boers who adopted a new geographic (Afrikaner) identity, deftly created a new identity for themselves as *awlad al-balad,* emphasizing their link to the soil and disengaging its former owners—their "black" ancestors. The parallels with the Afrikaner ends with the adoption of the continental identity stripped of its "blackness." Another path was taken by the Brazilians, whose "Africanity," like that of the northern Sudanese, was selectively adopted.[73] The ensuing generations of hybridized Sudanese thus took upon themselves the mandate of a "civilizing mission" that equated blackness with the darkness of the *jahiliyya* and sought to Arabize/lighten and Islamize/enlighten the inhabitants of Sudan. Through campaigns of conquest, conversion, and commerce, which condoned the rape and looting of subjugated communities, a small number of settlers were able to produce and reproduce a new community that overrode any previous claims to the land by either the indigenous inhabitants or the settlers. The indigenous inhabitants were either exterminated or defeated and disenfranchised, while the settlers were assimilated as the privileged elite of the hybridized polity bent on constructing the territory in their own image. With control over the waters and access to its mineral wealth, the settlers of the first millennium claimed native "rights" by virtue of their representing the multiple entities that made up the old *bilad as-Sudan.* The northern Sudanese constructed "Arab" identities and genealogies and reconstructed Sufi Islam, adapting it to indigenous frameworks of beliefs. They also Sudanized/nativized the religion, thereby selectively appropriating elements from the culture of the settler and the native to create a new synthesis that would privilege the hybridized Sudanese and marginalize both the indigenous communities and Arab settlers.

In Brazil, in an interesting parallel to the emergence of a "geography-based" ethnic identity in northern Sudan, the descendants of Portuguese settlers, indigenous communities, and imported African slaves reconstructed a new identity based on their Latin American colony and emerged as "Brazilians," with a "civilizing mission" to Europeanize/lighten/whiten and Christianize/enlighten the natives and imported African slaves.[74] In the Sudan, too, the dominant sociopolitical discourse emphasized the geographic factor while deemphasizing the "blackness" that comes from having Sudanic ancestry. Like the Portuguese colonists, they glorified their mixed heritage but claimed the higher political ground by invoking religion to consolidate their hegemony over their subjects. Therefore, in both Sudan and Brazil, a person of dual or triple heritage who assimilates into an Arab or European genealogical framework becomes a self-empowered entity and claims superiority over the native /enslaved communities.

True to the logic of conquest, the vanquished lose access to land and other resources and become dependent on their masters, whom they emulate in the struggle to survive in such asymmetrical relations. The Brazilians cast off their identification with the Portuguese empire[75] and established their own republic where Christianity, Native American belief systems, and African traditional religions all coexisted.[76] The primacy of the Euro-Brazilian (like that of the Arabized Sudanese) was maintained through the construction of the ideology of *luso-tropicalismo,* within which coexisted—rather lopsidedly the glorification of the "inherent flexibility "of the itinerant Portuguese.[77] Conquest, commerce, and conversion into the "settler" way of life provided the triad upon which the Brazilian as well as the Afro-Arab Sudanese ruling elites erected their hegemonic rule over those they dispossessed and displaced in order to claim their status as the "children of the union between newcomers and old inhabitants," which endowed them with the self-arrogated right to own not only the land but those who lived on it as well. In both Sudan and Brazil, the encounter between settlers and natives began much earlier than it did in the United States and South Africa.

The Euro-African encounters in these two countries occurred much later, and their constructed racial and Christian (Protestant) ideologies rested on the separation of the European from the African and regarded the inevitable admixture—miscegenation—as a threat to their hegemony. Both master-slave and settler-native social relations were regarded as aberrant in the US and South African cases, despite the frequency of their occurrences.[78] In the era of colonial empire building, both the Sudanese and Brazilian elites developed ideologies that celebrated their "mixed" status but nevertheless sought to represent the settler as superior to the native. *Indigenismo* and forced native labor policies stood in stark contrast to the ideologies celebrating "native cultures" in the past as does the discourse of hybridity.[79] Rather than the campaigns of Arabization and Europeanization spearheaded by Arab and Portuguese settlers, the United States and South Africa pursued, with equal vigor, the campaigns of segregation, enslavement, and social degradation of persons of mixed parentage, including the offspring of the ruling elite.[80] The Sudanese and Brazilians, on the contrary, acknowledged biological links between master and slave and glorified the mixing as a special feature that created an ideal hybrid endowed to rule over those "less civilized."[81] While the Brazilians continue to associate "whiteness" with superiority, the Sudanese have redefined "their own color scheme, which favors the mixed mold as the ideal, relegating both black and white to a lesser order."[82]

The dominant social and political ideologies of the United States and South Africa regarded racial mixing as a threat that would stain their claim to superiority—based on the conventional equating of European ancestry with whiteness. Any person known to have kinship with natives or imported African slaves was officially categorized as a being of lesser worth and was labeled either "coloured" (South Africa) or "negro" (United States). The growing number of hybrid persons did nothing to narrow the gap between the practices of masters, who demanded sexual services from their slaves, and the official decree of the government and of the church. The flexibility of the Brazilians and the Sudanese created amorphous borders that make it difficult to distinguish the descendants of slaves from those of the masters, whereas the harsh boundaries of the United States and South Africa led to alliances of all shades of "peoples of color" united against supremacists.[83] Such clarity can be obtained in the Brazilian and Sudanese case only by giving primacy to the geographies of conflict based on identifying the origin and development of the wars over resources. The mathematics of resource allocation, distribution, and politics of exclusion may, in this case, be less fuzzy than trying to follow the numerous threads that narrate the ethnic, racial, and religious conflicts that followed the battles over resources.[84] In Sudan, the millennial competition for resources produced a multicultural hybrid polity whose constituents were held together by conquest and coercion as well as by kinship between the conqueror and the vanquished. The unaddressed grievances of the dispossessed have led to multiple conflicts over membership in the polity and attendant rights to access to the nation's resources.

Conclusion

The wars of conquest for the waters of the Nile in antiquity have been replaced by the new geoeconomic wars of the twenty-first century, which are fought with sophisticated weapons on the ground while politicians discourse over how to name the atrocities and whether and how to hold the perpetrators accountable. As the demand of the south for an equitable share of its regional wealth was addressed, the simmering conflict over land and water exploded in the west, producing a spiraling violence in Darfur and its borderlands. Global concerns over access to the new oil fields of Sudan led to unprecedented international discourse on the causes and consequences of the geowars, which were conveniently attributed to hostilities between "black Africans" and "Arabs." The geographies of conflicts were once again redrawn as the regime in Khartoum launched systematic campaigns of violence to quell the rebellion in the west, center, and east.

As the twenty-first century dawned, Sudan's geography of conflict had become so immured in the detritus of centuries of slave and cattle raids and intercommunal bloodletting justified by the ideologues of racial/religious supremacy or racial distinctiveness that the commonly shared fate of being Sudanese receded into the past, and hearts hardened as peace agreements lost their relevance.[85] While a partial peace was negotiated between the rebels of the south and the government ruling from Khartoum, new wars broke out in the west and east threatening to inundate the power base of the legatees of the *awlad al-balad.* In 2005, peace loomed on the horizon for the war-weary populations of the south, and legitimacy was building up for the regime, which remained locked in a deadly war against rebels in the western regions of Darfur, echoing the past demands of their southern conationals for power sharing and wealth sharing.[86]

Will Sudan come to terms with its past and reach a consensus that the country "belongs to all," regardless of geographic location, ethnicity, or creed? Or will the "supremacists" and their ideologues hold sway over the ravaged land and preside over the "end of Sudan" as the giant nation whose Sudanic polity is distinguished by its African roots, with branches from contiguous Arab areas whose kinship has been nurtured in the past by the waters of the Nile, and whose future holds promises from oil proceeds? Will the theocratic division of the land into the *dar al-harb* and the *dar al-Islam* become a "gulf between the political realm and the rest of society," reducing "the concept of citizenship" to a mere "slogan?"[87] Or will the "genocidal" aspects of the wars of the twentieth century against the south and the center be reenacted in the west and east in the twenty-first century?[88] Will peace in the south yield more destruction of the dispossessed, or will it provide a model to be emulated for a successful reclaiming of rights of wealth and power sharing in a multinational Sudan?

Notes

1. Colin Flint, *The Geography of War and Peace: From Death Camps to Diplomat* (Oxford: Oxford University Press, 2005), p. 5.
2. Wendy R. James, "Social Assimilation and Changing Identity in the Southern Funj," in Yusuf Fadl Hasan (ed.), *Sudan in Africa: Studies Presented to the First International Conference Sponsored by the Sudan Research Unit, 7–12 February 1968* (Khartoum: Khartoum University Press 1971), p. 198.
3. Mohamed Suliman, "Ethnicity from Perception to Cause of Violent Conflicts: The Case of the Fur and Nuba Conflicts in Western Sudan," paper presented at the CONTICI International Workshop, Bern, Switzerland, July 8–11, 1991.
4. In this chapter, we address the "geographies of conflict" by discussing how the "spatial ontology" of Sudan sheds light on the gaps between territorial locations, professions of specific ideologies, and geographic identities—all of which lead to conflicting claims over territory and identity. We use the term ontology here to refer to "the entities and processes invoked in an explanation." For a detailed discussion of "civilizational," "ideological," and "naturalized" geopolitics, see John Agnew and Stuart Cordridge, *Mastering Space: Hegemony, Territory and International Political Economy* (London: Routledge, 1995), pp. 13, 46–77.
5. For details, see John Garang, *John Garang Speaks,* edited and introduced by Mansour Khalid (London: Kegan Paul International, 1987), p. 61.
6. Ibid.
7. Wendy R. James, "Social Assimilation and Changing Identity in the Southern Funj," p. 207.

8. For an excellent analysis of the politics of identity in Sudan, see Amir H. Idris, *Sudan's Civil War: Slavery, Race and Formational Identities* (Lampeter, ON: Edwin Mellen Press, 2001), pp. 4–5. See also Catherine Besteman, *Unraveling Somalia: Race, Violence and the Legacy of Slavery* (Philadelphia: University of Pennsylvania Press, 1999), pp. 51–52.

9. This omission remains an egregious one, especially in light of the roles of Nuer/Dinka "prophets" and Nuba *kujurs* in mobilizing opposition to the Khartoum regime, which interestingly enough have been integrated as literary "devices" to enhance dramatic fictional and journalistic accounts. For examples of such portrayals, see Deborah Scroggins, *Emma's War* (New York: Pantheon Books, 2002); and Philip Caputo, *Acts of Faith* (New York: Alfred A. Knopf, 2005).

10. See the late Alexander Naty's pioneering study "Memory and the Humiliation of Men," in Wendy James, Donald L. Donham, Eisei Kurimoto, and Alessandro Triulzi (eds.), *Remapping Ethiopia: Socialism and After* (Oxford: James Currey Publishers, 2002), pp. 59–73.

11. The most comprehensive definition of this subregion, providing valuable insights for those interested in understanding not only the causes of conflict but also the avenues to peacemaking and peacebuilding within communities and between communities and states, is John Markakis, *Resource Conflict in the Horn of Africa* (London: Sage Publications, 1998), p. 8.

12. For an excellent overview of francophone Africa, see Victor T. Le Vine, *Politics of Francophone Africa* (Boulder, CO: Lynne Rienner Publishers, 2004).

13. Terje Tvedt, *The River Nile in the Age of the British: Political Ecology and the Quest for Economic Power* (London: I. B. Taurus, 2004).

14. Kelly C. Raymond, *The Nuer Conquest: The Structure and Development of an Expansionist System* (Ann Arbor: University of Michigan Press, 1985), pp. 196–197; Peter P. Garretson, "Vicious Cycles: Ivory, Slaves, and Arms on the New Maji Frontier," in Donald Donham and Wendy James (eds.), *The Southern Marches of Imperial Ethiopia: Essays in History and Social Anthropology* (Cambridge: Cambridge University Press, 1986), pp. 64–65.

15. The one exception, from the Sudanese perspective, would be the loss of Halaieb to Egypt, which has been contested for almost a century. See Gabriel Warburg, *Islam, Sectarianism and Politics in the Sudan Since the Mahdiyya* (Madison: University of Wisconsin Press, 2003).

16. French colonial rulers asserted their rule over the smaller sultanates located in the western peripheries of Sudan's power center, while Belgian and German aspirations to Equatorial Sudan were skillfully countered by British diplomats through diplomatic channels, military campaigns, and informal proxies, such as the British East India commercial enterprises. For details, see Robert O. Collins, *Land Beyond the Waters* (New Haven: Yale University Press, 1972), pp. 137–172.

17. Jok Madut Jok, *War and Slavery in Sudan* (Philadelphia: University of Pennsylvania Press, 2001), pp. 57–65, 157–179.

18. Mohamed Suliman, in his illuminating analysis of the extraeconomic role of the *jellaba*, literally "the bringer of goods," underscores their less visible but politically effective impact on the emergence of the modern Sudanese state. He argues, "Their political talent has been underestimated on many occasions, and when challenged they have re-gained their hold on the state, either by the power of the gun, acting as Dr. Jekyll or Mr. Hyde according to the situation." For further details, see "Civil War in the Sudan: The Impacts of Ecological Degradation," in Girma Kebbede (ed.), *Sudan's Predicament: Civil War, Displacement and Ecological Degradation* (Aldershot, UK: Ashgate, 1999), p. 91.

19. Robert O. Collins provides a comparative framework for our understanding of the economic role of the Sudanese *jellaba,* the counterparts of the Indian banyan who traded in East Africa, while the *zariba* magnates' impact on indigenous society was akin to that of the Europeans in the Kenyan highlands. See Collins, "Sudanese Factors in the History of the Congo and Central West Africa in the Nineteenth Century," in Yusuf Fadl Hasan, *Sudan in Africa,* p. 156. For a concise discussion of the impacts of two infamous empire-building slaving magnates, Al-Zubayr Rahma Mansur and Rabi Fadl Allah, see pp. 161–164.

20. The "horsemen" of yesteryear wreaked havoc and left a legacy of mistrust and fear that has continued to scar relations between Sudanese cultivators and mounted nomads since the seventh century.

21. The political acumen of personalities such as Zubayr al-Rahma, who used not only coercion but also diplomacy and trade to gain alliances with ruling Zande kings in Equatoria and membership in influential clans in Bahr al-Ghazal, needs to be recognized. The marriages contracted with the daughters of ruling elites or the influence gained by joining the clan of powerful "prophets" showed the fallacy of the African-Arab divide. His lieutenant, Rabih Fadlalla, also known as Rabih Zubayr, even went so far as to claim the sultanate of Bornu until his death in a battle with French forces.

22. Benedict Anderson's discussion of the rise of "Creole pioneers" and the rise of an imagined nationalism deracinated from its roots in distant metropoles has some relevance to an understanding of the discourse over the political identity of the land. Modern Sudanese nationalism is a hybrid of the visions and experiences of the African-Arab encounter. For an interesting discussion on the universality of membership in the *umma* versus territory-based nationalism, see Benedict Anderson, *Imagined Nationalism: Reflections on the Origins and Spread of Nationalism* (London: Verso, 1991), pp. 53–54.

23. P. M. Holt, "The Islamization of Nilotic Sudan," in Michael Brett (ed.), *Northern Africa: Islam and Modernization* (London: Frank Cass, 1973), pp. 13–14.

24. The marginalization of the Beja Congress (BC) relative to the other opposition movements/fronts begs the question of why the conflicts in this region have not been given the necessary attention. Contiguity of this area with Eritrea has led to some important developments that affect the way the conflicts over resources have been addressed. See BBC News, "Fighting Erupts in Eastern Sudan," June 21, 2005, available at http://news.bbc.co.uk/go/pr/fr/-1/hi/world/africa/4114374.stm.

25. This eastern region has historically been divided between the adherents of the Khatmmiya and its founding family—the Mirghani dynasty—and those of the Mahdiyya and its founding family—the Mahdi family. Competition for political power by these two sectarian movements have overshadowed the impact of other movements, such as the Sudanese leftists and workers' unions, both in the far north and northeastern sections of the country. For details, see Tim Niblock, *Class and Power in Sudan: The Dynamics of Sudanese Politics, 1898–1985* (Albany: State University of New York Press, 1987); and Ahmad A. Sikainga, *"City of Steel and Fire": A Social History of Atbara, Sudan's Railway Town, 1906–1984* (Portsmouth, NH: Heinemann, 2002).

26. Ghada H. Talhami, *Suakin and Massawa Under Egyptian Rule: 1865–1885* (Washington, DC: University Press of America, 1979), pp. 220–228.

27. For an excellent study on the industrialization of the region and the vanguard role played by its workers, unions, and nationalists in the making of modern Sudan, see Sikainga, *City of Steel and Fire,* pp. 38–39, 88–89.

28. That the Nuba and the peoples of the southern Blue Nile should not be prisoners of geography was reiterated numerous times by the late Yousif Kuwa Mekki,

who supported a united Sudan but also affirmed the right of southern Sudanese to use "a democratic process to secede from Sudan." See "Appendix 1: Clarifications on the SPLM Peace Position with Regard to the Nuba Mountains," in Suleiman Musa Rahhal (ed.), *The Right to Be Nuba: The Story of a Sudanese People's Struggle for Survival* (Lawrenceville, NJ: Red Sea Press, 2001), p. 122.

29. The conventional wisdom is to regard the Mahdiyya as the manifestation of Islamic resistance to European rule. A closer examination of the internal socio-historical and economic factors would indicate that the Mahdist state owes its genesis more to uncoordinated Sudanic defiance in the face of the efforts to treat the land and its inhabitants—slavers and slaves alike—as the uncontested resources of the Egyptian viceroys of the Ottoman Turks. The most concerted resistance—and not necessarily the most successful one against European rule—was the decade-and-a-half-long political campaign waged by Sultan Ali Dinar Zakariya of Dar Fur from 1898 to 1916. See Jay Spaulding and Lidwien Kapteijns (eds.), *An Islamic Alliance: 'Ali Dinar and the Sanusiyya, 1906–1918* (Evanston, IL: Northwestern University Press, 1994).

30. Mark Duffield, *Maiurno: Capitalism and Rural Life in Sudan* (London: Ithaca Press, 1981), p. 16.

31. John A. Works, *Pilgrims in a Strange Land: Hausa Communities in Chad* (New York: Columbia University Press, 1976), p. 3. For details on the three types of Hausa migrants—peddlers, pilgrims, and colonial conscripts—as aids to the Tirailleurs Sénégalais in Chad, Oubgani-Chari, Cameroon, and Madagascar, see pp. 4–15.

32. Mark Duffield, "The Fallata: Ideology and the National Economy of the Sudan," in Norman O'Neill and Jay O'Brien (eds.), *Economy and Class in the Sudan* (Brookfield, VT: Aldershot, 1988), p. 124.

33. Steven Wöndu and Ann Lesch, *Battle for Peace in Sudan: An Analysis of the Abuja Conferences, 1992–1993* (Lanham, MD: University Press of America, 2000), pp. 92–93.

34. For details, see John Garang's broadcasts on Radio SPLA of May 26 and 27, 1985 (John Garang, *John Garang Speaks* [London and New York: KPI Ltd., 1987], pp. 49–61), which addressed the downtrodden, the elite, and women in the discourse of the nation, aimed at unifying all Sudanese against the Khartoum regime's policy of "divide-and-rule," p. 49. For details on the government's *al-mashru' al hadhari* (civilizing mission) intended to guarantee the hegemony of the ideologues of Arabism and Islamism, see Alex de Waal and A. H. Abdel Salam, "Islamism, State Power and Jihad in Sudan," in de Waal (ed.), *Islamism and Its Enemies in the Horn of Africa* (Bloomington: Indiana University Press, 2004), pp. 89–106.

35. Garang, *John Garang Speaks,* p. 61.

36. Ibid., p. 67.

37. Ibid., p. 93.

38. Unfortunately, Western scholarship and popular writing continues to ignore this expropriation of the native by the settler, who after their millennial blending have developed claims to lands granted to them by various chiefs, sultans, and colonial officers. Modern travelogues extolling the virtues of the desert Arab as well as their mistreatment of disenfranchised indigenous communities record the existence of raids and counterraids without identifying the root of the problem—competing demands for shared resources to land, water, and pasturage. See Michael Asher, *A Desert Dies* (New York: St. Martin's Press, 1986), pp. 279–280.

39. The multiple wars waged in the western region of Darfur and eastern Sudan, along with the long war waged in the south and in the borderlands inhabited by the Nuba and Ingessana peoples, are consequences of centuries-old disenfranchisement and mistreatment at the hands of the hegemonic elites of Khartoum.

40. The communities whom we have come to know as Ingessana and Nuba did not until very recently refer to themselves by these names, which were given to them by outsiders. These communities appropriated the names in the mid–twentieth century, when notions of "blackness," "negritude," and pride in "Africanity" constructed a shared identity from their experiences of denigration by and subordination to the dominant ideology of the hegemonic group espousing Arabism. For a detailed discussion of the concept of Africanity, see Jacques Maquet, *Africanity: The Cultural Unity of Black Africa* (New York: Oxford University Press, 1972), pp. 54–55.

41. Francis Deng, "Abyei: A Bridge or a Gulf? The Ngok Dinka on Sudan's North-South Border," in Jay Spaulding and Stephanie Beswick (eds.), *White Nile, Black Blood* (Lawrenceville, NJ: Red Sea Press, 2000), pp. 137–147.

42. Yousif Kuwa Mekki, "Things Were No Longer the Same," in Rahhal, *The Right To Be Nuba*, pp. 29–30. See also Ahmad Sikainga, "Military Slavery and the Emergence of a Southern Sudan, 1884–1954," in Spaulding and Beswick, *White Nile, Black Blood*.

43. L. P. Kirwan, "Greek and Roman Expeditions to the Southern Sudan," in John Mack and Peter Robertshaw (eds.), *Culture History in the Southern Sudan: Archaelogy, Linguistics and Ethnohistory* (Nairobi: British Institute in Eastern Africa, 1982), pp. 71–74. See also Robert O. Collins, *The Waters of the Nile* (Oxford: Oxford University Press, 1990), pp. 3–4.

44. For details on the role of notable black Sudanese soldiers in the nineteenth century, see Richard Hill and Peter Hogg, *A Black Corps d'Elite: An Egyptian Sudanese Conscript Battalion with the French Army in Mexico, 1863–1867, and Its Survivors in Subsequent African History* (East Lansing: Michigan State University Press, 1995), pp. 123–144. See also George Reid Andrews, *The Afro-Argentines of Buenos Aires, 1800–1900* (Madison: University of Wisconsin Press, 1980), pp. 81–101.

45. E. A. DeCosson, *Fighting the Fuzzy-Wuzzy: Days and Nights of Service with Sir Gerald Graham's Field Force at Suakin* (London: Greenhill Books, Lionel Leventhal, 1990).

46. Janet J. Ewald, *Soldiers, Traders, and Slaves: State-Formation and Economic Transformation in the Greater Nile Valley, 1700–1885* (Madison: University of Wisconsin Press, 1990), pp. 123–126.

47. Hugo D'Aybaury produced a documentary film portraying the cultural revival of the Nuba as well as their armed mobilization in alliance with the SPLM/A. For details, see *The Right to Be Nuba* (New York: Filmmakers Library, 1994).

48. Alex de Waal, "The Right to Be Nuba," in Rahhal, *The Right to Be Nuba*, pp. 2–5.

49. One of the most notable returnees was Jayli wad Adam, a claimant to the title of *makk* in the Jebel Taqali, who had forcibly been taken by the *ansar* to the Ethio-Sudanese borderlands. Sultan Ali Dinar also abandoned the Mahdists and returned to claim his throne; and numerous displaced/detribalized slave soldiers, such as the former veteran of the Mexican wars and convert to the Mahdist cause Faraj Azazi, also returned to their birthplaces. The two former notables faired better than the latter, who was considered a threat to the young Ali Dinar and executed.

50. Holt and Daly, *Short History of the Sudan*.

51. *Area Handbook for The Republic of the Sudan* (Washington, DC: Department of the Army, Foreign Areas Studies Division, 1960), p. 44.

52. The Comprehensive Peace Agreement, signed on January 9, 2005, in Nairobi, was the culmination of numerous peace agreements drafted from 2002 to 2004. For full details, see Machakos Protocol, July 20, 2002; Framework Agreement on Security Arrangements During the Interim Period Between the Government of Sudan (GOS)

and the Sudan People's Liberation Movement/Army (SPLM/A), Naivasha, Kenya, September 25, 2003; Framework Agreement on Wealth Sharing During the Pre-Interim and Interim Period Between the Government of Sudan (GOS) and the Sudan People's Liberation Movement/Army (SPLM/A), Naivasha, Kenya, January 7, 2004; Protocol Between the Government of Sudan (GOS) and the Sudan People's Liberation Movement (SPLM) on the Resolution of the Conflict in Abyei, Naivasha, Kenya, May 26, 2004; Protocol Between the Government of Sudan (GOS) and the Sudan People's Liberation Movement (SPLM) on Power Sharing, Naivasha, Kenya, May 26, 2004; Agreement on Permanent Ceasefire and Security Arrangements, Implementation of Modalities During the Pre-Interim and Interim Periods Between the Government of Sudan (GOS) and the Sudan People's Liberation Movement/Army (SPLM/A), Naivasha, Kenya, December 31, 2004; Agreement on Implementation Modalities Between the Governemnt of Sudan (GOS) and the Sudan People's Liberation Movement/Army (SPLM/A), Naivasha, Kenya, December 31, 2004.

53. Bona Malwal's words of a decade ago come to mind. A seasoned veteran of southern opposition, he held that the option of secession was necessary to check northerners' hegemonic ambitions. He pointed out that without shifts in attitude, it was imperative that "people of the south . . . should have a say over their future." He argued that "there are endless anecdotes that portray the deep racism that characterizes the northern view of the south. . . . How can John Garang, the naked Dinka from the cattle camp, think he can rule Sudan? . . . These attitudes reveal what is at the heart of the Sudanese conflict: unadulterated racism . . . [where] the religious element . . . is nothing more than an excuse for the north to perpetuate its long-standing racist, Arab rule over the country." For details, see Bona Malwal, "Sudan's Political and Economic Future: A Southern Perspective," in Charles Gurdon (ed.), *The Horn of Africa* (New York: St. Martin's Press, 1994), p. 97.

54. Human Rights Watch, *Sudan: Oil and Human Rights* (New York: Human Rights Watch, 2003), pp. 58–79

55. See Robert O. Collins, *The Waters of the Nile: Hydro-politics and the Jonglei Canal, 1900–1988* (Oxford: Oxford University Press, 1990).

56. For a comprehensive discussion of the resource wars and their victims, see Human Rights Watch, *Sudan: Oil and Human Rights*.

57. Sulayman Nyang and Douglas Johnston, "Conflict Resolution as a Normative Value in Islamic Law: Application to the Republic of Sudan," in Douglas Johnston (ed.), *Faith-Based Diplomacy: Trumping Realpolitik* (Oxford: Oxford University Press, 2003), pp. 218–226.

58. For details, see Ian Cunnison, *Baggara Arabs: Power and Lineage in a Sudanese Nomad Tribe* (Oxford: Clarendon Press, 1966), p. 6 (emphasis added).

59. United Nations, *Report of the International Commission of Inquiry on Darfur to the United Nations Secretary-General* (Geneva: United Nations, January 25, 2005), pp. 158–161.

60. The conflicts in the Nuba Mountains, Abyei, Blue Nile, and Red Sea Hills clearly indicate the lack of fit between the geographic designations and the communities in question. The Comprehensive Peace Agreement signed between the GOS and the SPLM/A in January 2005 is an excellent beginning to redress this nomenclature, which continues to camouflage the roots and, subsequently, the requisites to the resolution of the multiple conflicts in Sudan, which include north-north and south-south conflicts in addition to the protracted north-south wars and west-center crisis that currently engage the world's attention.

61. Abdias Do Nascimento, *Mixture or Massacre? Essays in the Genocide of a Black People* (Buffalo: Afrodiaspora, Puerto Rican Studies and Research Center, State University of New York at Buffalo, 1979), pp. 57–91.

62. Helena Holgersson-Shorter, "Authority's Shadowy Double: Thomas Jefferson and the Architecture of Illegitimacy," in Alexandra Isfahani-Hammond (ed.), *The Masters and the Slaves: Plantation Relations and Mestizaje in American Imaginaries* (New York: Palgrave Macmillan, 2005), pp. 51–66.

63. Jennifer D. Brody, *Impossible Purities: Blackness, Femininity, and Victorian Culture* (Durham, NC: Duke University Press, 1998), pp. 14–58.

64. Thomas Holt, "Explaining Racism in American History," in Anthony Molho and Gordon S. Wood (eds.), *Imagined Histories: American Historians Interpret the Past* (Princeton: Princeton University Press, 1998), pp. 107–119.

65. A number of authors have nevertheless produced groundbreaking works on the transformation of historical and anthropological identities that urgently need to be taken up by political analysts dealing with conflicts arising out of the absence or violation of citizenship rights. Mahmood Mamdani's query into the settler-native divide in eastern and central Africa is notable for posing the question of hybrid identity in contemporary Africa. For details, see "When Does a Settler Become Native? Reflections on the Colonial Roots of Citizenship in Equatorial and South Africa," University of Cape Town Inaugural Lecture, New Series 208, May 13, 1998. A pioneering historical work that has relevance for the resolution of the conflict in Sudan is Ahmad Alawad Sikainga's *Slaves into Workers: Emancipation and Labor in Colonial Sudan* (Austin: University of Texas Press, 1996). G. P. Makris has also produced a remarkable work that has tapped into the historical currents that have shaped the modern sociopolitical identities of Sudan's subalterns. See G. P. Makris, *Changing Masters: Spirit Possession and Identity Construction Among Slave Descendants and Other Subordinates in the Sudan* (Evanston, IL: Northwestern University Press, 2000). Comparative perspectives of transformation of hybridized identities are also provided by Livio Sansone, *Blackness Without Ethnicity: Construction of Race in Brazil* (New York: Palgrave Macmillan, 2003); Jill Lane, *Blackface Cuba, 1840–1895* (Philadelphia: University of Pennsylvania Press, 2005); Robert C. Lieberman, *Shaping Race Policy: The United States in Comparative Perspective* (Princeton: Princeton University Press, 2005).

66. Abdou Maliqalim Simone, *In Whose Image? Political Islam and Urban Practices in Sudan* (Chicago: University of Chicago Press, 1995), pp. 109–128.

67. Mark Duffield, "The Fallata: Ideology and the National Economy in Sudan," in Norman O'Neill and Jay O'Brien (eds.), *Economy and Class in Sudan* (Aldershot, UK: Avebury, 1988), pp. 122–129. See also John A. Works, *Pilgrims in a Strange Land: Hausa Communities in Chad* (New York: Columbia University Press, 1976), pp. 169–183.

68. Sharif Harir, "'Arab Belt' Versus 'African Belt': Ethno-political Conflict in Dar Fur and the Regional Cultural Factors," in Sharif Harir and Terje Tvedt (eds.), *Shortcut to Decay: The Case of the Sudan* (Uppsala: Scandinavian Institute for African Studies, 1994), pp. 161–163.

69. The inequality of the descendants of African slaves of Sudan has parallels to the plight of the Afro-Brazilians, especially in the emergence of the phenomenon of spirit possession and African-centered religions. See Makris, *Changing Masters,* pp. 117–138; Livio Sansone, "From Africa to Afro: Use and Abuse of Africa in Brazil" (Amsterdam: South-South Exchange Programme for Research on the History of Development [SEPHIS] and Council for the Development of Social Science Research [CODESRIA], 1999), pp. 7–25.

70. The term is borrowed from Jacques Maquet's classic work on Rwanda, *The Premise of Inequality in Ruanda: A Study of Political Relations in a Central African Kingdom* (London: Oxford University Press, 1961).

71. Luis Vaz de Camões, *The Lusiads,* translated by William C. Atkinson (Middlesex, UK: Penguin Books, 1952).

72 Sansone, *Blackness Without Ethnicity,* pp. 56–58.

73. Peter Wade, *Race and Ethnicity in Latin America* (London: Pluto Press, 1997), pp. 34– 35.

74. For a discussion of the Portuguese colonial vision, see Vaz de Camões, *The Lusiads.*

75. Anderson, *Imagined Communities,* pp. 59–60.

76. See Gerald Bender, *Angola Under the Portuguese: The Myth and Reality* (Berkeley: University of California Press, 1978), pp 3–18.

77. Lieberman, *Shaping Race Policy,* pp. 28–34, 42–53.

78. The divide between settler and native was not so clearly demarcated, since "other natives" were used to quell both indigenous and international communities. See Hill and Hogg, *A Black Corps d'Elite;* Myron Echenberg, *Colonial Conscripts: The Tirailleurs Sénégalais in French West Africa, 1857–1960* (Portsmouth, NH: Heinemann, 1991).

79. Annette Gordon-Reed, *Thomas Jefferson and Sally Hemings: An American Controversy* (Charlottesville: University Press of Virginia, 1997), pp. 152–157.

80. The role of the "mixed" Euro-African or Euro-American represented yet another problem of identity in Portugal's colonies in Africa. See Peter Karibe Mendy, *Colonialismo Português em Africa: A Tradição de Resistência na Guiné-Bissau* (Lisbon: Instituto Nacional de Estudios e Pesquisa, 1994), pp. 282–296.

81. Francis M. Deng, "Sudan's Turbulent Road to Nationhood," in Ricardo R. Laremont (ed.), *Borders, Nationalism, and the African State* (Boulder, CO: Lynne Rienner Publishers, 2005), p. 49.

82. Anthony Marx, *Making Race, Making Nations: A Comparison of South Africa, the United States, and Brazil* (New York: Cambridge University Press, 1998).

83. Jeremy Black, "Geographies of War: The Recent Historical Background," in Colin Flint (ed.), *The Geography of War and Peace* (New York: Oxford University Press, 2005), pp. 19–25.

84. The paradox of the misnamed "comprehensive" peace agreement of 2005 has been aptly captured as having the potential to "hold the Sudan's self-destructive forces in check. But the fear is that while the southern peace may have legitimized the Khartoum government in the world's chancelleries, making it a negotiating partner, even an ally of the West, it has also given it license to carry on killing its own people in western Sudan—and now the east as well, where a rebel group recently opened up a new front." See *The Economist,* December 3–9, 2005, p. 25.

85. Steven Wöndu and Ann Lesch, *Battle for Peace in Sudan: An Analysis of the Abuja Conferences, 1992–1992* (Lanham, MD: University Press of America, 2000). See also Taisir M. Ali and Robert O. Matthews (eds.), *Durable Peace: Challenges for Peacebuilding in Africa* (Toronto: University of Toronto Press, 2004).

86. Celestin Monga, *The Anthropology of Anger: Civil Society and Democracy in Africa* (Boulder, CO: Lynne Rienner Publishers, 1996), p. 188.

87. Gérard Prunier, *Darfur: The Ambiguous Genocide* (London: Hurst, 2005), p. 164.

4

Regional and
International Involvement

The previous two chapters have furnished an overview of the geography, demography, and ecology of conflicts in Sudan. These chapters underscored the coincidence of racial, religious, and resource cleavages in giving substance and complexity to the turbulence that has marked the Sudanese multinational state. In the postcolonial period, Sudan's crises of identity became regionalized and internationalized through the intervention of diverse actors. Chapters 4 and 5 analyze how the north-south dimension of the conflict attracted regional and international actors against the background of major issues, events, and actors.

From the 1960s, the internationalization of the north-south conflict mirrored efforts by external actors to alter the international norms and strictures that insulated them from playing meaningful roles in conflict resolution. The United Nations' principles of sovereign equality, noninterference, and respect for boundaries, which were also domesticated by the Organization of African Unity (OAU) and, now, the African Union (AU), placed severe limits on external involvement in the search for solutions to Sudan's conflicts. But external engagement in the period up to the signing of the Comprehensive Peace Agreement in January 2005, and the ongoing negotiations over Darfur, demonstrate the persistence and resilience of external actors in transcending the limits of those international strictures and norms. In large measure, because of its intractability and longevity, the postcolonial trajectory of the north-south divide in Sudan also epitomizes a profound pattern of engagement by regional and international actors unparalleled in African conflicts.

Chapters 4 and 5 examine how the evolution of the north-south conflict shaped the modes of regional and international intervention. They reveal how political contests and alliances in the north have interacted with those in the south to provide opportunities for outside entry and participation. External intervenors have always had mixed motives for doing so, as their competing interests and ideologies featured prominently in the manner in which they defined the nature of the problem and the means by which they resolved it. In effect, these chapters proceed from the assumption that the regional geography of conflict emanating from the structures of conflict discussed in the previous chapters was decisive in scrambling the multiple alliances that became an essential component in the attempts to resolve the conflicts.

The Primacy of the North-South Problem

The dominant north-south fissure found explicit postcolonial definition in the asymmetrical nature of the independence agreement of 1956 that deepened northern Islamic hegemony over the largely Christian south. On the eve of independence, southern grievances were captured in the epic mutiny of southern army and police units that began in Torit, in the Equatoria region, in the summer of 1955 and engulfed the three southern provinces. The mutineers targeted symbols of northern domination, notably army officers, administrators, and merchants. The mutiny lacked strong organization and was a spontaneous uprising of disgruntled troops, but it subsequently formed a significant point of reference for the coalescence of southern political movements. Most analysts treat the mutiny as the beginning of the southern struggle against northern dominance.[1]

The hasty transition to independence, driven in part by the mutiny, left unresolved two fundamental constitutional questions that were to shape the contours of the postcolonial conflict: Would the new state be federal or unitary, and would it be officially secular or Islamic in character? Afraid of continued domination by the Muslim-controlled northern governments, most southern politicians favored federalism, but the northerners pushed for a unitary government, perceiving federalism as the beginning of southern separatism. Shortly after independence, the central government, at the behest of northern political parties, dissolved the Constituent Assembly to prevent it from deciding on the question of federalism. Instead, the three southern provinces were offered token representation in the central government institutions.[2]

The immediate postindependence period was marked by a weak parliamentary system controlled by the Egyptian-leaning National Unionist Party (NUP), later renamed the Democratic Unionist Party (DUP), and the Mahdist Umma Party. The coalition governments used their first years in power to put an Islamic stamp on the nation, forcibly closing missionary schools and centers and expelling missionaries from the south. After the military government of General Ibrahim Abboud overthrew the civilian government in November 1958, Islamization of the south was sanctioned by the Missionary Societies Act of 1962, which led to the harassment of missionaries and the closing of missionary schools in the south. The government further accused the missionaries of endangering the integrity and unity of the country by encouraging the south to resist Arabization and Islamization.

General Abboud's policy of Arabization and Islamization in the south galvanized the southern leadership into military and political movements that found inspiration in the 1955 mutiny. In 1961, William Deng, a Dinka exiled in the Congo, founded the Sudan African National Union (SANU), a political movement that started to advance the objective of self-determination. At the same time, some southern leaders organized the Anyanya (cobra poison) guerrilla forces, which launched the rebellion against the central government. Between 1960 and 1963, the Anyanya rebels grew numerically by recruiting and training new members. They also attacked strategic military targets and influenced political activities throughout the country. In its formative years, though, the Anyanya lacked coherent political and organizational structures and had only tenuous links with the southern political elite. The government responded by increasing the presence of the Sudan Defence Force to meet the challenge of the Anyanya and, increasingly, to exact revenge on villagers sheltering the rebels. By early 1964, most of Sudan's 18,000-strong army was involved in major operations against rebel forces in the south.[3]

The civilian government in Khartoum made overtures to SANU and Anyanya in early 1965 in an attempt to reduce military pressure and find a political settlement. However, the move by the central government sparked intense rivalries within the political and military elements of the southern movement, manifested in events that were to be replayed in subsequent years. Two groups, the Southern Front and the People's Progressive Party, split from SANU in 1965 in response to the government's peace gestures. The government also convened a constitutional conference in March 1965 to which it invited Sudan's near and distant African neighbors as observers. The participation by Ghana, Uganda, Tanzania, Nigeria, Algeria, Egypt, and Kenya represented the first instance of regional involvement in the civil war, a development that helped move the conflict from being a purely Sudanese affair to being a growing African concern. At the Khartoum conference, southern delegates proposed several possible solutions to the conflict, including outright separation, a plebiscite in the south, and local control of administrative structures under a federal constitution. However, the northern political parties, in collaboration with the government, were adamantly opposed to any form of self-determination, federation, or regional autonomy.[4] It was no surprise that the conference did not achieve much, though it did, as noted, bring new players into the conflict.

In the latter half of the 1960s, as governmental instability persisted in Khartoum and the south held firm to its demands, the Anyanya guerrillas stepped up their attacks on government positions, significantly increasing the number of refugees fleeing into neighboring countries. Facing sustained onslaught from the south, the government accused Uganda and Congo-Kinshasa of complicity in the rebellion. In July 1965, a government-led delegation to Ethiopia, Uganda, Kenya, and Tanzania sought guarantees that neighboring countries would respect the principle of nonintervention. Sudan's neighbors pledged neutrality in the conflict even as refugees grew to be a new source of strain that would enmesh some of these countries deeply into the course of Sudan's civil war.[5]

A ray of optimism shone on the Sudanese political process in 1967 when the Umma government of Sadiq al-Mahdi announced elections for the south to fill seats in the Constituent Assembly. Although al-Mahdi subsequently entered into a political alliance with Deng's SANU, what seemed a political gamble was, in fact, largely meant to strengthen the Umma Party against its northern opponents rather than genuinely to address southern concerns. Moreover, north-south tensions deepened when the army killed Deng. As Mohammed Omer Beshir noted,

> The murder of William Deng represented a great setback in North-South Relations. Only those opposed to a peaceful solution or to his leadership would have benefited from it. Deng's decision to return to the Sudan in 1965 to attend the Round Table conference and his participation in that event, in the Twelve-Man Committee and in the National Constitutional Commission had all made a positive contribution to the search for a solution to the Southern problem.[6]

After Deng's death, moderate southern parties, including SANU and the Southern Front, unsuccessfully used their participation in the Constituent Assembly to reinvigorate the campaign for southern autonomy and their opposition to the adoption of an Islamic-based constitution. Unable to prevail, representatives of southern parties walked out of the Constituent Assembly in 1969.

The string of political failures emboldened radical southern movements in their military campaigns, but they were still unable to muster a common front. From 1967 on, there was a proliferation of southern "governments" that dramatized the scale of the southerner's political fragmentation. In July 1967, Aggrey Jaden founded the Southern Sudan Provisional Government (SSPG). A rival group, the Nile Provisional Government, was formed in March 1969 to oppose Jaden's SSPG group. Yet another faction formed the Anyidi Revolutionary Government in July 1969, ostensibly to provide more military muscle and organization to the rebellion. Similarly, dissatisfied with the leadership of the Anyanya, Joseph Lagu formed a breakaway faction, the Anyanya National Organization, in a bid to exercise more control over the prosecution of the military campaign.[7] It should be noted that the infighting among the southern rebel movements anticipated the splits that were witnessed in the late 1980s and 1990s. It was during this period of profound southern disorganization that Colonel Ja'far al-Numeiri led a coalition of military officers, communists, and socialists, which overthrew the civilian government and proclaimed a new Revolutionary Council in May 1969.

The Rise and Fall of the Addis Ababa Agreement, 1972–1983

Before the advent of Numeiri, sectarianism and political instability in the north prevented the emergence of a consensus about resolving the array of identity issues raised by the south. Paradoxically, however, northern disunity also gave the northern establishment (the traditional parties and the military) reasons to procrastinate on meeting southern grievances. The key to this paradox was that northerners were fundamentally in agreement about the two core issues that animated relations with the south: Islamization and unitarism. Thus, while the south universally opposed Islamization from the outset, as Johnson shows,

> The sectarian nature of Northern political parties meant that mobilization of votes in the North was conducted essentially along the lines of religious affiliation. This is one reason why the Islamization of the South has been a constant policy of all governments dominated by the sectarian parties. In the 1950s Islamization and Arabization were presented as necessary policies to create national unity. By the 1960s, however, the position of the major parties had evolved to advocacy of an Islamic state.[8]

Similarly, the northern establishment opposed federalism or devolution of power even as some of the parties made opportunistic and rhetorical commitments toward this end when seeking southern support. As a result, within the wider scheme of northern political calculus, the southern problem was useful in two respects: northern parties could invoke it to shore up their unity in the service of Islamization and unitarism, and they could mobilize and use southern grievances to fight northern sectarian battles.

Also important in the immediate postcolonial period was the absence of a coherent southern movement that would furnish leadership to advance southern demands. This was largely due, first, to the sinecures of southern participation in the central government, which nullified to some extent the perception of marginalization; and, second, to the relative inexperience of southerners in forging a cohesive political program. By the late 1960s, however, there began to emerge a clear delineation between moderate political forces willing to work in central government institutions in Khartoum and radical groups that strove to define the conflict in military terms.

Although riddled with factions, as was the case in previous administrations, the Numeiri government's initial approach to the southern problem was to promise a political solution that would take southern uniqueness into consideration. Numeiri also issued a declaration that outlined plans for a regional self-government, appointed a southerner to head the portfolio of southern affairs, and promised amnesty to rebel movements.[9] There was, nonetheless, limited movement on Numeiri's agenda for the south for almost two years as he fought to consolidate his power. When the communists attempted a coup in July 1971, Numeiri found an opportunity to purge them from government and reverse his dalliance with socialism at home and abroad. Following the onslaught against the communists, Numeiri needed new allies to bolster his rule, particularly since his government had also alienated key northern parties. At the moment of profound vulnerability, Numeiri found southern partners willing to engage in negotiations. These occurred between February and March 1972, culminating in the Addis Ababa Agreement.

Numeiri's principal southern partner, Lagu, had successfully transcended the divisive politics in the south, creating a political movement, the South Sudan Liberation Movement (SSLM), which had put a stamp of organization and unity on the fractured political and military movements. As leader of the expanded Anyanya Armed Forces, Lagu formed the SSLM partly to marginalize exiled political leaders who did not have any military presence in southern Sudan. In 1969, he formed the Anyanya High Command Council and, in 1971, announced the formation of the SSLM, for the first time uniting southern Sudanese armed factions.[10]

At the height of unifying the military and political high commands, Lagu benefited from propitious regional and international environments. One of the salient shifts in the regional geography of the conflict was the availability of arms to the Anyanya after the end of the civil war in the Congo, particularly as defeated Congolese rebels indiscriminately sold their arms to willing buyers. Equally germane, the Anyanya received arms and logistical support following the coup in Uganda that brought the sympathetic regime of Idi Amin to power. Idi Amin allowed the Anyanya to transit supplies through Uganda and to conduct their activities from the Ugandan border areas. The Ethiopian imperial regime also gave military support to the Anyanya in retaliation for the Sudanese support for the Eritrean secessionist movements. Ethiopian and Ugandan military support for the Anyanya underscored the regionalization of the conflict and laid the infrastructure for what emerged in the 1990s as the Frontline States, a zone of neighbors sympathetic to the southern cause. Internationally, the Israelis were the major supporters of the Anyanya through arms airlifts, particularly after the Numeiri government aligned with militant Libya and Egypt.[11]

On the eve of the Addis Ababa talks, Anyanya's military fortunes started to change radically, reflecting the uncertain structures of alliances that Sudanese actors were to face in the future. But by the time Numeiri signed agreements with Idi Amin and Haile Selassie in 1972 to reduce Ugandan and Ethiopian support for Anyanya, and Western countries had started to draw closer to Numeiri after his break with the communists, Anyanya had built a credible military and political organization that made a difference in the bargaining with the north.

The diplomatic engagement of Ethiopia as the seat of the OAU provided legitimacy and credence to conflict resolution within the rubric of inherited boundaries. African countries had previously obtained only a token diplomatic presence during the constitutional conference in Khartoum in 1965, but Numeiri's decision to designate Ethiopia as the venue and Emperor Haile Selassie as the mediator in 1972 deepened the continental engagement in an internal conflict.[12] Long before the invocation of African solutions to African problems, the conclave at Addis Ababa epitomized the spirit of indigenous problem solving. Emperor Haile Selassie's stature in African politics gave him the weight to intervene frequently when the talks reached deadlocks. Facing Eritrean secessionism, it was useful for Haile Selassie to support a peaceful resolution of the Sudan conflict within the context of unity and inherited boundaries. The Ethiopian venue also allowed the key participation of the World Council of Churches and the All Africa Conference of Churches as co-mediators, representing a moral victory for Christian churches that had been persecuted in the south by previous northern governments. These actors also gave broad international stature to the mediation.[13]

The negotiations between the government and the SSLM resulted in the 1972 Addis Ababa Agreement, which provided for autonomy for the south, including the establishment of a Southern Regional Government and a National Assembly at Juba. Although the agreement gave the Southern Regional Government the power to raise revenue from local taxation, most of its revenues derived from the central government. On security matters, the agreement granted amnesty to rebel soldiers and their absorption into the Southern Defence Corps, which comprised 6,000 southern and 6,000 northern troops. The agreement, however, left considerable ambiguity about the timing of the integration of armed forces: while the government expected integration in five years, the SSLM wanted integration to occur after a five-year period.[14]

The Addis Ababa Agreement seemed to be an innovative solution to the north-south conflict, winning acclaim for Numeiri as Sudan's Lincoln,[15] but in reality, it continued to mirror the profound regional power imbalances. During the negotiations, some southern leaders presented a program of federalism that was rejected by the Numeiri government. In the end, the government's position prevailed and the notion of limited autonomy was embodied in the agreement. Similarly, the central government's control of military integration deepened the animosity between Anyanya forces and the government and led to violence during the implementation process. More ominous, in 1973, the agreement was appended to a national constitution that gave strong executive powers to Numeiri, subjecting the agreement to the uncertainties of Numeiri's personal rule. In essence, as Terje Tvedt notes, the Addis Ababa Agreement created a semiautonomous state that was dependent on the political will and decisions of Numeiri: "Seen from the south, Numeiri was the man who had given the southerners peace and regional autonomy, or more precisely, he was seen as the only leader in Khartoum who could safeguard that peace, and was given support on that understanding."[16] In the same vein, Nyaba describes this period as one in which the "south became a sub-system of the Numeiri regime . . . an island of liberal democracy in an ocean of one party dictatorship and the personal rule of Numeiri . . . which lacked or was denied the economic power and resources to develop the region."[17]

For southern elites, managing the quasi-autonomous institutions in Juba presented more constraints than opportunities, particularly in the context of administrative inexperience, weak economic resources, and interethnic strife. Although the Addis Ababa arrangements gave southerners the first opportunity to govern themselves in modern institutions, the High Executive Council (HEC) brought to the fore the rivalries that had bedeviled southern politicians over the years. As the initial façade of unity dissipated, the southern elite embarked on mobilization along ethnic, sectional, and regional lines. As it turned out, Numeiri took advantage of these weaknesses and transformed the HEC into a subsystem of his presidency in which he dismissed sitting leaders and appointed new ones at will.[18]

From 1972 to 1983, southern politics revolved around the personalities and ethnic identities of Joseph Lagu, an Equatorian, and Abel Alier, a Dinka.[19] During the leadership of Alier (1972–1978), there were claims of bureaucratic and economic dominance by the Dinka at the expense of the Equatorians, who had been instrumental in the guerrilla struggle. Intense competition for jobs between the returning exiles and those who remained in the south strained the resources of a weakly funded administration. Alier's tenure was also marked by the interventionism of Numeiri in southern affairs, severely restricting the authority of the regional institutions. In 1978, Lagu quit the armed forces and successfully contested Alier's presidency of the HEC, but the change in regime did not improve the quality of governance or reduce Numeiri's hand in southern affairs.

Even while Numeiri intervened heavy-handedly to reduce the authority of the southern administration, he embarked on a concerted bid to woo back his previous northern enemies into the government. After relying on the south, particularly the ex-Anyanya forces in the presidential guard, to fend off two Muslim-led coup attempts, in 1975 and 1976, Numeiri expediently changed course. Conscious of the dangers of dependence on the "southern constituency," Numeiri reached out to his Islamist opponents, Sadiq el-Mahdi's Umma Party and Hassan Turabi's Muslim Brothers Islamic Charter Front (ICF), later renamed the National Islamic Front (NIF). As part of the terms of the 1977 "National Reconciliation," Numeiri made concessions to the sectarian parties that were to have a grave impact on the implementation of the Addis Ababa Agreement. The key elements of the agreement included the incorporation of members of the sectarian parties into the structures of government; a pledge to review the provisions of the 1973 constitution that gave Christianity equal status to Islam; opposition to a secular constitution in preference for an Islamic one; and government willingness to revisit the provisions of the Addis Ababa Agreement that "weakened national sovereignty."[20] As Alier has observed,

> The national reconciliation agreement of President Nimeiri and El Saddiq in 1977 brought with it policies which were not consistent with the terms of the Addis Ababa Agreement. Following the reconciliation, statements from Nimeiri further undermined Southern confidence. It was no longer uncommon to hear remarks from responsible officials of government that suggested that the Addis Ababa Accord was "neither a Koran nor a Bible," meaning that it could be changed either slightly or substantially or even thrown overboard.[21]

In a critical move, Numeiri appointed Turabi as attorney general, a strategic position that gave him considerable influence in shaping Islamic reforms in Sudan.[22]

The internal rapprochement in Khartoum coincided with Sudan's deepening links with the United States. Since the Ethiopian revolution of 1974 that brought the Marxist-oriented regime of Mengistu Haile Mariam, Sudan had become the major regional counterweight to Soviet encroachment in the Horn of Africa. Washington, in turn, repaid Numeiri with economic and military support. In the early 1980s, the administration of US president Ronald Reagan gave military and economic assistance to the Numeiri government, increasing its confidence domestically and regionally. Deepening relations with the United States also affected Ethiopian-Sudanese relations, which had improved markedly since the Addis Ababa Agreement. As Numeiri turned for support to the United States and moderate Arab states, the Ethiopian Mengistu government became primarily reliant on the Soviet Union. In this position, Ethiopia reemerged as the most stable regional ally of the anti-Sudanese forces, beginning with a collection of southern guerrillas, known collectively as the Anyanya II, who had repudiated the Addis Ababa Agreement.[23] Anyanya II was formed in the mid-1970s by elements of the original Anyanya I who were disgruntled with the terms and implementation of the Addis Ababa Agreement. As tensions mounted between the Numeiri government and the southern administration in the early 1980s, the

Anyanya II forces operating from Ethiopia kept alive the flame of southern rebellion.

The Addis Ababa Agreement came under additional pressure from economic and resource conflicts between the south and north that grew in intensity in the late 1980s. With the bulk of Sudanese resources (oil, water, and fertile soils) based in the south, the regional administration tried to assert control over the management of these resources. After Chevron announced the discovery of oil in the Bentiu area in Upper Nile in 1978, the Numeiri government moved quickly to exclude the regional government from oil affairs. The government introduced the Regional Government Bill of 1980 that sought to redraw the borders of the south, contrary to the 1972 agreement. The bill was vehemently opposed by the south and, to deflect the opposition to the new boundaries, Numeiri announced retention of the 1956 borders. As a compromise, the government decreed the creation of a new entity called the Unity region to administer the oil fields. Amid mounting misgivings in the south about Numeiri's economic intentions, one of the ministers in the Alier administration tried to exert control over economic policy, precipitating Numeiri's dissolution of the quasi-autonomous southern institutions, in October 1981.[24]

The dissolution of Alier's government was the prelude to Numeiri's abrogation of the terms of the Addis Ababa Agreement. In June 1983, Numeiri decreed the creation of three new southern regions with separate governments—Equatoria, Upper Nile, and Bahr al-Ghazal. Although supported by Lagu and some southerners who desired more decentralization of power away from Juba, the decree proclaimed the annulment of the autonomous status for the south. Because most southerners read the redivision as a draconian bid by the central government to further control an already weakened autonomous government, they responded overwhelmingly by rejecting the move.[25] The political expression of this rejection was the formation of the Sudan People's Liberation Movement/Army (SPLM/A) in July 1983 under John Garang, which sought to liberate all of Sudan from northern elite rule.

The SPLM/A arose from a confluence of events that related to the inadequate implementation of the Addis Ababa Agreement. The slow absorption of former Anyanya troops into the national army and the frustration by the absorbed units over pay and lack of facilities created resentment among southern units that occasionally erupted in mutinies. In May 1983, military grievances, notably the failure to pay salaries and attempts to reshuffle and transfer soldiers from the south, eventually led to a mutiny in Bor, eliciting a violent response from the central government. Garang took advantage of the abortive government offensive to lead the mutineers into Ethiopia to join the Anyanya II rebels, signaling the beginning of Sudan's second civil war. With more mutinies and desertions in the south following Numeiri's abrogation of the Addis Ababa Agreement, Garang began a long process of consolidating his control over the SPLM/A under Ethiopian tutelage. In its July 1983 manifesto, the SPLM announced its intention to fight for a "New Sudan" of social, economic, and political equality. Abjuring the separatist agenda promoted by some of the Anyanya II forces, the SPLM highlighted the importance of a national context where all Sudanese would be free to develop their cultures. It also underlined that although the south shared common grievances with the west and east, successive northern governments had camouflaged these issues by seeking to construct a Sudanese identity based primarily on the Arabic language, Arab culture, and Islam.[26]

With the resumption of war, Numeiri's political position in the north became increasingly tenuous, so in September 1983, in desperation, he introduced Islamic *sharia* laws, injecting a combustible element in the north-south equation. Two years later, Numeiri was overthrown through a popular revolt led by the National Alliance for National Salvation (NANS), a coalition of northern professionals and civic activists that coalesced around the platform of ending economic regression and the decay of state institutions and returning to a democratic order.[27] A Transitional Military Council (TMC), which took power in 1985, pledged to organize elections in one year and invited civilians to join its cabinet. The SPLM, however, rejected the invitation to participate in the transitional institutions, because Numeiri's military had hijacked the popular will and because the TMC refused to revoke the September *sharia* laws. Instead, the SPLM sought to reach out to moderate elements in the NANS to find a formula for healing the north-south wounds. At a meeting in March 1986 at Koka Dam, Ethiopia, the SPLM met key parties to the NANS, including representatives from the Umma Party. Noticeably absent were the DUP and NIF. The participants issued the Koka Dam Declaration, in which they made a commitment to hold a constitutional conference on national questions. The SPLM also pledged to order a cease-fire in the war provided the TMC repealed the 1983 *sharia* laws, abrogated military pacts that compromised national sovereignty, lifted the state of emergency, and replaced the 1985 transitional constitution with the 1956 constitution.[28]

The Koka Dam Declaration was overshadowed by the end of the term of the transitional government and the beginning of electoral contests among northern parties. Some of the northern signatories shied away from the declaration in the face of concerted opposition from the Umma Party and the NIF, which had gained organizational strength under Numeiri. Furthermore, the elections of 1986 brought an unstable coalition government with no sufficient mandate to engage the SPLM. Without a governing majority, the government of Prime Minister Sadiq al-Mahdi and his Umma Party was condemned to shaky alliances with the DUP and the NIF. Although al-Mahdi met Garang in July 1986 and promised to repeal the *sharia* laws, he soon reneged after his coalition partners vehemently opposed the Koka Dam Declaration.[29]

Predictably, the failure of the Koka Dam talks led to an intensification of the war. Between 1988 and 1989, the SPLA garnered major military victories over government forces in southern Sudan, capturing the former provincial capitals of Torit, Nasir, and Bor. More significant, through these victories, the SPLA cut government supply lines and secured the Ethiopian border. In response, the al-Mahdi administration declared a full-scale war on the SPLM/A and reinforced its war efforts by arming ethnic militias in the south. In Equatoria province, the government supported militias to attack civilian Dinka populations in Jonglei and Lake provinces. The government also recruited Anyanya II, who declined to join the SPLA in the Nuer ethnic districts of Upper Nile province. In addition, exploiting the perennial conflicts among pastoral groups, the government provided arms to the nomadic Arab ethnic groups to protect the nomadic migratory routes of the Baggara Arabs to the south. These militias also rustled cattle from the Dinka in Bahr al-Ghazal province. Although Prime Minister al-Mahdi described the militias as defenders of democracy, the policy of indiscriminate armament of these groups compounded the ethnic and resource wars that were to convulse Sudan in the 1990s and beyond.[30]

A ray of hope for peace occurred at the end of 1988 when the DUP, marginalized in the governing coalition by the Umma Party and the NIF, reached out to the SPLA at the encouragement of Egypt. Drawing on the growing northern disenchantment with the escalating war, DUP leader Mohammed Osman al-Mirghani entered into direct talks with Garang in Addis Ababa. These talks produced an agreement that modified key provisions of the Koka Dam Declaration. Specifically, the SPLA dropped its demand for the dissolution of the government and agreed to a suspension of *sharia laws* pending the outcome of a constitutional convention. In early 1989, the army bought into these terms and asked the al-Mahdi government to open negotiations with the SPLA. Afraid of the new developments, the NIF pulled out of the government, leading to a new coalition between Umma and the DUP that sought to engage the SPLA. To preempt a scheduled meeting between al-Mahdi and Garang, General Omar al-Bashir led Islamists in the army supported by the Turabi's NIF to stage a coup in June 1989. In the aftermath of the coup, Bashir's program of forced Arabization and Islamization of Sudan effectively halted the prospects of peace.

Toward Abuja, 1989–1993

The Addis Ababa Agreement and its institutional edifice were brittle because they were erected on the foundation of personal rule that was in itself insecure. Numeiri's penchant for vacillation followed the familiar pattern of northern politicians, opportunistically using southern grievances when it suited their political objectives. The failure was also an attribute of southern unpreparedness for governance in the face of countervailing pressures of regionalism and ethnicity. Although the spirit of collective action unleashed by the Anyanya movement waned in the aftermath of the Addis Ababa Agreement, it was left to the SPLM/A to translate southern aspirations into more solid organizational structures. There was also a vital change in the domestic landscape that arose from the recognition among some northern actors about the national context of the southern problem, a recognition that was captured in the belated bid by the Umma and DUP to address the SPLM/A's concerns. The fractious nature of northern political parties continued to impede a national consensus on the south, but the attempts at building bridges across the racial and cultural divide were significant in changing the perceptions of the parties toward the conflict. The formation of a multiparty National Democratic Alliance (NDA) in 1989 and its revitalization in 1995 was an instance of building bridges with implications for altering ways to resolve the conflict.

The triumphant rise of the NIF from the ashes of the Addis Ababa Agreement posed weighty dilemmas for the search for a settlement to the north-south conflict, but in most respects, it also helped clarify the positions and actors to the conflict. Where factionalism and sectarianism had long marked northern politics, allowing parties to hide under ambiguous programs about the future of the nation, the NIF's single-mindedness in advancing the Islamic agenda furnished a measure of coherence to the policymaking arena. While militarism and Islamism plunged the country into renewed civil war, the NIF articulated a radical vision that sharpened both northern and southern opposition movements toward the quest for common objectives. After taking over power, the NIF government enacted *sharia* laws into the constitution, exempting the south from only five of the 186 articles of the 1991 Penal Code. In taking the position that implementation of *sharia* was God-ordained and not subject to validation or invalidation by political consensus or dissension, the Bashir government alienated a large segment of NIF's previous allies in the north.[31]

The Addis Ababa Agreement drew regional and international actors into the conflict, helping to further rupture the walls of sovereignty that had shielded the conflict from outsiders. The roles of external actors as mediators and providers of diverse resources multiplied as geopolitical shifts in alliances affected the course of the conflict. External participation in the conflict presented numerous vistas and constraints to the Sudanese parties, at once offering resources to parties to strengthen their organizational capacity, but at same time subjecting them to the vagaries of external dependence. As the SPLA's experience with domestic changes in Ethiopia in the early

1990s was to reveal, unanticipated changes in the patron's domestic climate could yield dramatic effects on the survival of the client.

In early 1989, the humanitarian crisis confronting the south galvanized international efforts toward the Sudanese conflict. Even before the fall of the al-Mahdi government, press reports of widespread famine and starvation in the south had led to an agreement between the Sudanese and the United Nations for the establishment of Operation Lifeline Sudan (OLS) in April 1989, a program to open emergency relief corridors via the air, the sea, river barges, and the railroad. To implement the program, the SPLA and the government had reached a tentative six-month cease-fire. The implementation of the OLS program was facilitated by the intense pressure exerted on the al-Mahdi government by the new administration of George Bush, who signaled the intention of the United States to phase out military and economic aid because of Sudan's links with Libya.[32]

The military junta of Bashir made commitments to the United Nations and the United States about continued support for the humanitarian effort, but to underscore its control of the domestic agenda, it refused pressures to engage the SPLM/A within the structures established by the DUP. Instead, in September 1989, the government organized a National Dialogue on Peace, composed of prominent individuals, as an alternative to the constitutional conference envisaged under the Koka Dam and DUP-SPLM/A agreements. Boycotted by the SPLM/A, the conference recommended that Sudan should have a federal system based on Islamic laws. To protect minority rights, the conference recommended that non-Muslims resident in the north should be exempted from Islamic laws.[33] The SPLM/A response to the new gesture was to resume the war. Because the resumption of the war threatened to jeopardize the OLS program, the United States tried to prod both sides to respect the terms of the cease-fire.

Former US president Jimmy Carter rode on the wave of US pressure on both sides to attempt a diplomatic initiative that would break the stalemate at the end of 1989. In addition to his stature and prestige, Carter was well placed to lend weight to the peace initiative because of his humanitarian involvement in the eradication of Guinea worm disease and river blindness. In August and December 1989, Carter presided over talks between the government of Sudan and the SPLM/A in Nairobi, Kenya. Although Carter sought to get the parties to agree to a constitutional conference as a way to resolve the conflict, the negotiations deadlocked on two issues: the government's insistence on exemption of the south from some, but not all, Islamic laws in a federal system; and the SPLM/A insistence on a secular and broad-based national unity government. Carter proposed the suspension of Islamic laws for three months until the conclusion of a constitutional convention reached a final decision, but the government rejected it, bringing the initiative to an end.[34]

After the collapse of the Carter talks, the Bashir government approached the United States to intervene in a new initiative in March 1990, led by the assistant secretary of state, Herman Cohen. With the SPLM/A gaining more ground on the battlefield, Bashir expressed interest in engaging the SPLM/A, a message his government articulated to the United States through key third parties: Francis Deng, then of the Brookings Institution, and former Nigerian president Olusegun Obasanjo. Cohen's bargaining strategy was to induce the government to withdraw half of its troops from the south in exchange for the withdrawal by SPLM/A forces from areas that it had occupied. These withdrawals were meant to build confidence for an all-parties constitutional conference that would decide on a federal system. But in the initial rounds of talks with the parties, Cohen found severe disagreement. While the government was willing to roll back its military forces (instead of total withdrawal), the SPLM/A thought the terms favored the government. Furthermore, Bashir rejected the idea of an all-party conference, preferring a bilateral meeting with Bashir. According to Cohen,

> Garang was suspicious of Bashir's offer to "sit down man-to-man" and work out a settlement. He called the proposal totally unacceptable because of its undemocratic nature. . . . Garang said he would accept only a conference that included representatives of all civil society, including banned political parties and labor unions. In effect, he would be willing to grant a military cease-fire, interrupting the SPLA's favorable military momentum, in return for a representative conference.[35]

Through several rounds of separate meetings with Bashir and Garang in April and May 1990, Cohen was unable to get the parties to narrow their differences. The onset of the Gulf War to reverse Iraq's invasion of Kuwait in August 1990 impeded further talks as the Khartoum government became stridently anti-American. Externally, the Bashir government moved more closely to Libya and Iran, alienating its erstwhile Middle Eastern allies such as Egypt, Saudi Arabia, Kuwait, and the Emirates. Internally, the regime became more repressive and began to impede the efforts of OLS. Although an internationally weak Sudan tried to reengage Cohen in the talks, two critical events—the SPLM/A's loss of Ethiopian support and internal split within the movement—worked against the resumption of talks.

Since its formation, the SPLM/A strategic dependence on the Mengistu regime in Ethiopia for training and safe havens had made a big difference in its military capacity. The Sudanese government had, in turn, reciprocated by supporting anti-Mengistu dissidence. After the fall of the Mengistu government in May 1991, the victorious Ethiopian People's Revolutionary Democratic Front (EPRDF) stopped the flow of arms to the SPLM/A and closed its camps. Although the SPLM/A had obtained new supply routes through Uganda and had gained arms from southern Africa, the Ethiopian loss was significant to reverse the military gains it had made since 1989.[36]

The split in the SPLM/A followed closely on the loss of Ethiopia support. Although Garang had successfully crafted a more formidable military organization than the previous Anyanya, this success came at the price of centralization and authoritarianism. Other than channeling and contesting grievances about the movement to Garang directly, the SPLM/A had not evolved any institutional organs for the rank and file. In 1991, two Nuer commanders, Lam Akol (Shilluk) and Riek Machar (Nuer), raised the issue of enhancing democracy in the SPLM/A and tried to mobilize disaffected factions to depose Garang. In August 1991, Akol and Machar, constituted as the SPLM/A-Nasir (from the name of their headquarters), denounced Garang's dictatorship and human rights violations, and pledged to fight for the independence of southern Sudan. Serious fighting between Garang and rebel forces in September and October 1991 resulted in large numbers of civilian casualties, and even though there were attempts at reconciliation, the split could not be reversed. More important, as the Akol and Machar faction began to receive weapons and ammunitions from the Khartoum government, healing the split became much more difficult.[37]

The ethnic fissures in the SPLM/A invariably strengthened the government's military hand. With its new allies in the south, the Sudanese army recaptured most of the territory controlled by the Nasir faction in Equatoria and Jonglei provinces. The government also captured the SPLA's headquarters at Torit.[38] At the same time, the Bashir government obtained military and financial assistance from Iran, considerably giving it the military edge in the conflict. Against the backdrop of these changes on the ground, the Bashir government sent emissaries to Nigeria's president, Ibrahim Babangida, who was also chairman of the OAU, to launch a new peace initiative, culminating in the Abuja peace talks between May 1992 and May 1993.

Babangida's initiative coincided with the OAU's efforts to develop mechanisms for the mediation of internal conflicts. Nigeria's leading position in Africa seemed to enhance its stature as a mediator. Besides, since the government in Khartoum claimed to be besieged by "imperialist and neo-colonialist" forces against its Islamic orientation, it saw Nigeria (with its large Muslim population) as a mediator that would preempt intrusive external actors and lend broad legitimacy to an "African solution." Equally significant, Nigeria's experience in overcoming its own civil war in the 1960s put it in a position to intervene in Sudan. Bashir underscored these views: "Babangida is the logical mediator because of his sincerity on issues concerning the African continent, Nigeria's experience in solving problems of internal conflict, as well as the fact that he is the current OAU chairman."[39]

The SPLA saw Nigerian mediation as an opportunity to mobilize African pressure on the government particularly after the military offensive that had weakened its forces. With the loss of Ethiopian support and the internecine strife, the SPLA was ready to negotiate. As Collins notes, "Weakened by disaffection and desertions, Garang had little choice but to negotiate. He was at a disastrous disadvantage, particularly when he was encouraged to do so by the United States and the new head of the Organization of African Unity

(OAU), the Nigerian president Ibrahim Babangida, whose intercession could not be ignored by either belligerent."[40]

The first phase of the Abuja talks began at the end of May 1992 and lasted for ten days. In preparation for the talks, the Nigerian mediators had committed the parties to an agenda that comprised three major phases: the first phase to deal with substantive issues of national identity, citizenship, and fundamental rights; the second phase to make power- and resource-sharing arrangements; and the third phase to set up interim arrangements and modalities for drafting a permanent constitution.[41] In addition, they proposed comprehensive debates on each item of the agenda followed by the establishment of committees to reconcile the parties' positions. Throughout the negotiations, Nigerian mediators drew lessons from their civil war as they tried to sell the formula of federalism, secularism, and multicultural-ism: "In Nigeria, no religion is imposed on anyone. We have no state reli-gion. We are a multi-religious country and Nigerians will resist the impo-sition of any religion as we cherish and respect our freedom of worship."[42]

Although the two SPLA delegations agreed to temporarily bury their differences in negotiations over self-determination, the government refused to budge on the key provisions of its agenda, insisting on an Islamic state and the unity of the Sudan. Thus, at the end of the talks in June 1992, the parties signed a communiqué stating that Sudan is a multiethnic, multilin-gual, and multireligious country and also pledged to work toward an "insti-tutional-political arrangement to cope with and to encourage such diversi-ties as is the case in Nigeria."[43] But the communiqué glossed over the primary areas of disagreement and, as Ann Lesch and Steven Wöndu show, "there was scant hope that the parties would alter their substantive posi-tions. Rather, the communiqué saved face for President Babangida and the mediating team."[44]

Following the adjournment of the Abuja talks, the Nigerian mediators tried to involve Kenya and Uganda in the peace process to bolster collec-tive pressure on Bashir's government.[45] In February 1993, President Muse-veni convened a meeting in Entebbe between Garang and the government in which they pledged to return to Abuja and exclude Machar's SPLA-Nasir faction from the negotiations. But when the talks resumed in April 1993, the parties could not find common ground on the contentious questions of secularism, the structure of political relationships between north and south, and the interim arrangements. Strengthened by additional military victories over the SPLA, the government was less inclined to budge from its previ-ous positions. To emphasize its growing confidence, in May 1993, the gov-ernment engaged in parallel negotiations in Nairobi with Machar's faction, further deepening the southern split.[46]

After the breakdown of Abuja II, Nigerian mediators, bereft of leverage and new ideas, withdrew from the negotiations. As Gill Lusk notes, the "party most put out" by the "predictable impasse at Abuja" was Nigeria, "which needed a diplomatic success, at a time of great uncertainty over its transition to civilian rule."[47] Abuja's demise and the escalation of the civil war in the "famine triangle" of the Upper Nile and Bahr al-Ghazal shifted the focus of attention from negotiations to alleviating the plight of an estimated 2 million people facing the threat of famine in the south. With the war impeding the OLS program, the US ambassador to Sudan, Donald Petterson, tried to mediate an agreement between Garang and Machar in June 1993.[48] Petterson's mediation enabled the UN to resume humanitarian assistance, but Khartoum vehemently objected to the creation of demilitarized safe havens in the south. Although UN and voluntary agencies advocated for negotiations on demilitarized zones that would allow noncombatants to resume economic activities, the government considered the establishment of safe zones as a pretext for external actors to intervene in its internal affairs and to "internationalize and complicate the southern Sudan issue."[49]

The US-brokered cease-fire did not end the factional fighting because of the inability of both parties to overcome their mutual antagonisms. Having boosted its military alliance with the SPLA dissidents, the government mounted a coordinated air and ground offensive against Garang forces along its supply routes on the Ugandan border, while in Upper Nile province the SPLA dissidents advanced on SPLA territory. By the end of the summer 1993, the government wrestled control of strategic towns from the SPLA and compromised its ability to sustain an effective guerrilla strategy.[50] On the occasion of the August celebration of Armed Forces Day, an exuberant Bashir could claim that Garang, "the vanguard of Islam's enemies, has been defeated in the battlefield despite his weapons and equipment. The rebels have dispersed from around him and his movement is torn apart because he has forgotten the concerns of the homeland and yielded to the whims of agents who want to humiliate this nation and force it to retreat to serve their cheap worldly purposes."[51]

Garang tried to compensate for losing ground in the field by lobbying for diplomatic support, finance, and arms in Africa, Europe, and the United States. At the regional level, in particular, Garang mobilized support from Kenyan and Ugandan governments worried about the impact of Khartoum's military successes and the spread of Islamic fundamentalist influence to Muslim minorities in their own countries.[52]

Conclusion

From the mid-1960s, the north-south dimension of the Sudanese conflict invariably attracted regional actors who began to have stakes in its evolution and resolution. To a large measure, the regional geography of the Sudanese conflict was decisive in steadily drawing neighbors into intramural debates on citizenship, power sharing, and resource allocation. Most of the post-independence governments invoked the norms of sovereignty in keeping outsiders from these debates, but since national questions remained open and violently contested, regional and international actors found intervention opportunities. Thus, the roundtable talks in Khartoum in 1965 started the regionalization of the north-south conflict and laid the basis for legitimation of subsequent external involvement in the quest for peace.

The roles of regional and international actors deepened with the escalation of the north-south conflict. From the late 1960s, the clarification of leadership and organizational questions in the south afforded regional and international actors more latitude in influencing the course of the conflict. Likewise, the civil war, mirrored in northern fragmentation, whittled national coherence, opening avenues for regional and international interveners to be profound participants in the search for solutions. As both the southern and northern parties drew upon external resources to prosecute the war and pursue peace efforts, they became increasingly subject to changing international and regional circumstances. Chapter 5 details the convergence of regional and international actors under the rubric of the Intergovernmental Authority on Development to prod the parties toward a negotiated settlement.

Notes

1. For diverse discussions of this early phase of independence, see Joseph Oduho and William Deng, *The Problem of the Southern Sudan* (London: Oxford University Press, 1963); Oliver Albino, *The Sudan: A Southern Viewpoint* (London: Oxford University Press, 1970); Dunstan Wai, *The African-Arab Conflict in the Sudan* (New York: Africana, 1981); Francis M. Deng, *War of Visions: Conflict of Identities in the Sudan* (Washington, DC: Brookings Institution, 1995); Douglas Johnson, *The Root Causes of Sudan's Civil Wars* (Bloomington: Indiana University Press, 2003).

2. Tim Niblock, *Class and Power in Sudan: The Dynamics of Sudanese Politics, 1898–1985* (Albany: State University of New York Press, 1987).

3. The history of Anyanya is well documented in Elias N. Wakoson, "The Dilemmas of South-North Conflict," in Francis Deng and P. Gifford, *The Search For Peace and Unity in the Sudan* (Washington, DC: Woodrow Wilson Center Press, 1987), pp. 90–106.

4. Raphael K. Badal, "Political Cleavages Within Southern Sudan: An Empirical Analysis of the Redivision Debate," in Sharif Harir and Terje Tvedt (eds.), *Shortcut to Decay: The Case of the Sudan* (Uppsala: Scandinavian Institute of African Studies, 1994), p. 107.

5. David W. McClintock, "The Southern Sudan Problem," *Middle East Journal* 24, no. 4 (autumn 1970): 466–478.

6. Mohamed Omer Beshir, *The Southern Sudan: From Conflict to Peace* (London: Hurst, 1975), p. 38.

7. For an excellent discussion of the proliferation of southern parties, see Timothy Niblock, *Class and Power in Sudan, 1889–1985* (Albany: State University of New York Press, 1987), pp. 273–274.

8. Johnson, *The Root Causes of Sudan's Civil War,* p. 35.

9. Omar el-Hag Musa, "Reconciliation, Rehabilitation, and Development Efforts in Southern Sudan," *Middle East Journal* 27, no. 1 (winter 1973): 1–6.

10. Niblock, *Class and Power in Sudan,* pp. 273–274.

11. Ibid., p. 274; Johnson, *The Root Causes of Sudan's Civil War,* pp. 30–31.

12. For analysis of the choice of Ethiopia, see Abel Alier Kwai, *Southern Sudan: Too Many Agreements Dishonoured,* 2nd ed. (Reading, UK: Ithaca Press, 1992), pp. 91–92.

13. Hizkias Assefa, *Mediation of Civil Wars: Approaches and Strategies—the Sudan Conflict* (Boulder, CO: Westview Press, 1987).

14. Johnson, *The Root Causes of Sudan's Civil War,* pp. 41–42.

15. For this description, see Peter K. Bechtold, "Military Rule in the Sudan: The First Five Years of Jafar Numayri," *Middle East Journal* 29, no. 1 (winter 1975): 27.

16. Terje Tevdt, "The Collapse of the State in Southern Sudan After the Addis Ababa Agreement: A Study of Internal Causes and the Role of the NGOs," in Harir and Tevdt, *Shortcut to Decay,* p. 77.

17. Peter A. Nyaba, *The Politics of Liberation in South Sudan: An Insider's View* (Kampala: Fountain Publishers, 1997), p. 19.

18. Tevdt, "The Collapse of the State," p. 76.

19. Tvedt has observed that the two "represented different political and administrative networks, different types of leadership, different provinces and different ethnic groups. The degree of conflict between these two men from 1972 to 1981, when Nimeiri dismissed Alier's administration, in important respects reflected the degree to which the Southern political elite and administration was unable to control the centrifugal forces within itself, especially in a situation when these contradictions were fueled by Khartoum's tactics." Tevdt, "The Collapse of the State," p. 72.

20. Alier, *Southern Sudan,* pp. 256–260.

21. Ibid., p. 262.

22. Gabriel Warburg, *Islam, Sectarianism, and Politics in Sudan Since the Mahdiyya* (Madison: University of Wisconsin Press, 2003), pp. 189–190.

23. Alier, *Southern Sudan,* pp. 91–92.

24. Johnson, *The Root Causes of Sudan's Civil War,* pp. 43–58.

25. For the chronology of events leading to the dissolution of the Alier administration, see Alier, *Southern Sudan,* pp. 101–122.

26. John Garang, *The Call for Democracy in Sudan,* 2nd ed. (London, Kegan Paul International, 1992), pp.125–129.

27. Warburg, *Islam, Sectarianism, and Politics in Sudan,* pp. 191–193.

28. Alier, *Southern Sudan,* pp. 290–291.

29. Ibid.

30. Sharif Harir and Terje Tevdt, "Recycling the Past in the Sudan," in Harir and Tevdt, *Shortcut to Decay,* pp. 58–59; Peter Woodward, *The Horn of Africa: Politics and International Relations* (New York: St. Martin's Press, 2003), pp. 54–56.

31. Bona Malwal, "The Roots of the Current Contention," in Deng and Gifford, *The Search for Peace and Unity in the Sudan,* pp. 9–14.

32. Herman Cohen, *Intervening in Africa: Superpower Peacemaking in a Troubled Continent* (New York: Macmillan, 2000), pp. 64–67.

33. Ahmed T. el-Gaili, "Federalism and the Tyranny of Religious Minorities: Challenges to Islamic Federalism in Sudan," *Harvard International Law Journal* 45, no. 2 (summer 2004): 531–532.

34. For an analysis of the Carter initiative, see Cohen, *Intervening in Africa,* p. 74.

35. Ibid.

36. Douglas H. Johnson, "The Sudan People's Liberation Army and the Problem of Factionalism," in Christopher Clapham (ed.), *African Guerrillas* (London: James Currey, 1998), pp. 62–64.

37. For discussions of the SPLA split, see P. A. Nyaba, *The Politics of Liberation in South Sudan: An Insider's View* (Kampala: Fountain Publishers, 1997); Peter Kok, "Sudan: Between Restructuring and Deconstruction of State Systems," *Review of African Political Economy* 23, no. 70 (1996): 558–560.

38. "Intensification of War in South," and "Fall of Southern Towns to Government Forces," *Keesing's Contemporary Record of World Events,* March 1992, pp. 38799–38800, 38854–38855.

39. "Sudanese Leader Stresses Achievement of National Peace," BBC Summary of World Broadcasts, August 19, 1991. See also the comments of the information minister: "We are studying the Nigerian experiment in the federal system to benefit from it in proceeding towards federation in Sudan."

40. Robert O. Collins, "Africans, Arabs, and Islamists: From the Conference Tables to the Battlefields in the Sudan," *African Studies Review* 42, no. 2 (September 1999): 113–114.

41. For a detailed analysis of the Abuja talks, see Steven Wöndu and Ann Lesch, *Battle for Peace in Sudan: An Analysis of the Abuja Conferences, 1992–1993* (Lanham, MD: University Press of America, 2000); Collins, "Africans, Arabs, and Islamists," pp. 113–114.

42. Cited in Wöndu and Lesch, *Battle for Peace in Sudan,* p. 113.

43. "Sudanese Peace Talks: Report on Delegations' Joint Communiqué," BBC Summary of World Broadcasts, June 8, 1992; "Sudan: Government, Rebels Agree on 'Multi-cultural, Multi-religious' Solution," *Arab Press Service Organization* 36, no. 23 (June 6, 1992).

44. Wöndu and Lesch, *Battle for Peace in Sudan,* p. 65.

45. During Abuja II, Nigerian interior minister Tunji Olagunju, chairman of the peace talks, proposed joint mediation during a visit to Kenya and Uganda, but the Sudanese government turned it down because it exceeded the terms of reference of the Abuja negotiations. As a government spokesman, Ali al-Haj, observed, "Attempts to settle the problem of the civil war outside the framework of direct talks is an infringement on Sudanese sovereignty and has to be rejected." See "Sudan Against Peace Talks Summit: Report," Agence France-Presse, May 14, 1993.

46. For a summary of Abuja II and the aftermath, see Wöndu and Lesch, *Battle for Peace in Sudan,* pp. 96–119; "Sudan Against Peace Talks Summit: Report," Agence France-Presse, May 14, 1993; "Nigeria Seeks Compromise Formula in Sudan Peace Talks," Reuters, May 1, 1993; "Garang Views Formula for Two Confederal States," FBIS-NES-93-125, July 1, 1993, p. 14; "Communiqué Issued at the Adjournment of Talks Between SPLA and Government, May 7–25 1993," Nairobi, May 1993.

47. Gill Lusk, "Abuja Fails Again," *Middle East International* 451 (May 28, 1993): 12.

48. Manoah Esipisu, "U.N. Launches Food Airlifts to Southern Sudan," Reuters, June 12, 1993; Pauline Jelinek, "Civil War in Southern Sudan Destroys Life for the People," *Calgary Herald,* June 15, 1993, p. C7; "Sudan: Pressure on Garang," *Middle East International* 452 (June 11, 1993): 13–14.

49. "Sudan Opposes Creation of 'Safe Areas' in Southern Sudan," Xinhua News Agency, June 5, 1993.

50. Mark C. Huband, "Thousands Flee New Fighting in Famine-racked Southern Sudan," *Washington Post,* August 18, 1993, p. A 27; Horace Awori, "Sudan:

SPLA Faces Toughest Test Yet," Inter Press Service, August 13, 1993; Horace Awori, "Sudan: Council of Churches Asks U.N. to Intervene in Civil Strife," Inter Press Service, August 17, 1993; "Rebel In-fighting Fuels Government Offensive," *Africa Research Bulletin,* August 1–31, 1993, pp. 11127–11128.

    51. "Sudan: Bashir's Army Day Speech: Claims Victory over SPLA Leader Garang," BBC Summary of World Broadcasts, August 17, 1993.

    52. John West, "Sudan Government's Offensive May Alarm Neighbors," Reuters, August 12, 1993.

5

IGAD Initiatives,
1993–2005

Chapter 4 focused on regional and international involvement to resolve the north-south conflict between the 1960s and 1980s. Before and after the Addis Ababa Agreement, internal political dynamics wrought consequences for the region, propelling external actors to intervene. But while the intensity of the conflict established the stakes of external actors in the search for a settlement, most of the peace initiatives after the Addis Ababa Agreement were sporadic and without solid institutional leadership. The Abuja peace initiatives marked the start of a significant shift in regional ownership of the conflict, furnishing an African institutional anchor. Nonetheless, despite the importance of Nigeria's leadership, Abuja remained geographically distant from the center of the conflict. The Intergovernmental Authority on Development (IGAD) emerged to fill the gap of a proximate regional institutional base as the principal focus for peace initiatives throughout the 1990s.

In analyzing IGAD's twelve-year effort in Sudan, this chapter demonstrates the opportunities and challenges that African regional actors faced during the process, specifically problems of mediation without adequate clout and leverage and the management of multiple African and international actors that equally laid claims to conflict resolution. Over the course of the protracted peace process, IGAD depended on a wide array of organizational, diplomatic, and economic resources from Western donors—the IGAD Partners Forum (IPF)—in sustaining the negotiations and insulating the IGAD efforts from competition, primarily from the Libya-Egypt initiatives. The latter initiatives injected a combustible continental Arab-African fissure on the conflict resolution process. Thus, in addition to dealing with the complex internal stakes and parties to the north-south conflict, the IGAD mediators managed regional and international actors, innovating as the conflict evolved and learning the limits of regional ownership and the content of African solutions. The Machakos-Naivasha agreements that ended the north-south conflict partly reflected IGAD's persistence and tenacity but, more pertinent, they underscored the coalescence of regional and international efforts in conflict resolution—efforts that started with the Addis Ababa Agreement and are continuing with the crisis in Darfur.

The Road to the Declaration of Principles

The rise of the NIF (later renamed the National Congress Party, NCP) gave a measure of coherence to northern politics, submerging the formerly discordant voices that had contributed to perennial instability. For the most part, Bashir and Turabi symbolized and solidified the two central pillars of the NIF—Islamism and militarism—furnishing a measure of authoritarian control on the previously sectarian nature of politics. The NIF's fundamentalist and authoritarian streaks, however, also helped in the aggregation of international opprobrium that decisively shaped the IGAD intervention. At the moment of growing international weakness, Bashir invited his IGAD neighbors to mediate the conflict. For the south, the 1991 internal rupture in the SPLA signified the brittleness of unity schemes that are constructed oblivious to the disintegrative forces of ethnicity and regionalism. Although the SPLM/A continued to make appeals to southern unity in dealing with the north, there was a shift in emphasis toward building a broad-based national alliance, which was captured in the multiparty National Democratic Alliance.

In the aftermath of the collapse of the Abuja peace talks, there was mounting international pressure for sanctions against the Bashir government. The Clinton administration took the lead, starting in 1993, to isolate Sudan, citing human rights abuses, support for international terrorism, and export of Islamic fundamentalism. Following accusations of Khartoum's complicity in the June 1993 bombing of the World Trade Center in New York and its growing cooperation with Iran and Iraq, the US State Department designated Sudan as a supporter of international terrorism, triggering a ban on all bilateral trade and foreign assistance, except humanitarian and disaster relief. In August 1993, the International Monetary Fund (IMF) added to the economic pressure by suspending Sudan's membership because it failed to repay its debt.[1]

Washington's designation of Sudan as a supporter of terrorism reinforced Khartoum's isolation by fellow Arab League members—notably Algeria, Egypt, and Tunisia—concerned about the spread of fundamentalism. In addition, Bashir lost vital economic support from oil-rich Gulf states after Khartoum supported Iraq's invasion of Kuwait in 1991. In other signs of increasing isolation, the Joint Assembly of the Africa Caribbean Pacific–European Community (ACP-EU) voted in October 1993 to freeze aid to Sudan under the Lomé Convention, while individual EU states reduced their engagement with Sudan. Mounting external pressure compounded an economy reeling under the strain of war, decreased agricultural production, soaring inflation, and high unemployment. In January 1994, government estimates showed that Sudan, which had also been hit by a devastating drought, was spending more than a million dollars a day on the army in the south and had a foreign debt estimated at more than US$17 billion, ranking it among the most indebted countries in the world.[2]

The confluence of Sudan's international isolation and domestic economic pressures led to the IGAD initiative. Departing from its previous tasks of coordinating regional responses to famine and environmental issues, IGAD (by then called the Intergovernmental Authority on Drought and Development, IGADD) began to mediate. This took place at the invitation of President Bashir during the annual summit in September 1993 in Addis Ababa. Bashir's motives for asking IGAD's intervention did not significantly differ from the previous invitation to the Nigerians at Abuja. The African nature of IGAD mechanisms, Bashir suggested, would prove to the world that "Africans have become mature enough to resolve their own problems . . . and are no longer in need of a foreign guardian." He also pointed to the need to preempt foreign intervention, stating that IGAD would be neutral and transparent, but "without loopholes through which colonialism could penetrate on the pretext of humanitarianism."[3] A foreign ministry statement also saw IGAD's proximity as an added advantage: "Their [IGAD] countries sharing the same borders with the Sudan, being fully knowledgeable of the root causes of the problem, are better placed to help bring about the desired peaceful settlement."[4] Beyond the issues of proximity and knowledge, however, Bashir had other motives, as Wöndu and Lesch argue:

> First, it was the right thing to say in that [IGAD] fraternity. Second, he did not expect them to take up the challenge so soon after Nigeria had failed. Third, by proposing that Sudan's immediate neighbors in IGAD form the mediation committee, Bashir calculated that its best friends would dominate the deliberations. The four-state IGAD Standing Committee on Peace in Sudan was to be chaired by Kenyan Daniel Arap Moi, with Presidents Meles Zenawi of Ethiopia, Isaias Afewerki of Eritrea and Yoweri Museveni of Uganda. According to Khartoum's arithmetic, Eritrea and Ethiopia were governed by former insurgents indebted to Sudan for the support they received during their struggle against Mengistu. Uganda's sympathy for the SPLM could be neutralized. Kenya was considered neutral and would be paralyzed by the responsibilities of the chair.[5]

Despite Bashir's mixed motives, IGAD took him up on the offer, perceiving its access to the principal Sudanese parties as a source of leverage to halt the escalating war and its spillover regional effects. Sudan's neighbors hoped that Sudan's membership in IGAD would provide them with a credible means of exerting collective pressure without seeming to be overly interventionist. As Abdelwahab El-Affendi has observed, "The motive of IGAD leaders in taking the task of mediation was first to integrate and contain Khartoum in the interest of regional stability."[6]

At the Addis Ababa summit in September 1993, IGAD established a four-nation mediation committee composed of Kenyan president Daniel arap Moi, Eritrean president Issaias Afewerki, Ethiopian president Meles Zenawi, and Uganda's Yoweri Museveni. A ministerial committee from the four nations was later designated to lead the mediation under Moi's chairmanship. The idea of a mediating committee endowed the initiative with a collective character and facilitated decisionmaking and consultation.[7]

For the SPLA, IGAD as a regional interstate initiative first elicited misgivings that gradually gave way to expectations that collective pressure would bring Khartoum to the negotiating table. These concerns stemmed from the SPLA's wariness that as an interstate organization, IGAD would perhaps be more inclined to curry favor with the government.[8] With the new momentum for peace, international supporters of the southern cause made attempts to reconcile the SPLA factions, culminating in the October 1993 agreement between Garang and Machar, mediated by the chairman of the US House Foreign Affairs Subcommittee on Africa, Harry Johnston. These efforts proceeded from the premise that fratricidal rifts would further weaken the bargaining position of the south. Furthermore, unity would reclaim the international legitimacy of the southern cause that had been shattered by the SPLA's human rights atrocities and its attempts to impede relief efforts.[9]

The October 1993 congressional reconciliation talks produced an eight-point Washington Declaration that committed Garang and Machar to an immediate cessation of hostilities; cooperation in relief work; the search for a common position on the right of self-determination for southern Sudan, Nuba Mountains, and other marginalized areas; and opposition to the "policies of the NIF government in Khartoum, and other subsequent regimes that deny the right to self-determination of the people of southern Sudan, Nuba Mountains, and other marginalized areas."[10] Despite the Washington Declaration, the real test for southern unity hinged less on forging common negotiating positions than on resolving the deep-seated leadership differences between Garang and Machar that resumed soon after the Washington meeting.[11]

IGAD's ministerial committee's first foray into the negotiations was through proximity consultations with the parties over the agenda in January 1994. These talks attempted to gradually force a compromise around specific items prior to the narrowing of substantive differences. Garang and Machar jointly presented three basic items for negotiations: a cease-fire to facilitate humanitarian relief; the right of self-determination through a referendum to be conducted in southern Sudan, the Nuba Mountains, and the marginalized areas; and comprehensive interim arrangements for the transitional period. For its part, the government reaffirmed its commitment to negotiate on "controversial issues," but was reluctant to include cease-fire negotiations and self-determination as separate items on the agenda.[12]

During the first round of talks, which began on March 22, 1994, IGAD mediators proposed a compromise agenda that would first negotiate a cease-fire, then agree on the constitutional principles that would guide the resolution of the civil war, and finally make the necessary political and security arrangements for the interim period. But the government representatives rejected the agenda and threatened to walk out if the mediators placed self-determination on the agenda. Despite the previous consensus by Garang and Machar to include self-determination in the negotiations, Machar backed the government's position. Nonetheless, the first round secured agreement on the formation of a negotiating subcommittee of SPLA factions, the government, and the UN to deal with issues of relief aid. In April 1994, the subcommittee, in a confidence-building measure, agreed to open up air corridors to seventy-three relief sites, create five land passages, and immunize children in the war zone.[13] After fruitless rounds of talks over the agenda in May 1994, the mediators prepared a draft Declaration of Principles (DOP) that the delegates were asked to review in preparation for detailed talks in July 1994. Through this strategy, the mediators devised a formula that became the basis for future negotiations.

The DOP embodied all the contentious questions about the conflict. Given the polarization of Sudan, the first principle upheld the right of self-determination as an inalienable right to people whose particular circumstances justified its application. By the same token, though, the mediators gave priority to national unity as a principle that would be created through a national consensus. To forge a national consensus, the parties had to agree on an interim period during which they would create conditions for national unity. Among these conditions would be the separation of state and religion, a system of multiparty democracy, respect for fundamental human rights, and political decentralization through a loose federation or confederation. After a sufficient interim period, the people of the south and other disadvantaged groups would decide by referendum whether to continue the unity arrangement or adopt alternative arrangements such as secession. Central to the realization of these arrangements, the parties would commit themselves to a peaceful resolution, a commitment that was to be demonstrated in the mutual declaration of a sustainable cease-fire monitored internationally.[14]

Between May and July 1994, various Western diplomatic initiatives solidified around a new grouping, the Friends of IGAD (later renamed the IGAD Partners Forum), whose goal became to shore up the leverage of the mediators.[15] On a visit to Khartoum in April 1994, the US ambassador to the United

Nations, Madeleine Albright, warned that Sudan was running the risk of "continuing along the path of international isolation if it did not change its attitude on human rights in the war in the south and support for terrorism." While Khartoum pleaded for the United States to remove Sudan from the list of terrorist states, Albright reiterated that she was more "convinced than ever that the international community must maintain its vigilance toward Sudan."[16] Following Albright's mission, President Clinton appointed Ambassador Melissa Wells, in June 1994, as special envoy to Sudan to assist the IGAD peace efforts.[17] A European diplomatic bid launched by "Friends of Sudan and Uganda," under the leadership of Austrian president Thomas Klestil, resulted in a secret meeting between Museveni and Bashir in Muerzsberg, Austria, in May 1994, where they resolved to ease bilateral tensions and "remove all obstacles to a peace settlement for southern Sudan."[18]

When the IGAD talks resumed in July 1994, the southern parties endorsed the DOP, but the government rejected the DOP because the issues of self-determination and secularism were not negotiable. The most the government would negotiate was an interim period in the south based on federalism. The government further blamed the IGAD mediators of overreaching their mandate by placing the DOP on the table: "The issues of self-determination and religion and state are not within the competence of IGAD group."[19] At the start of the fourth round in early September 1994, Khartoum replaced its chief negotiators with Ghazi Salih al-Din, a militant minister of state for presidential affairs, signaling an even harder-line position at the negotiating table in Nairobi. Moi opened the talks with a warning that unless there was "convincing evidence" that the talks would show results, "we are not prepared to preside over them as people continue to get killed, maimed, or property destroyed."[20] Neither the threat nor the moral exhortation, however, could bridge the diametrically opposed positions of the parties. Al-Din castigated IGADD for issuing the DOP:

> The separation of state from religion is impossible because Sharia law embodies Islamic values. Sharia and custom as they stand are irreplaceable, but predominantly non-Muslim state legislation may provide for alternative laws vis-à-vis Sharia penal provisions in the south. The government has in no time before agreed to the principle of self-determination for the south in the sense that a new sovereign and independent state should be created. Self-determination or any other term that might cloak separation is a non-issue and the government is not ready to dwell upon it. The government suggested during the previous rounds of talks a "mechanism" through which the people of southern Sudan could express their political future within a United Sudan. Self-determination-alias-separation of southern Sudan is bound to elicit a chain-reaction afflicting the rest of Africa. This is an eventuality that the founding fathers of the OAU consciously tried to avoid.[21]

The September negotiations and a subsequent IGAD head of state summit failed to convince Khartoum of the wisdom of the DOP. The atmosphere was soured further when Eritrea and Uganda blamed Sudan for the breakdown of the talks and called for international sanctions against Khartoum. Subsequently, despite frantic efforts by Kenya to revive the initiative, Sudan insisted on the removal of self-determination and secularism from the IGAD agenda and the withdrawal of Uganda and Eritrea from the IGAD negotiating committee.[22]

Conflict and Confrontation: Toward the Frontline Strategy

Bashir outlined two objectives after the collapse of the September 1994 talks: to resolve the war in Southern Sudan "through the barrel of a gun . . . [and] to bring peace from within the country without the SPLA."[23] The obduracy elicited countervailing measures among IGAD states—Eritrea, Ethiopia, and Uganda—which became conduits of military, political, and diplomatic support to the SPLA. The Clinton administration led what it described as the Frontline States strategy, which entailed expanding economic and diplomatic sanctions against Sudan and strengthening the military capability of regional states to meet the escalation of the civil war. In engaging the Frontline States, the United States deepened Sudan's external isolation and narrowed its internal options.

Launched in early 1995, the Frontline strategy aimed to deter Sudanese support for terrorism and extremism, end the north-south civil conflict, encourage the restoration of political and human rights, and end the humanitarian crisis.[24] Washington's economic and military support to Eritrea, Ethiopia, and Uganda, in turn, became critical to the SPLA's execution of the guerrilla war. Eritrea first broke diplomatic relations with Sudan in December 1994, citing Khartoum's destabilization policies. Uganda followed suit by severing diplomatic relations with Sudan in April 1995.[25] Similarly, relations between Sudan and Ethiopia deteriorated following allegations of Khartoum's complicity in an assassination attempt on the life of Egyptian president Hosni Mubarak in Addis Ababa in summer 1995.[26]

A critical part of the Frontline strategy was to craft a credible domestic alliance against the Bashir government, particularly after the futile search for reconciliation between Garang and Machar, who had renamed his faction the Southern Sudan Independence Movement (SSIM). In the absence of southern unity, collaboration between the SPLA and northern opposition groups in the NDA presented an opportunity for new avenues of internal pressure. To solidify the NDA, Eritrea organized a meeting between the SPLA and leading opposition groups—the Umma Party, the Democratic

Unionist Party, and the Sudanese Allied Forces—in December 1994. This meeting adopted the Asmara Declaration, which stressed national unity but left the door open to southern independence in case of violation of the principles of multiracialism, multiculturalism, and separation of state and religion.[27] In January 1995, Afewerki turned over the Sudanese embassy in Asmara to the NDA, noting that

> those who argue for patience, saying there are moderates in the National Independence Front, or that a split is likely between the NIF and the military, are deceiving themselves. The stability of the region depends on the regime's defeat. There is no more room for diplomacy, and no compromise. Eritrea will provide any type of support for the people of Sudan. The sky is the limit. . . . We believe that it's an obligation on the part of Eritrea because the Sudanese people supported us during our struggle for independence.[28]

The international isolation campaign also peaked in January 1996 when the UN Security Council adopted Resolution 1044 condemning Sudan's threat to regional peace. Furthermore, the United States withdrew all its embassy personnel from Khartoum, citing concern about threats from extremist groups. In April 1996, the Security Council imposed limited sanctions that included limits on the travel of government officials abroad and a ban on international conferences in Khartoum.[2]

The Frontline strategy compromised IGAD's mediating hand, heightening Sudan's misgivings about IGAD's evenhandedness. With a bulk of IGAD at war with Sudan, what remained of the IGAD initiative was essentially a nominal and lone Kenyan affair. In these circumstances, other competitive mediators tried to come up with their own initiatives. Filling the vacuum of a fraying IGAD was a welter of mediators from the Carter Center, Iran, Libya, Malawi, and South Africa, seeking unsuccessfully to restart the talks. Even the Friends of IGAD were themselves incapable of breaking the impasse, torn as they were between the United States, which favored a hard line, and Europeans, who still believed in a peaceful solution.[30]

In the face of regional and international isolation, Bashir focused on consolidating his internal position by organizing presidential and legislative elections in March 1996—elections that solidified his presidency and Turabi's leadership as speaker of the national assembly. Equally pertinent, the government held peace talks with Machar's SSIM, culminating in the signing of a peace charter, in which Machar relinquished his demands for southern autonomy. Although the agreement declared that the "unity of the Sudan with its known boundaries shall be preserved," it provided for a referendum "as a means for realizing the aspirations of the citizens of the south . . . after full establishment of peace, stability, and reasonable level of social development."

In addition, even though Islamic *sharia* law would continue to be the basis of national legislation, the south would retain the right to enact special legislation to "complement federal law."[31] Bashir subsequently broadened the internal peace initiative in April 1997 by including five additional southern groups in a peace charter that promised a cease-fire and a four-year interim period leading to a referendum on self-determination in the south.

At the end of 1996, a multipronged SPLA-NDA offensive from the Eritrean and Ethiopian borders signaled the growing impact of the Frontline strategy. Posing the greatest challenge to the government since 1994, the offensive led to the capture of a string of towns and garrisons adjacent to the Ethiopian, Eritrean, and Ugandan borders. Washington provided $20 million in "defensive" weapons to Eritrea, Ethiopia, and Uganda toward these efforts.[32] The NDA also got a political boost when Sadiq al-Mahdi, the Sudanese prime minister who was overthrown by the Islamists in 1989, escaped to Eritrea in May 1997 and supported the NDA's military campaign, claiming that Khartoum stood on the brink of collapse.[33] By summer 1997, the coalition's impressive military gains tilted the balance of power on the battlefield, leading to Garang's claims about the end of the war.[34]

Although the government responded by searching for allies in the Arab world against what it characterized as conspiracy from a regional African-Christian alliance, the deteriorating military position forced Bashir back to the negotiations. At an IGAD summit in July 1997, Moi injected new life into the IGAD initiative, nudging Bashir to finally accept the DOP as the basis for negotiations. Following the summit, the IGAD ministerial committee moved quickly to build on the momentum, obtaining agreement for resumption of high-level talks in October 1997. At these negotiations, the IGAD mediators tried to force negotiations on the details of the DOP, but from the start, the talks made little progress, with the parties deeply divided on the familiar bones of contention: self-determination and secularism.[35]

On the eve of the adjournment of the talks in November 1997, the United States announced sweeping new sanctions against Khartoum that included a freeze on Sudanese assets in the United States and a ban on financial transactions because of Khartoum's sponsorship of international terror and destabilization of neighbors.[36] The timing of the sanctions reflected Washington's low expectations for the success of IGAD negotiations, but it became a salient propaganda coup to Sudan, which accused Washington of sabotaging the talks by "feeding Garang's intransigence."[37] US sanctions strengthened the Frontline strategy of containment, a policy that US secretary of state Madeleine Albright reiterated on a visit to Eritrea, Ethiopia, and Uganda in December 1997. Meeting Garang and members of the NDA in Kampala, she lauded their role in laying "the groundwork for a new Sudan in which people of all faiths and cultures can focus on reconstruction."[38]

The Egyptian-Libyan Initiative

The Frontline strategy was a double-edged sword, bringing pressure to bear on Sudan, but not generating significant movement on the peace front. The US sanctions of November 1997 epitomized IGAD's dependence on a key ally for a carrot-and-stick strategy that had uncertain outcomes on the negotiations, heightening the tensions between militarism and mediation. Further complicating IGAD's position was the gradual decline in two underpinnings of the Frontline strategy—the regional consensus on Sudan's destabilization role and the internal coherence of the NDA. The first component was predicated on maintaining the broad-based alliance that had converged around the theme of Khartoum's role in exporting Islamic fundamentalism, while the second was based on maintaining a precarious amalgam of northern and southern opposition around the goal of getting rid of the Bashir government. Starting in late 1997, these pillars frayed at the seams as Egypt, a key regional actor, reconsidered its policy toward the government and as the NDA began to disintegrate.

Egyptian reconciliation with the Khartoum government began in October 1997, ending a two-year period of animosity. Following high-level diplomatic exchanges, the two countries normalized relations in February 1998, at which time Sudan's minister of state for foreign affairs, Mustafa Osman Ismail, emphasized their mutual security interests:

> We believe that Egyptian-Sudanese relations are old and eternal relations. Hence they should always be sincere and warm and realize the interests of the Nile Valley peoples. We consider all that has befallen relations between the two countries in the past period as a mere summer cloud which is in the process of dispersing and dissipating through our constant principles, particularly as we are facing issues of destiny threatening the unity of the Nile Valley, its wealth, and its achievements. In other words, there is a danger to our nationalist and strategic issues, and this necessitates our sitting down together to talk and consult so as to transcend these issues, which are not really simple and which could happen because basically differences do occur in one country and even in one house. The real challenge lies in mustering the ability to sit around a table to tackle these differences.[39]

The Cairo-Khartoum rapprochement was inspired by traditional Egyptian fears that the disintegration of Sudan's territorial integrity could cause chaos at the mouth of the Nile and compromise Egypt's water allocations. Moreover, as *Africa Confidential* noted, "Having considered Sudan its backyard since the pharaoh's time, Cairo is angry that Ethiopia, Eritrea, and Uganda host the NDA. . . . Cairo's moves also reflect its (and Arab governments') fear of partition."[40]

Egypt subsequently allied with Libya to mediate between the northern factions, the NDA, and the Khartoum government, efforts that gradually grew into a frontal assault on the IGAD initiative. In November 1997, Cairo and Tripoli proposed a constitutional conference, composed of the government and northern opposition parties, that would "restore Sudanese and Arab unity." At its convention in Asmara in January 1998, the Umma Party, a key player in the NDA, made only fleeting reference to the unity between the NDA and Garang. Instead, most of its speakers emphasized the importance of Islam in politics and the potential loss of Sudan's mineral riches if southern Sudan became independent. Although reiterating support for the IGAD initiative, the convention noted that "the initiative in its old context has been overtaken by circumstances and will no longer be effective unless it is developed with the participation of all the parties to the conflict in Sudan, and unless its agenda deals with, in addition to the issue of peace, the issue of the country's regime and the widening of IGAD membership to include Egypt, South Africa, Zimbabwe, and another Arab or Islamic country."[41] A delegation of another NDA northern faction, the Sudanese Democratic Unionist, made similar demands during a February 1998 visit to the Netherlands, claiming that "the African element in Sudanese negotiations is dominant at the expense of the Arab element and we suggested the addition of Arab elements to this [IGAD] partnership, including UN envoy Lakhdar Brahimi, a man known for his Arab endeavors, so that it would include both an Arab and an African element."[42]

The demands for expansion of IGAD were overshadowed in the spring of 1998 by the resurgence of famine in southern Sudan. With aid agencies reporting that warfare and drought threatened 350,000 southerners with death by starvation, the attention focused on negotiating a cease-fire between the combatants to permit the delivery of food and medical supplies. During an IGAD foreign ministers meeting with the IPF in Rome in March 1998, the latter took more of a leadership role in the peace process by designating the Italian undersecretary for foreign affairs, Rino Serri, to negotiate a cease-fire that would alleviate human suffering and provide a conducive climate for the resumption of IGAD talks.[43]

Serri's intervention was a temporary move to defuse mounting tensions between Egypt-Libya and IGAD. Although the IPF were suspicious of the North African attempts to marginalize the IGAD states, they were not keen on alienating the Egyptians, in particular. When IGAD states refused to enlarge the peace process to accommodate Egypt, Egypt threatened to launch a parallel peace initiative. But these threats also forced the IGAD mediators to hasten their diplomatic efforts to restart the negotiations. A new round of talks opened in May 1998 in Nairobi, with the IGAD mediators assembling a broad spectrum of international actors at the opening session, including the UN secretary general, Kofi Annan, and IPF representatives. Although the parties continued to disagree on the questions of secularism and cease-fire terms, they made progress on the issue of self-determination by accepting to respect the principle of self-determination for the south on the basis of an international referendum.[44] As the humanitarian situation deteriorated in the south, the UK, which had normalized diplomatic relations with Khartoum, forced negotiations on a cease-fire. Like the previous Italian intervention, the British minister in the foreign office, Derek Fatchett, brokered a three-month cease-fire agreement between the government and the SPLA in mid-July 1998 that provided for "corridors of tranquility" to permit relief aid in the south.[45]

On the eve of new IGAD talks in Addis Ababa in early August 1998, Khartoum announced a "complete and comprehensive ceasefire in all the war zones," as a goodwill gesture. IGAD mediators invited OAU secretary-general Salim to lend his weight to the Addis Ababa talks, but not even Salim's presence could make a difference at the table. In three days of talks, IGAD mediators could not bridge the gaps on the long-standing issues.[46] More important, the collapse of the Addis Ababa talks coincided with an escalation in the Ethiopia-Eritrea border war. With the two IGAD partners embroiled in a border war, Egypt stepped up its efforts to become the critical player in the conflict, inviting all the leaders of the NDA to a convention in Cairo in August 1998.[47] In a declaration in Cairo, the NDA underlined the special ties binding Egypt and Sudan and the legitimate interests they each had in the other's affairs, and affirmed that the "continued existence of Khartoum's terrorist regime represents a real danger that threatens Sudan's and Egypt's security and stability." The declaration also renewed the northern NDA's clamor for the inclusion of Egypt into IGAD and reiterated its commitment to "Sudanese unity, racial, religious, and cultural diversity."[48]

Pressure for a More Professional IGAD

The structural contexts that had given credence to IGAD's intervention—Khartoum's international and regional vulnerability, and the coherence of the NDA—came under increased strain from new trends that converged to force changes in the approach to mediation. The most vital shift in the power equation that affected IGAD mediation was oil exploration in southern Sudan. In December 1998, a consortium of Malaysian, Canadian, Chinese, and British companies completed the construction of a pipeline to carry crude oil from the Nuer areas of Western Upper Nile to refineries and export terminals in the north. The daily yield of 150,000 barrels, beginning in 1999, provided a $450,000 million windfall that dampened the weight of external economic pressures.[49]

Oil revenues boosted Khartoum's investment profile and struggling economy at a time when pressure was mounting on the Clinton administration from domestic constituencies and in Europe to reassess its Sudan policy. The administration's position was compounded by its cruise missile bombing of the Al-Shifa pharmaceutical plant in August 1998 in retaliation for Sudan's involvement in the manufacture of chemical weapons and its links to fugitive Islamic militant Osama bin Laden. In a tacit admission that it did not have enough evidence to back the missile attack, Washington later decided to unfreeze the assets of the Saudi businessman who owned the factory. In March 1999, leading US humanitarian agencies asked the Clinton administration to reestablish diplomatic contacts with the Sudanese government to forge a comprehensive cease-fire along with IGAD Partners; to support and reinforce efforts by the IGAD Partners Forum to establish a timetable for a serious peace process; and to persuade the SPLA and its regional allies to increase their commitment to the peace process. In response to these pressures, President Clinton appointed former US representative Harry Johnston, in May 1999, to be a special envoy to Sudan to focus international attention on the human rights situation and to strengthen the IGAD peace process.[50]

At the regional level, the most decisive change was the rapprochement between Sudan and Eritrea in May 1999. Bashir and Afewerki agreed to restore diplomatic ties, halt negative media campaigns, and abstain "from hosting or organizing international or regional conferences with the aim of adopting policies or coordinating activities that target the security and stability of neighboring countries."[51] Bashir made similar overtures to Ethiopia, culminating in the normalization of relations in the spring of 1999, and later that year, the Carter Center mediated an agreement between Kampala and Khartoum, weakening the draconian arm of the Frontline coalition.[52]

The IPF responded to the changing circumstances by seeking to inject a modicum of professionalism in IGAD mediation. The IGAD mediating committee under the leadership of Kenyan foreign ministers had, for the most part, been responsible for managing the mediation. Yet the constant changes in foreign ministers had subjected the mediation to uncertainties that stymied continuity. Within a period of five years, Nairobi had had four foreign ministers heading the mediation committee, all with varying levels of competence. The IPF, providing a bulk of the financial and technical assistance, brought pressure to bear on Kenya to appoint a special envoy from the foreign ministry to speed up the peace process and prevent the long delays and postponements that had come to characterize the mediation.

At a forum in Oslo in March 1999, the IPF criticized IGAD for the slow pace of the negotiations and warned that "the current aid flow from the donor community to Sudan would be difficult to maintain in the long run, without an accelerated and strengthened political process toward peace." The IPF proposed "urgent enhancement" of the IGAD peace process, specifically calling for financial support to a "dedicated secretariat" to support a new Kenyan special envoy to "mount a concentrated and continuous mediation effort."[53] The pressure for a special envoy led eventually to the establishment of an IGAD secretariat in the foreign ministry led by Daniel Mboya, Kenya's former ambassador to Khartoum. Mboya's appointment, however, did not make much difference in the IGAD talks in July 1999, where the focus was to try to build on the successes achieved previously and to reduce the outstanding differences.[54]

In light of the impasse, the Sudan government tried to reengage Egypt and Libya in a further bid to coax northern NDA parties out of their alliance with the SPLA. Following the reconciliation between the government and al-Mahdi's Umma Party in May 1999, Bashir spoke of a comprehensive national settlement that would bypass "IGAD's bilateral solution."[55] Libya's Qaddafi echoed the theme of comprehensiveness by calling for an "inclusive conference for all Sudanese where they can resolve their differences."[56] As a result, Libya and Egypt pressured the NDA to abandon IGAD, as al-Mahdi acknowledged:

> I don't call it pressure. All of Sudan's neighbors are very much interested in what is taking place in the country. . . . Egypt is bound to be interested in a peaceful resolution of Sudan's problems. This does not mean that Egypt wants to exert pressure, but to play a role in finding a solution to the problem. Libya has developed a new African policy line. Is it conceivable for Libya to resolve African conflicts without doing anything about the conflict in Sudan? Therefore, I believe that Egypt and Libya are showing great interest in events in Sudan in order to find a solution to the conflict from the viewpoint of their security and relationship with the peoples of the region. The unusual thing would be if there was a lack of Egyptian or Libyan interest in the events in Sudan.[57]

In a Tripoli meeting of the NDA at the end of July 1999, the parties agreed to Qaddafi's proposal for a conference on national dialogue in a declaration that called for immediate cessation of all military operations by all sides; immediate cessation of media propaganda by all sides; the start of direct talks between the government and the opposition through an inclusive national conference to reach a comprehensive political solution to the problem, which takes into account the unity of Sudan and secures the recognition of the ethnic, religious, and cultural diversity of the Sudanese people; and the establishment of a preparatory committee in charge of drawing up plans for a national conference. Subsequently, Egypt and Libya set up a joint committee to garner international support for the initiative.[58] Sudan quickly jumped onto the Egyptian-Libyan initiative, as the foreign minister, Mustafa Ismail, remarked, "We are prepared to cooperate and we hope the initiative will have an outcome that will help in accommodating other initiatives. We are certainly committed to the IGAD initiative and Egypt's efforts but we hope that there will be coordination that will advance the Libyan initiative."[59] The

SPLA, however, rejected the Egyptian-Libyan plan with Garang warning that "parallel tracks" would obliterate IGAD's progress.[60]

Even as it gathered momentum, the Egyptian-Libyan initiative faced three challenges. First, its success depended on whether the divided NDA could marshal a consensus to carry through the major provisions of the plan, especially the appointment of representatives to the preparatory committee. By mid-October 1999, factions allied with the SPLA, citing the government's continued bombing of the south and east, blocked the formation of an NDA team.[61] Second, most IGAD states were unwilling to entertain the Egyptian-Libyan initiative, seeing it as competitive rather than complementary. Third, in trying to supplant the IGAD initiative, Cairo and Tripoli had to contend with the United States. Visiting Nairobi in October 1999, Secretary of State Albright supported IGAD: "We do not support other processes that some are suggesting, the Egyptians, the Libyans. We believe that through the work of IGAD, Kenya's leadership in it, our support in it, we can hope to make some significant steps in the future that might lessen the horror, dying, and slavery that is taking place in Sudan."[62]

Despite the mounting criticisms, Egypt and Libya proceeded in November 1999 to create a Joint Egyptian-Libyan Committee for National Accord in Sudan to work out an agenda for action, including ways of coordinating with IGAD.[63] More discreetly, the new US special envoy, Harry Johnston, attempted a compromise in meetings with NDA leaders in Cairo and Kampala toward the end of 1999. Johnston proposed that although the United States adhered to the IGAD initiative, it favored the participation of all the opposition forces in a peace process that excluded Libya. Toward this end, the United States would commit to the expansion of the IGAD initiative with the Sudanese opposition participating collectively in a unified delegation under the leadership of the SPLA, while Egypt would obtain observer status in IGAD.[64] At a meeting in Kampala in December 1999, the NDA leadership rejected the compromise proposal, stating that "the Sudanese opposition could not countenance to be put under U.S. tutelage."[65]

In December 1999, Bashir dissolved parliament and declared a three-month state of emergency following an escalating power struggle with the speaker of parliament, Turabi. Presented as acts of national salvation to avert imminent threats to the coherence of the state, these measures consolidated Bashir's power and began Turabi's political marginalization.[66] Egypt and Libya lauded Turabi's demise as the end of political extremism that would improve the chances of a comprehensive agreement consistent with their initiative. In February 2000, Libya, Egypt, and Sudan reaffirmed support for their initiative, pledging periodic meetings, under the chairmanship of the three foreign ministers, to review and bolster the steps to achieve peace and national accord in Sudan.[67]

IGAD Under Siege, January 2000–November 2001

Despite campaigns to discredit the IGAD process and replace it with the Egyptian-Libyan initiative, IGAD mediators persisted relentlessly. The push for a more professional IGAD mediation structure, which began in mid-1999, culminated in donor commitment to a continuous mediation effort by the IGAD secretariat. Under Mboya's leadership, the secretariat created two negotiating committees to deal sequentially with key aspects of the conflict: a political committee to deal with the governance components of the DOP, and a transitional issues committee. Reports from these committees were then presented to ministerial plenary sessions. This method allowed the fragmentation of the agenda and the fashioning of compromises around core issues. In another departure, the IGAD secretariat enlisted external experts and IPF representatives who participated as observers. Previously, as El-Affendi shows, the IGAD mediation had been beset with severe organizational problems:

> The mediators relied mainly on improvisation, and were singularly unable to structure the talks to avoid sliding the talks into the usual deadlock; it was not all clear why the talks had been called at all before some progress had been made on resolving these contentious issues. . . . The talks were normally scheduled to take one week (Monday to Friday) to fit the busy timetables of ministers involved, but often broke up after only three days. The format was varied occasionally to include separate discussions with the parties, but the norm was plenary sessions that degenerated very quickly into [shouting] matches. Little footwork was undertaken prior to the working sessions to ascertain shifts in positions, devise, and promote possible compromises or prepare working papers to guide the discussions.[68]

Mboya convened committee negotiations in Nanyuki (outside Nairobi) in early 2000. The political committee intermittently deliberated on the separation of religion and state and the boundaries of southern Sudan. The mediators strove for a breakthrough on the vexing question of secularism, hoping that a breakthrough would generate sufficient momentum to tackle the rest of the political issues.[69] But even under the new negotiating framework, both sides came no closer to a compromise than previously. In March 2000, the SPLA suspended its participation in the IGAD talks following government air attacks against southern civilians.[70] The collapse renewed US efforts to push for a merger of the IGAD and Egyptian-Libyan initiatives. During a visit to Khartoum in March 2000, Johnston indicated that the United States would reconsider its ambivalence toward the North African plan: "Although the U.S. was committed to the IGAD peace initiative, it would not ignore the interests of Egypt and Libya and the opposition National Democratic Alliance (NDA)." In addition, Johnston suggested that the United States supported self-determination but not the separation of the south: "Going to a referendum for self-determination without resolving issues like power-sharing or the judiciary would be an invitation to the separation of the south."[71] More significant, Garang gave a new lease on life to the Egyptian-Libyan initiative on a visit to Cairo in May 2000:

> The SPLM believes these two initiatives must be coordinated or merged in order to achieve a solution that can neither be accused of being predominantly African (IGAD) nor principally Arab (the Egyptian-Libyan proposals). Sudan's problems can't be solved without active Egyptian participation. Similarly, the Egyptian-Libyan initiative can't succeed without the IGAD nations taking part. Combining the two can be achieved in several ways. The IGAD blueprint, for example, contains certain elements that are absent in the Egyptian-Libyan plan, and the opposite is also true. A new combined initiative can overcome the shortcomings of both its constituent parts. The Egyptian-Libyan plan contains eight points lacking in the IGAD initiative, particularly in the area of preparing the conditions conducive for the success of negotiations. This and other elements can be incorporated in a new combined plan. We've already asked the nations taking part in both peace plans to form a joint technical committee to look into ways a merger can be achieved. Those nations should also bear the responsibility for activating the combined initiative. We can help by putting forward our ideas and recommendations, but advancing the process itself is primarily the responsibility of its sponsors.[72]

Emboldened by the position of Garang, Egypt exerted pressure on IGAD to decide on a merger or risk marginalization; as the Egyptian foreign minister, Amr Musa, observed, "It was now up to the IGAD mediators to state whether they want amalgamation or coordination. Now that Garang has come on board, the Libyan-Egyptian initiative should proceed as the main initiative."[73]

A resurgent Egyptian-Libyan initiative placed the IGAD Partners in a delicate diplomatic position of mediating between the two competitors. Saddled with the tasks of professionalizing IGAD, the Partners seemed unprepared to plunge into an intramural Arab-African conflict. In June 2000, the Partners met in Oslo to seek a compromise between IGAD and Egypt but ran against Egyptian opposition for amalgamation. A row between Kenya and Egypt in Oslo over the terms of amalgamation deepened the animosity between the Arab north and Africa over their respective intentions in Sudan, with Kenya complaining of Egyptian heavy-handedness. More poignantly, the Egyptian delegate warned that Cairo would not accept self-determination of the south and would use all means to prevent it. Caught in between these pressures, the IGAD Partners announced their continued support to the IGAD secretariat, but in a departure from previous endorsements, they gave IGAD mediators three months to come up with an agreement.[74]

Procedural wrangles characterized the negotiations as Mboya and his team tried anxiously to meet the donor's deadline. When the talks finally resumed in September 2000, the mediators proposed a secular federal framework that would permit individual states to implement Islamic laws. They also adopted a new negotiating tack: forcing the parties to give specific responses to the issues of secularism and self-determination. After deliberating on each item, the mediators asked both parties to commit in writing their agreements and disagreements before proceeding to the next agenda. The mediators' attempts to sequence the negotiations and seek closure did not produce any movement on the contested items. At the end of the September 2000 talks, the parties recorded intractable disagreement on secularism, forcing the mediators to seek agreement on self-determination and interim arrangements. But in October 2000, IGAD mediators were unable to convene new talks, as Khartoum increasingly looked to solidify its military gains and national reconciliation with northern parties in the NDA. In a national reconciliation conference in Khartoum in October, Bashir urged the northern parties to disengage from the NDA, abandon the military struggle, and embrace peace before being defeated. In a sign of the government's successful efforts at co-opting the NDA, al-Mahdi ended four years of exile and returned to Khartoum pledging to pursue a national political agenda.[75]

The altered domestic context gave the government the upper hand in deflecting further pressures from IGAD mediators. An IGAD heads of state summit in Khartoum, on November 23, 2000, illustrated IGAD's quandary and the doubts that began to emerge about its efficacy. Not only did Moi boycott the summit, but deep divisions among the mediators came to the fore, in particular with Eritrea's Afewerki charging that "only Eritrea was qualified to broker peace in the Sudan."[76] The growing divisions in IGAD exposed the organization to closer scrutiny from the IGAD Partners. At a meeting in London in October 2000, the Partners made a major appraisal of the IGAD peace process, concluding that there was very little confidence in the initiative:

> The Secretariat often works in a cumbersome, time-consuming manner; the decision-making is time consuming, difficult, and inflexible; the secretariat's efficiency is adversely affected by its reliance on consensus decisions of the envoys of the four mediator countries; the IGAD mediator countries have different relationships with the two Sudanese parties to the conflict; the mediators all have a vested but different interest in the Sudanese conflict and each wants a different result from the peace process; the Special Envoy seems to lack the necessary authority to effectively pursue his mandate. Important initiatives from the Special Envoy are overruled; during the negotiations, the secretariat acts as a cautious or passive observer rather than as active mediators; and not challenging the positions of the parties. On involving the other Sudanese stakeholders to the conflict, the secretariat's attempts to consult the opposition National Democratic Alliance (NDA) encountered political obstacles that required, but did not receive, resolution at the senior political levels of IGAD.[77]

As the IGAD initiative faltered, Egypt reaffirmed the integrity of the North African initiative. In January 2001, Egyptian foreign minister Amr Musa denounced the IGAD efforts and noted that only Egypt was in a position to resolve the conflict:

> If IGAD wants a piece of this cake then it should agree to amalgamate its initiative with the Libyan-Egyptian one. Otherwise IGAD will remain as a deadwood unfit even for burning. Everyone should know that IGAD's partners in European and world capitals will not solve the Sudanese problem via the IGAD initiative alone. The joint Libyan-Egyptian initiative for a comprehensive settlement is still the correct one. The Egyptian role in the issue is important and there can be no solution without it.[78]

From Confrontation to Accommodation: The Bush Administration, September 11, and the Path to Machakos and Beyond

The IPF's indictment of IGAD's organizational inadequacies and the Egyptian-Libyan bid to wrest the Sudan problem out of IGAD's hands occurred against the backdrop of changes in the US government, from the Clinton to the Bush administration, that radically altered the parameters of engagement with Khartoum. The September 11, 2001, attacks in the United States further deepened the engagement and, in turn, transformed the fortunes of IGAD as a relevant actor in the quest for a negotiated settlement. Regionally, Sudan mended its relationships with all its IGAD neighbors. The parties to the conflict were also reinvigorated in different ways, with Khartoum gaining more confidence in its growing oil revenues, while southerners found unity in a new reconciliation bid between Garang and Machar in January 2002.

Clinton's departure signaled a shift from the core confrontation premises of the Frontline strategy to a policy of accommodation and evenhandedness toward Khartoum. The Center for Strategic and International Studies (CSIS) produced an influential report in February 2001 that tried to reconcile competing positions within the new US government. Warning that rising oil production in the south had shifted the military balance of power in Khartoum's favor and diminished the prospects of military victory by the SPLA and its allies, the report urged Washington to lead a multilateral push to halt the war. The report castigated the Clinton policy of economic sanctions and suggested that Washington become an impartial broker through the resumption of diplomatic relations with Khartoum. In calling on the United States, Norway, and Britain to spearhead a new peace initiative based on the DOP, the report was skeptical of the competing regional initiatives: "Although the IGAD peace initiative has had certain achievements on which any future initiatives should build, IGAD cannot be relied on to persuade Sudan's warring principals to enter into serious negotiations. The

Egypt/Libya initiative is essentially intended to checkmate IGAD, specifically on the issue of self-determination of the south. A new, robust extra-regional mediation agency is required if a credible peace process is to begin in Sudan."[79]

As the Bush administration reviewed its Sudan policy, IGAD Partners prevailed on Moi to reinvigorate the peace bid through high-level intervention. Following Moi's visit to Khartoum, the two sides agreed to convene an emergency IGAD summit conference on the IGAD initiative in Nairobi in June 2001. But despite heightened hopes for a breakthrough, the summit foundered on old animosities as the IGAD mediators were unable to bridge the differences. At the height of the summit, Bashir refused to meet Garang despite pleas from IGAD mediators. The most Moi could pry from the parties was the appointment of permanent negotiating teams to the IGAD secretariat to continue the talks.[80]

With chances for a political dialogue under IGAD looking remote, the flurry of diplomatic activities in summer 2001 shifted invariably to Cairo and Tripoli. Egypt and Libya abandoned the previous position of seeking a merger with IGAD, contending that the latter was irrelevant. The NDA convention in Cairo in late June 2001 billed itself as the "last chance to reach a concrete proposal for coordinating the two initiatives." The NDA chairman, Mohammed Al-Mirghani, commented that the "integration of the Libyan-Egyptian initiative with that of IGAD was imperative so that the Sudanese issue does not become an Arab versus African issue." But he could not prevail because of continued pressure from Egypt and Libya, who were adamantly opposed to southern self-determination.[81]

In summer 2001, Egypt and Libya formally handed the government and opposition parties a nine-point plan to resolve the conflict. Its provisions were: Sudanese unity; recognition of ethnic, religious, and cultural diversity; the need for pluralist democracy; the guarantee of basic freedoms and human rights; citizenship as a basis for rights and duties; the need for decentralized rule of law; urgent cessation of violence; and the pursuit of a foreign policy that guaranteed national interests and respected good neighborliness. Key to its implementation was the proposal to form an interim national government representing all political forces that would organize a national conference to revise the constitution and hold elections.[82] Khartoum unconditionally accepted the nine-point Egyptian-Libyan plan and called on the two countries to "take all the necessary measures for the implementation of the articles of the initiative."[83] The SPLA and its NDA allies greeted the plan with cautious optimism, agreeing to it in principle and pledging to attend a proposed follow-up conference, but they reiterated the inclusion of three core principles: self-determination, secularism, and the need for "formal unification" of the Egyptian-Libyan and IGAD initiatives.[84]

The September 11, 2001, terrorist attacks occurred at a time when the IGAD process had lost steam and a northern Africa initiative had been stymied. The attacks altered Sudanese-US relations in a more propitious direction as Khartoum sought to break out of pariah status as a former supporter of Al-Qaida, and the Bush administration was eager to engage Sudan in the new war on terrorism. These changes also coincided with the convergence of interests among IGAD Partners about harmonizing the multilateral efforts toward a credible peace process in Sudan. Where formerly the European Union and the United States had pursued contradictory policies toward Sudan and IGAD, there now emerged a transatlantic consensus on achieving a settlement. International pressure for the revitalization of the peace process also led to the appointment of Lieutenant General Lazarus Sumbeiywo, a close ally of Moi, as the head of the IGAD secretariat.[85]

US leadership of the peace process was reflected in the Bush administration's appointment of former senator John Danforth as special envoy to Sudan in September 2001. In a visit to Sudan, Danforth presented a limited confidence-building plan focusing on facilitating a temporary cease-fire, delivering humanitarian aid, ending aerial bombardment of civilians, and prohibiting slave raiding in the Nuba Mountains. In January 2002, when Danforth brought the SPLA and government representatives to Buergenstock, Switzerland, this first direct US mediation formalized a six-month renewable cease-fire agreement in the Nuba Mountains that would be supervised by international monitors. Danforth also persuaded the government to accept an international investigation into allegations of abduction and slavery.[86] Danforth expressed optimism that the Nuba Mountains cease-fire agreement would form the basis for a comprehensive cease-fire and resumption of the IGAD talks. He also sought to bridge the gaps between Sudan's African and Arab neighbors in the search for peace.[87]

Spurred on by the Danforth initiative, Garang and Machar patched up their differences in a new unity deal, signed in Nairobi in January 2002, in which they pledged to merge military units, end hostilities, and conduct military operations against the government. Subsequently, Sumbeiywo assembled mediators from Eritrea, Ethiopia, and Uganda, assisted by observers from the United States, the UK, Norway, and Italy, for renewed talks with the two warring parties starting in May 2002. Even though the talks coincided with the escalation of heavy fighting in the south, Sumbeiywo and the IGAD secretariat proposed an agenda based primarily on the DOP, culminating in the Machakos Protocol signed in July 2002.

The Machakos Protocol was a breakthrough in two key areas. First, the SPLA agreed that *sharia* would remain the source of legislation in the north, while the south would be governed by a secular administration. Second,

Khartoum accepted an internationally monitored referendum that would be held after a transition period of six and a half years, in which the south would decide whether to secede or continue to exist within a united federal Sudan. In addition, the parties agreed to "give unity a chance," that is, prioritize unity as the most desirable outcome of the referendum.[88] At heart, the Machakos Protocol represented a mutual renunciation of previously "non-negotiable" items: for the government, the Islamization of southern Sudan; and for the SPLA, the secularization of the entire country.

The Machakos Protocol also constituted a framework for negotiations of the outstanding issues and outlined the basic tenets of the final peace agreement. Soon after the signing of the protocol, there were additional hopes for peace when Garang and Museveni met in Kampala in August 2002. But soon the climate of mutual trust was ruptured when the SPLA captured Torit in September 2002, leading to the government's withdrawal from the negotiations. For the mediators, the resumption of hostilities underscored the urgency of negotiating credible cease-fire arrangements that would solidify the climate for negotiating the remaining issues.

Contributing to the peace momentum was the passage of the Sudan Peace Act by the US Congress in October 2002. Although initially conceived by congressional proponents of punitive economic sanctions against the Sudanese government, the final Sudan Peace Act sought to support an "internationally sanctioned peace process." One of its core provisions was a request to the US president to submit a six-monthly report to Congress assessing whether both Sudanese parties were "negotiating in good faith"; failure to comply, particularly by the government, would have triggered economic sanctions. The Sudan Peace Act afforded more sticks than carrots to the Sudanese government. While keepin up the pressure, however, it also held out the possibility of the normalization of relations.

Through the intensified efforts of the mediators, the government returned to the negotiating table in October 2002, leading to a Memorandum of Understanding (MOU) on Cessation of Hostilities in all areas of Sudan by all forces, including allied forces and affiliated militias. In February 2003, the parties signed an addendum to the cessation of hostilities to strengthen the implementation of the MOU. A significant provision of the addendum was the creation of a Verification and Monitoring Team (VMT), which comprised the two parties plus personnel and aircraft from the existing Civilian Protection Monitoring Team (CPMT), IGAD, AU, Observer Nations, and other nations acceptable to the parties. The parties agreed to permit the VMT free access to areas where complaints had been filed, and the VMT was required to notify the MOU committee of the results of any such mission. In a confidence-building IGAD summit in Nairobi in April 2003, Bashir and Garang expressed their confidence in the mediators, reiterated the need to maintain the momentum toward a comprehensive peace agreement, promised high-level negotiations, and agreed to facilitate the delivery of humanitarian assistance.[89]

During the spring and summer of 2003, negotiations focused on political, security, and wealth-sharing arrangements. The mediators also encouraged parallel talks outside the IGAD framework to begin discussions on the issue of the three contested areas: Nuba Mountains, Abyei, and Southern Blue Nile. But the pace of talks slackened, largely because of the outbreak of hostilities in Darfur, plunging Khartoum into a new crisis that partly distracted from the IGAD negotiations. In July 2003, the talks almost collapsed when Bashir rejected a compromise draft text of almost all the issues submitted by the mediators, ostensibly because its provisions favored the SPLA. Nonetheless, serious talks resumed in September 2003, when the first vice-president of Sudan, Ali Osman Mohamed Taha, and Garang met face-to-face in Naivasha. These meetings had significant implications for the conduct of the negotiations, deepening the chemistry between the two leaders, boosting the parties' ownership of the peace process, and reducing the role of IGAD mediators.[90]

By September 2004, when the parties concluded negotiations on security arrangements without the IGAD mediators, both sides described the peace process as "irreversible." Yet as the negotiation of details pertaining to a formal cease-fire agreement and modalities to implement the protocols seemed to drag on endlessly, the United States used its presidency of the UN Security Council to convene a Security Council session in Nairobi, in November 2004, to press the parties to conclude a comprehensive peace accord by the end of 2004. Despite looming pressures for sanctions against Sudan because of its atrocities in Darfur, the Security Council emphasized the peace dividends that both parties would derive from finalizing the IGAD peace talks. In a declaration signed in Nairobi, Taha and Garang pledged to resume direct talks in Nairobi to sort out the remaining differences. On January 9, 2005, both parties signed the Comprehensive Peace Agreement (CPA) in Nairobi, concluding the IGAD peace process.[91]

The CPA comprises the six protocols signed by the government and SPLA since the Machakos talks. In the protocol on power sharing, the parties agreed to establish a government of national unity inspired by democracy, respect for human rights, justice, devolution of power to the states and the government of southern Sudan, and good governance. The protocol also outlines the different layers of government and their compositions, and plans for general elections at all levels of government to be concluded by the end of the third year of the interim period. The wealth-sharing protocol details arrangements for sharing oil revenue and other national resources. Although revenue from Sudan's oil deposits will be divided evenly between north and south, communities in areas of oil production will have a say in oil contracts. In the Framework Agreement on Security Arrangements during the interim period, the parties agreed to an internationally monitored permanent cease-fire and subsequent verification of redeployment of government and SPLA forces, demobilization of considerable numbers of both armies, and the monitoring of the creation of new joint and integrated units. In the interim period, there will be three forces—government troops, SPLA forces, and integrated units made up of soldiers from both sides. In the protocol on the Resolution of Conflict in Southern Kordofan/Nuba Mountains and Blue Nile states, the parties reached an understanding on matters related to administration and popular consultations in the two areas. The protocol on the Resolution of the Conflict in Abyei provides for mechanisms for a referendum on whether Abyei will remain part of the north or become part of the south.

Conclusion

At the signing of the CPA, Museveni, as chair of IGAD, contended that the peace agreement underscored the power of geographical proximity: "We in IGAD region and Africa as a whole have created a viable partnership, which reduces chances for outsiders to jump into regional conflicts where they have very little knowledge about them."[92] Reminiscent of Bashir's invitation to IGAD in September 1993, this explanation obscures the multiple roles of diverse actors that had converged to promote the peace enterprise since its inception. Questions of ownership pervade most African peace processes, where local actors are often reluctant to be overshadowed by foreign and distant actors. Equally critical, successful agreements are easier to own than failed ones, particularly where, as in the IGAD case, there were many instances of failures and where the success invariably elicited celebrations about regional capacity.

A more accurate reading of the success of the decade-long IGAD talks is the convergence of multiple actors playing complementary, and oftentimes competitive, roles to steer a complex conflict into a maturity that allows the core parties to gradually rediscover points of agreements. Also, successful efforts in conflict resolution of internal conflicts such as Sudan are cumulative, building neatly on past successes and failures, as parties gradually learn the size and content of the political envelope, the limits of tolerance, and the possibilities of collective approaches. The power-sharing arrangements within the CPA embody some of what the Addis Ababa Agreement aspired to achieve, but in a changed circumstance where the south is more organized and ready to defend the gains that have been achieved at the negotiating table. More pertinent, the CPA does not fundamentally depart from the DOP; in fact, the core principles vindicate IGAD's basic framework of a Sudan that can, through creative political will, institutions, and leadership, hang together as a viable territorial and political artifice. By the same token, the

DOP recognized that absent these variables, southerners needed the geographical and political space to attempt to recreate their own sense of statehood, probably having learned from the mistakes of their predecessors.

Also, the less momentous peace initiatives and encounters, such as the Koka Dam Declaration (1986), the Political Charter (1996–1997), and the Asmara Declaration (1994), cannot be discounted in the wider corpus of experiences that now inform the spirit of the CPA. Some of these agreements provided the road map that has been captured in the CPA, a road map that has, over the years, remained essentially constant. Failure to implement these agreements was also instructive from the perspective of alliance formation and destruction. These previous agreements tested the durability of political alliances as northern and southern elites learned to live with each other, keep and break promises, and explore the possibilities of building institutions.

The circumstances of conflict contagion and the force of geography propelled IGAD to participate in the process that has culminated in the CPA. The longevity of the north-south conflict guaranteed that it would exact the energies of both African neighbors and the broader international community. IGAD's major contribution to the resolution of the Sudanese conflict lies in how it obtained the engagement of other salient actors into the conflict, how it innovated along the way, and how it persisted despite the odds. Likewise, IGAD was able to draw lessons from the cumulative African initiatives and experiences around the Sudanese conflict—in particular, the Addis Ababa Agreement and the Abuja negotiations.

Peter Woodward has raised a more vexing question of ownership in the Sudanese context: "There were worries that perhaps the whole process was one imposed on Sudan by the international community, and especially the USA. The danger might lie in the parties feeling a lack of ownership of the agreement, and with the international community turned away, one or other of the signatories might seek to disown aspects of it and pursue a different course of action."[93] Although Bashir described the CPA as an agreement that ends the war and marks a new contract for the Sudanese to share their wealth and defend their country, it is too early to judge whether the government commitment is halfhearted. The SPLA, too, will need to demonstrate its commitment by strictly adhering to the terms of the CPA. Nonetheless, the commitment of both parties and their allies to the agreement can only be measured in the implementation phase, a process that continues to unfold.

Notes

1. Norman Kempster, "Terrorism Case Puts Focus on Secretive Sudan," *Los Angeles Times,* June 26, 1993, p. 16; Don Scott, "Disaster in Sudan: Why Is West

Ignoring the Cries for Aid?" *Ottawa Citizen,* July 27, 1993, p. A7; "U.S. Review of Sudan Terrorist Link Gains Urgency," *Washington Post,* June 27, 1993, p. A 21; Kim Murphy, "Sudan's Road to Social Justice Paved with Fear," *Los Angeles Times,* August 16, 1993, p. 8; "Sudan Criticizes IMF for Suspending Its Membership," Xinhua News Agency, August 10, 1993.

2. For analyses of the poor state of the economy, see "Sudan: Economy," *Keesing's Record of World Events,* January 1994, p. 40091; "Anti-government Demonstrations," *Africa Research Bulletin,* October 1–30, 1993, p. 11202; "Unconvincing Transition?" *Africa Confidential,* October 22, 1993.

3. "Regional Politics: IGADD Summit," FBIS-AFR-93-181, September 21, 1993, p. 1. See also previous comments by the foreign minister in "Sudan: Foreign Minister Looks Forward to OAU Summit," BBC Summary of World Broadcasts, ME/1711/A, June 10, 1993.

4. "Statement by Dr. Hussein Suleiman Abu Salih, Minister of Foreign Affairs," March 1994.

5. Steven Wöndu and Ann Lesch, *Battle for Peace in Sudan: An Analysis of the Abuja Conferences, 1992–1993* (Lanham, MD: University Press of America, 2000), p. 153. An informant also revealed that "from the outset, Bashir thought Moi was pliable and malleable, but gradually this perception changed." Interview with author, Washington, DC, September 1997.

6. Abdelwahab El-Affendi, "The Impasse in the IGAD Peace Process for Sudan: The Limits of Regional Peacemaking?" *African Affairs* 100 (December 2001): 686.

7. "East Africa: Leaders Set Up Mediation Committee on Sudan," Inter Press Service, September 7, 1993; "IGADD Summit in Addis Ababa," BBC Summary of World Broadcasts, AL/1788/A, September 8, 1993.

8. Wöndu and Lesch, *Battle for Peace in Sudan,* note starkly: "Although SPLM leaders were initially uncomfortable with the composition of the Peace Committee and the way they were approached, they knew that they had no alternative" (p. 153).

9. Harry Johnston and Ted Dagne, "The Crisis in Sudan: The North-South Conflict," *Mediterranean Quarterly* 7, no. 3 (spring 1996): 3.

10. Washington Declaration, October 22, 1993. See also Gill Lusk, "SPLA Reconciliation," *Middle East International* 462 (November 5, 1993): 12.

11. "Minister on Garang Talks, U.S. Involvement," FBIS-NES-94-002, January 4, 1994, p. 15.

12. Horace Awori, "Sudan: SPLA Factions Agree on Common Agenda for Peace Talks," Inter Press Service, January 7, 1994; "Government Affirms Willingness to Meet Rebels," FBIS-NES-94-006, January 10, 1994, p. 16.

13. Horace Awori, "Sudan-Politics: Still Talking About Peace," Inter Press Service, May 23, 1994; "Sudanese Peace Open," *Daily Nation,* May 21, 1994; "'Warring Faction Refuses to Sign Treaty as Scheduled," *Daily Nation,* April 12, 1994; "IGADD Meeting on Aid Suspended," FBIS-NES-94-073, April 15, 1994, p. 16; "Government Delegation Issues Statement," FBIS-NES-94-072, April 15, 1994, p. 17; "Sudan: Peace Talks," *Africa Research Bulletin,* May 1–30, 1994, p. 11454; Wöndu and Lesch, *Battle for Peace in Sudan,* pp. 154–155.

14. "Draft Declaration of Principles," Nairobi, May 24, 1994. For a good analysis of the DOP, see Francis M. Deng, "Mediating the Sudanese Conflict: A Challenge for the IGADD," *CSIS Africa Notes,* No. 169, February 1995, pp. 1–7; InterAfrica Group, *IGADD Mediation of the Sudanese Conflict,* report by Inter-Africa Group resource persons, Addis Ababa, July 1994.

15. According to El-Effendi, "Impasse," "by 1998, the IPF's twenty-odd membership read like a who's who of major industrialized countries plus the European Union and a number of UN agencies."

16. "Al-Bashir, U.S. Envoy Meet: Foreign Minister Comments," FBIS-AFR-94-NES-064, April 4, 1994, p. 19; "Sudan: U.S. Warning," *Africa Research Bulletin,* April 1–30, 1994, p. 11415.

17. For initial accounts of Wells's mission, see "U.S. Envoy Arrives with Clinton Letter," FBIS-NES-94-113, June 13, 1994, pp. 19–20; "Foreign Minister on U.S. Relations," FBIS-AFR-94-119, June 21, 1994, pp. 15–16; "Wells Meets Southern Assembly Members," FBIS-NES-94-117, June 17, 1994, p. 14.

28. "Uganda, Sudanese Leaders Hold Talks in Austria"; "Talk Termed 'Tough, Productive'," FBIS-WEU-94-104, May 31, 1994, pp. 1–2; "Sudanese President Calls Talks with Uganda 'Successful,'" FBIS-WEU-94-104, June 1, 1994, p. 4.

29. See, for instance, the account in "U.S Reportedly Seeking to Partition Sudan," FBIS-NES-94-216, September 12, 1994, p. 27, which links IGADD initiatives to attempts to partition Sudan and, therefore, the "unity of Islam"; and "Al-Bashir on Iraqi, 'Jihad,' U.S. Imperialism," FBIS-NES-94-216, November 8, 1994.

20. "Speech by President Daniel arap Moi on the Occasion of Sudanese Peace Talks," September 6, 1994, Nairobi; "President Receives Report on the Sudan," *Daily Nation,* September 8, 1994.

21. "Sudan's Position on 'State and Religion' and 'Self-determination': Report on Government Position on the Fourth Round of IGADD Talks that Took Place in Nairobi, September 7, 1994," Nairobi, Embassy of Sudan, September 22, 1994. See also Nhial Bol, "Sudan-Politics: Any Prospect for Peace?" Inter Press Service, August 29, 1994; Horace Awori, "Sudan-Politics: Peace Talks in Danger," Inter Press Service, August 25, 1994; Horace Awori, "Sudan-Peace: Regional-sponsored Talks Collapse," Inter Press Service, September 8, 1994; "Sudanese Peace Talks Reach Stalemate in Nairobi," FBIS-AFR-94-174, September 8, 1994, p. 1; "Spokesman Suggests New Mechanism for Negotiations," FBIS-NES-94-169, August 31, 1994, p. 17.

22. Nhial Bol, "Sudan-Peace: Kenyan Envoy Visits War-torn South," Inter Press Service, November 1, 1994; "Kenyan Envoy Pays Visit, Meets with Officials," FBIS-NES-94-218, November 10, 1994, pp. 10–11; Nhial Bol, "Sudan-Politics: Khartoum Rejects Eritrea's Mediation Role," Inter Press Service, January 10, 1995; "Bashir Unhappy at IGADD's Partiality, Says Talks at Dead End," BBC Summary of World Broadcasts, September 22, 1994.

23. "Bashir Unhappy."

24. See "Testimony by E. Brynn on U.S. Policy Toward Sudan," U.S. Department of State Bureau of African Affairs, March 22, 1995. Speaking during the January 1995 independence celebration, Bashir called for a jihad against unbelievers of Islam and promised to train 1 million people to defend the country and faith. "Sudan: Call for Jihad," *Keesing's Record of World Events,* January 1995, p. 40348. See also Nhial Bol, "Sudan-Politics: Muslim Leader Declares War on Secularism," Inter Press Service, October 10, 1994.

25. Edmond Kizito, "Uganda-Sudan Dispute Worsens," Reuters, April 23, 1995; "Relations Between Sudan, Uganda Said to Be Worsening," FBIS-AFR-94-193, October 5, 1994, pp. 1–2.

26. "Sudan Isolation Deepens," *Africa Research Bulletin,* January 1–31, 1996, p. 1211; "Sudan: Deteriorating Relations with Ethiopia," *Keesing's Record of World Events,* January 1996, p. 40891.

27. Nhial Bol, "Sudan-Refugees: Eritreans Prepare to Go Home," Inter Press Service, October 31, 1994; Nhial Bol, "Sudan-Eritrea: Diplomatic Row Erupts over

Destabilization Claims," Inter Press Service, November 29, 1994; Nhial Bol and Charles Wachira, "Sudan-Eritrea: Khartoum Appeals to Asmara Not to Close Embassy," Inter Press Service, December 6, 1994.

28. "Eritrea: Afewerki on Relations with U.S., Sudan," FBIS-AFR-95-020, January 31, 1995, p. 5. See also Jim Fisher-Thompson "Eritrean President Makes Big Impression in Washington: Moose Comments on Isaias Visit," US Information Agency, February 15, 1995; Bol, "Sudan-Eritrea"; Bol and Wachira, "Sudan-Eritrea."

29. "Official Accuses Egypt of Involvement in Latest Ugandan Attack," BBC Summary of World Broadcasts, EE/D2474/ME, November 29, 1995; Nhial Bol, "Africa-Politics: Sudan Blames Neighbors as Rebel Offensive Rages," Inter Press Service, November 1, 1995; "Sudan Said to Mobilize Against Uganda," *United Press International,* November 9, 1995; Anna Borzello, "Uganda-Sudan-Politics: Your Enemy, My Friend," Inter Press Service, November 10, 1995.

30. For an account of these initiatives, see Bona Malwal, "The Jimmy Carter Initiative," *Sudan Democratic Gazette,* March 1995; "Friends of IGADD," *Africa Confidential,* March 31, 1995; "Pronk Attempts to Re-open Sudanese Peace Negotiations," *ANP English News Bulletin,* May 28, 1996; Moyiga Nduru, "Sudan-Politics: Khartoum Canvasses African Support Against Rebels," Inter Press Service, May 15, 1995.

31. "Sudan: Peace Agreement with Southern Rebel Factions," *Keesing's Record of World Events,* April 1996, p. 41034; "Government and Southern Rebel Movement Agree to Continue Cease-fire," BBC Summary of World Broadcasts, March 13, 1996; "Sudanese Rebel Movement Declares Cease-fire," BBC Summary of World Broadcasts, EE/D2551/ME, March 3, 1996.

32. Judith Matloff, "Sudan's Civil War Looking Less Civil War," *Christian Science Monitor,* January 31, 1997.

33. For good coverage of the rebel offensive and government reaction, see Gill Lusk, "Sudan: Opposition Offensive," *Middle East International,* January 24, 1997, pp. 8–9, 12; Lusk, "Sudan: Lull Before the Storm," *Middle East International,* February 7, 1997, p. 5; Lusk, "Sudan: Heavy Fighting," *Middle East International,* April 4, 1997, p. 12; Lusk, "Sudan: War in Slow Motion," *Middle East International,* June 27, 1997, p. 11.

34. "Our Goal Is to Topple the Khartoum Regime: Interview with John Garang, Head of the SPLA," *Swiss Review of International Affairs,* June 1997, pp. 23–24.

35. "Sudan: Government Rejects Proposal to End War Analysis: What Hopes for Peace in Sudan?" *Los Angeles Times,* November 13, 1997; Michela Wrong, "Peace Talks Postponed to April," Pan-African News Agency, November 11, 1997.

36. "New US Sanctions Announced," *Electronic Mail and Guardian,* November 7, 1997.

37. Yahya El Hassan, "Sudanese Leader Accuses U.S. of Sabotaging Talks," Pan-African News Agency, November 19, 1997. See also "Sudan Scoffs at New US Sanctions," *Mail and Guardian,* November 7, 1997.

38. "Albright and Museveni Hold Joint Press Conference," *New Vision* (Kampala), December 11, 1997.

39. "Sudanese Minister in Cairo to Discuss Ties," Agence France-Presse, January 12, 1998.

40. "Sudan: Cairo Competes," *Africa Confidential,* December 19, 1997, p. 8.

41. "Sudanese Umma Party Adopts 'Action Plan'," FBIS-NES-98-036, February 5, 1998. As Mahdi remarked, "How can Sudan's problems be tackled without all the relevant parties being part of this effort, and without taking the constitutional

transformation into account? Moreover, the IGAD mechanism in its current form cannot be sufficient because there are elements among Sudan's important neighbors, like Egypt, who must be included in this mechanism." See "Sudan: Al-Mahdi on Sudanese Opposition Goals," FBIS-NES-98-007, January 7, 1998.

42. "Sudan's al-Hindi on Results of Initiative," FBIS-NES-98-058, February 27, 1998. He added, "These IGAD states are not above suspicion because they are themselves states with upheavals, states involved in hostile activity toward Sudan, and it is impossible for them to be both adversary and authority."

43. "Italy: Official Previews Sudan Peace Mediation Talks in Nairobi," FBIS-WEU-98-089, March 30, 1998; "Sudan: Italian Delegation Wraps Up Visit to Sudan," FBIS-NES-98-096, April 6, 1998.

44. "Kenyan Foreign Minister Says 'Significant Progress' made in Talks May 8, 1998," Agence France-Presse, May 9, 1998; "Government, SPLA Agree to Referendum on Self-determination, More Talks," BBC Summary of World Broadcasts, May 8, 1998.

45. Matthew Bigg, "Agencies Skeptical About Sudan Ceasefire," Reuters, July 15, 1998; "Sudanese Rebels Begin Ceasefire to Help Famine Victims," Agence France-Presse, July 15, 1998; Christopher Lockwood, "Food Aid Follows Ceasefire," *Telegraph,* July 16, 1998.

46. "Sudan Peace Talks Deadlocked," BBC Summary of World Broadcasts, August 6, 1998; Ghion Hagos, "Delegations Clash at Peace Talks," Pan-African News Agency, August 5, 1998; Judith Achieng', "Politics-Sudan: Rebels Blame Khartoum for Failed Peace Talks," Inter Press Service, August 7, 1998; Lisa Bryant, "Sudan Opposition Talks," Voice of America, Correspondent Report No. 2-237210, August 17, 1998.

47. "Sudanese Opposition Leaders Open Meetings in Cairo," FBIS-AFR-98-227, August 15, 1998; David Hirst, "Mubarak Risks Taking Sides in Sudan," *The Guardian,* August 17, 1998, p. 14.

48. "Egypt: Sudan's Opposition NDA Issues Statement," FBIS-NES-98-230, August 18, 1998; "Sudan: Sudan's NDA Issues Cairo Declaration," FBIS-AFR-98-230, August 18, 1998.

49. "President Omar al-Bashir on Dialogue with the West," FBIS-AFR-99-001, January 1, 1999.

50. See also "USCR Criticizes U.S. Efforts in Sudan," Pan-African News Agency, March 23, 1999; "Sudan Says Ready for 'Serious, Frank' Dialogue with US," FBIS-AFR-1999-0317, March 17, 1999.

51. "Sudan-Eritrea: Reconciliation Agreement Signed," Integrated Regional Information Networks (IRIN), May 3, 1999; "Eritrea Tells Sudanese Opposition To Evacuate Embassy," FBIS-AFR-1999-0516, May 16, 1999.

52. "Ethiopia-Sudanese Leader Sees Improved Ties in Future," FBIS-AFR-1999-0331, March 31, 1999.

53. "Sudan: Hope for 'New Momentum' at IGAD Talks," Agence France-Presse, April 15, 1999.

54. "Sudan: Little Progress Achieved at Peace Talks," IRIN News Briefs, July 26, 1999; "Sudan Government, Rebels Meet Behind Closed Doors," FBIS-AFR-1999-0720, July 20, 1999. A government official signaled growing skepticism about IGAD: "IGAD is only a waste of time and is no longer a serious platform for negotiations."

55. "Sudan: Secret Government, Opposition Talks Reported," FBIS-AFR-1999-0430, April 30, 1999. See also "Sudanese Opposition Welcomes al-Turabi-al-Mahdi Meeting," FBIS-AFR-1999-0513, May 13, 1999; "Sudanese Oppositionist Praises Al-Turabi-Al-Mahdi Meeting," FBIS-AFR-1999-0504, May 4, 1999.

56. "Gadaffi Vows to Reconcile Sudanese Belligerents," Pan-African News Agency, June 20, 1999; "Gadaffi Accuses U.S. of 'Terrorism' Over Al-Shifa," FBIS-AFR-1999-0619, June 19, 1999; "Sudanese Opposition Leaders to Meet Egyptian and Libyan Officials," FBIS-AFR-1999-0615, June 15, 1999.

57. "Sudan's Al-Mahdi on Rapprochement Prospect," FBIS-AFR-1999-0618, June 15, 1999.

58. "Opposition Calls for National Dialogue Conference After Libyan Mediation," BBC Summary of World Broadcasts, August 5, 1999; "Egypt, Libya Set Ball Rolling for Sudan Peace Conference," Agence France-Presse, August 10, 1999.

59. "Foreign Minister Says 'Ball Is in the Opposition's Court,'" BBC Summary of World Broadcasts, August 10, 1999; "Sudan Hopes for Initiative to End Civil War," Xinhua News Agency, August 7, 1999; "Envoy in Cairo Discusses Peace Efforts, Relations with Egypt," BBC Summary of World Broadcasts, August 17, 1999; "Sudanese Minister Thanks Egypt, Libya for Initiative," FBIS-AFR-1999-0912, September 12, 1999; "Meeting to Prepare Sudanese Peace Talks Set for October," FBIS-AFR-1999-0912, September 12, 1999.

60. "SPLM Leader John Garang Tells Kenyan TV: Khartoum Authorities 'Evil,'" BBC Summary of World Broadcasts, August 14, 1999. See also "Sudanese Rebels Reject Peace Plan," BBC Summary of World Broadcasts, August 30, 1999; "Sudan: Rebel Leader Garang Says No Plans to Meet Bashir," FBIS-AFR-1999-0915, September 15, 1999; and Osman Njuguna, "Sudan: IGAD Endorsed as Suitable Forum for Peace Process," All Africa News Agency, August 6, 1999.

61. "Sudanese Opposition Alliance Issues Statement in Cairo," FBIS-AFR-1999-1022, October 22, 1999; "Sudan Rebels Said to Be in 'State of Conflict,'" FBIS-AFR-1999-1024, October 23, 1999.

62. US Department of State, Office of the Spokesman, "Press Availability of Secretary of State Madeleine K. Albright and Kenyan President Daniel arap Moi, State House Nairobi, Kenya, October 22, 1999."

63. "Egypt Says Its Sudan Plan Is Viable," BBC Summary of World Broadcasts, October 23, 1999; "Egypt and Libya Sign Accord on Sudan," Agence France-Presse, November 12, 1999.

64. "Albright's African Tour, US Policy Viewed," FBIS-AFR-1999-1103, November 1999.

65. "Sudan Oppositionists Object to Meeting in Washington," FBIS-AFR-1999-1214, December 14, 1999.

66. "State of Emergency Declared in Sudan," Associated Press, December 12, 1999; "Sudanese Government Says Emergency Not Coup d'ñtat," FBIS-AFR-1999-1213, December 13, 1999.

67. "North Africa; Sudan, Egypt, Libya Issue Joint Communiqué After Talks in Khartoum," *Africa News,* January 13, 2000; "Opposition Ummah Army Withdraws Confidence in Garang's Leadership," BBC Summary of World Broadcasts, March 24, 2000; "Mahdi's Withdrawal Dents Opposition Alliance," Pan-African News Agency, March 24, 2000; "Opposition Leader Mahdi Commends Egyptian-Libyan Peace Initiative," BBC Summary of World Broadcasts, April 13, 2000.

68. El-Affendi, "The Impasse in the IGAD Peace Process for Sudan," pp. 588–589.

69. Judith Achieng', "Politics-Sudan: Government, Rebels Agree to Revive Peace Talks," Inter Press Service, January 18, 2000; Chege Mbitiru, "Rebels Say Sudan Bombed Town as Peace Talks Resume," Associated Press, January 16, 2000; "Sudan Peace Talks End in Deadlock," Agence France-Presse, January 2000; "Government Delegation Arrives in Nairobi for Peace Talks with Rebels," BBC Summary of World Broadcasts, February 23, 2000.

70. "Peace Talks in Kenya Reportedly End in Deadlock," BBC Summary of World Broadcasts, March 1, 2000.

71. "Breakthrough in Sudan-U.S. Relations," Reuters, March 6, 2000.

72. "Garang: 'We Are Going to Activate the SPLA in Khartoum Proper,'" *Mideast Mirror* 14, no. 96 (May 22, 2000). See also "Garang Wants Northern Opposition Included in Regional Peace Initiative," BBC Summary of World Broadcasts, May 17, 2000; "Garang Said Not to Favor Partition from North," BBC Summary of World Broadcasts, May 19, 2000; "The Solution for Sudan—By John Garang," *Mideast Mirror* 14, no. 93 (May 17, 2000).

73. "SPLA Leader Suspends Participation at IGAD to Placate Egypt and Libya," *Sudan Democratic Gazette,* June 2000, pp. 4–5.

74. "The IGAD Peace Process: Between a Rock and a Hard Place," *Sudan Democratic Gazette,* September 2000, p. 5.

75. "El Mahdi Returns to a Tumultuous Public Welcome in Khartoum," *Sudan Democratic Gazette,* December 2000, pp. 5–7.

76. "As IGAD Unravels at the Helm, What Are the Prospects for Peace in Sudan? *Sudan Democratic Gazette,* December 2000, p. 12.

77. *Sudan Democratic Gazette,* December 2000, p. 12.

78. "Promoting Reconciliation: Has Egypt Derailed IGAD Peace Process on Sudan?" *Sudan Democratic Gazette,* February 2001, p. 10; "Libya-Egyptian Initiative Achieves Progress in Sudanese Conflict," BBC Summary of World Broadcasts, January 11, 2001.

79. Francis M. Deng and J. Stephen Morrison, *U.S. Policy to End Sudan's War: Report of the CSIS Task Force on U.S.-Sudan Policy* (Washington, DC: CSIS, February 2001), p. 7.

80. "Regional Summit on Sudan Issues Joint Communiqué," BBC Monitoring Service, June 2, 2001; "Kenyan President Says Sudanese to Have a Final Say on Peace," BBC Monitoring Service, June 2, 2001.

81. "Sudan: Opposition Groups Meet to Coordinate Peace Proposals," *Africa News,* June 28, 2001; "Libya's Gadaffi Arrives in Sudan for Talks on Arab Peace Plan," Agence France-Presse, July 17, 2001.

82. "Egypt, Libya Hand Government, Opposition Peace Bid Proposals," Agence France-Presse, June 26, 2001; "Sudan: Khartoum Accepts Libyan-Egyptian Peace Initiative," *Africa News,* July 7, 2001.

83. "Sudan Peace Plan Welcomed," *The Independent,* July 5, 2001; Mohamed Osman, "El-Bashir: Peace Initiative Does Not Mean Separating Religion from the State," Associated Press, July 22, 2001.

84. "Sudanese Opposition Backs Arab Peace Plan But Asks for More," Agence France-Presse, June 29, 2001.

85. Fred Oluoch, "Sumbeiywo: The Unsung Hero of Sudan Peace," *The East African,* January 17–23, 2005.

86. For analyses of the Danforth initiatives, see "Sudan Peace Talks Begin," Agence France-Presse, January 14, 2002; "US Peace Envoy Starts Sudan Mission," Agence France-Presse, November 14, 2001; "A Cease-Fire Is Set in Sudan War," *New York Times,* January 20, 2002; John Prendergast, "Senator Danforth's Sudan Challenge: Building a Bridge to Peace," *CSIS Africa Notes,* No. 5, January 2002; *International Crisis Group, God, Oil, and Country: Changing Logic of War in Sudan* (Washington, DC: ICG, 2002), pp. 169–175.

87. "Moi meets US Special Envoy to Sudan," *Nation,* January 14, 2002.

88. IGAD, "IGAD Secretariat on Peace in the Sudan, the Machakos Protocol, July 2002," Nairobi, 2002. See also Tabitha J. Sei, "The Intergovernmental Authority (IGAD) and the Sudanese Peace Process," in Korwa Adar et al. (eds.), *Sudan*

Peace Process: Challenges and Future Prospects (Pretoria: Africa Institute, 2004), pp. 15–36.

89. Emeric Rogier, *No More Hills Ahead? The Sudan's Tortuous Ascent to the Heights of Peace,* Clingendael Security Paper No. 1 (The Hague: Clingendael Security and Conflict Programme, August 2005), pp. 64–69.

90. Ibid., pp. 93–94.

91. Glenn Kessler, "Sudan, Southern Rebels Sign Accord to End Decades of War," *Washington Post,* January 10, 2005; International Crisis Group, *The Khartoum-SPLM Agreement: Sudan's Uncertain Peace,* ICG Africa Report No. 96 (Washington, DC: ICG, July 25, 2005).

92. Marc Lacey, "Sudan and Southern Rebels Sign Deal Ending Civil War," *New York Times,* January 10, 2005.

93. Peter Woodward, "Somalia and Sudan: A Tale of Two Peace Processes," *The Round Table* 93, no. 375 (July 2004): 477.

6

Flashpoint Darfur

The problem with the public discussion of Darfur and Sudan is not simply that we know so little; it is also the representation of what we do know.[1]

Repressive violence is justified in the name of law and order. It responds to the fear of minorities that the failure to react forcefully will be interpreted as a sign of weakness, and unleash vengeful hordes in murderous assaults.[2]

The assimilation in Sudan of Arab-Islamic culture was the signal achievement of the two great African kingdoms of Fur and Funj. Sudan's history is both rich and potent, and its rediscovery will help forge a more cohesive nation.[3]

Darfur is a geopolitical frontier within the larger Sudanese state. In the early years of the twenty-first century, Darfur has come to represent the specters of war, famine, pestilence, and death. These events—and the forces of wanton destruction—were in part precipitated by ill-fated government policies based on ideologies arising from the vestigial racism of a multiethnic state in denial of its slaving past. The shadow that looms over Darfur today is one with a long history. The inability (or unwillingness) of outsiders—international actors, the media, and humanitarian organizations—to fully comprehend and address the panoply of historical facts has created a barrier to understanding and accounting for the roots of the well-documented "crime against humanity."[4] The complex sociopolitical and economic history of Darfur defies facile efforts to reduce its past to the easily digestible bytes of an apocalyptic war between "Arab and African," with the "Black African" portrayed as a hapless victim of the "Arab" horsemen known as Janjaweed.[5]

The intricate socioeconomic, historical, and political interrelationships among the primary actors in the tragic theater of war in Darfur have been

overshadowed by gruesome acts of violence—systematic looting, the burning of farms, and the rape of women.[6] The massacre of civilians and the
torching of villages, against the backdrop of ominous shadows of men
mounted on camels and protected by hovering helicopters, were televised
internationally. The oral testimonies of these victims of the nightly raids by
both the government-sponsored militias and the rebels demonstrated that
Khartoum's response had gone beyond conventional neglect—both economic and political—of a peripheral district, to the waging of a "dirty
war."[7] The origins of the conflict in Darfur can be traced to the region's
forced incorporation into Anglo-Egyptian Sudan in 1916 and the marginalization and pauperization of its inhabitants since 1956. The characterization
of the events of 2003 as a starting point of the crisis, rather than as the outcome of almost a century of discontent[8] by an impoverished and humiliated
polity, has led to regional and international responses that fail to address the
socioeconomic and political roots of the conflict. The continued depiction
of a conflict pitting "African" against "Arab," "farmer" against" herder,"
"genocidal acts" against "genocidal intentions" only serves to obscure the
driving forces of the conflict: the demands of rival groups for a more equitable conceptualization of national citizenship with attendant rights to power
and wealth sharing.[9]

Today, as in the past, Darfur represents one of the quintessential traits
of Sahelian societies: a continual dynamic producing hybrid peoples and
groups. Darfur is a place where centuries-old socioeconomic and political
networks attest to the acculturation of Afro-Arab-Islamic values. These values and traits are more politically salient and resurface in contemporary
alliances, although it remains difficult to discern the indigenous communities from the settlers/invaders from the Arabian Peninsula and the kingdoms
of West and North Africa. Much like the modern republic of "Sudan," present-day "Darfur" replicates the paradoxes of the *bilad as-Sudan,* where neither the contemporary nomenclature nor the ethnic categories ascribed to its
inhabitants fit the geopolitical, economic, and social realities of its inhabitants. Historically, the term *dar Fur* refers to the "domain of the Fur," whose
ancestral homeland was limited to the central region of the Marrah Mountains before the northward and southward expansion of the Afro-Arab sultanate of Kayra from 1650 to 1873. By the late nineteenth century, the Fur-
dominated sultanate no longer exercised hegemony over its expanded *dar,*
which included the territories inhabited by the Zaghawa, the Masalit, the
descendants of the ninth-century Hillali invaders, and West Africans.[10] Nevertheless, the terms *Darfur,* and *Darfuri/Darfurians*[11] have, through a process
of ellipsis, come into frequent usage, implying the potential of a unifying eth-
noregional-territorial nationalism.[12] These terms ignore the footprints of history and the transformations of the Kayra sultans' estate-granting *hakura* system[13] in the era of Fur hegemony, as well as the episodic empowerment of

the former client/subject communities during the Turkiyya, the Mahdiyya, and the Condominium periods.

The unquestioning use of these Fur-centered terminologies by outsiders encourages a facile misreading of the factors militating against the emergence of a consensual and legitimate authoritative body that could allay non-Fur communities' fear of being dominated by the historically hegemonic Fur.[14] In fact, the historical record clearly shows how the fear of Fur domination operates as a subtext in the recent politics of the region. There are parallels in other parts of Sudan, in smaller communities, such as the Nuer, Murle, and Equatorians, whose fear of domination by the Dinka-led SPLA led to fragmentation within the rebels' ranks, which was astutely exploited by Khartoum politicians to the detriment of the peoples of the south.[15] Although ethnicity and territorial rights should be acknowledged as major factors in the Darfur crisis, the making and keeping of peace will rest on constitutional safeguards reining in the proven excesses of the region's ethnonationalists and radical Islamists. Darfur's history, especially from 1898 to 1916—under the last Kayra sultan, Ali Dinar—demonstrates a model of governance based on a pragmatic ideology akin to the secularism of the rule by medieval Islamic caliphates before the advent of puritanical movements. The pragmatic policies of the sultan on the role of religion and government, economic networks, and relations with contiguous and distant neighbors and international allies could yield valuable lessons for a region bereft of effective partners in its quest for a just and equal peace.[16]

With the transformation of Sudan into Africa's newest petrostate in the late 1990s and the production of oil in southern Darfur, this frontier zone became even more politically polarized following intensified fighting on the multiple war fronts in the Nuba Mountains and in south and eastern Sudan. In the western periphery of Darfur, the conflicts over resources became ethnocentric, fueled by ideologies of Africanism that redefined warring groups as either Zurga/Ifrigiya (black/African) or Arabi (nonblack/non-African), delegitimizing the traditional accommodation of the local Afro-Arab Muslims. This polarization of identities occurred in tandem with raids and counterraids intended to construct and/or demarcate territories into either *al hazim al zurga* (African belts) or *al hazim al arabi* (Arab belts), marking a total negation of the triple heritage, African-Arabic-Islamic, of Darfur's communities. The division of the multiethnic communities into two artificially constructed camps belied a long history of socioeconomic and political interaction, economic interdependence, and intercommunal marriages between those who now claimed to be only African or only Arab—ignoring the fact that the multiple identities had overlapped since the seventeenth century. Islam had provided Darfur's sedentary, pastoral, and trading communities with membership in the *umma,* which had been integrated into the indigenous forms of governance of the autonomous sultanate of Darfur until the early 1900s. With the subordination of Darfur to the hegemonic rule of the Nile Valley, Islam's role as a unifying thread diminished and the ethnic cleavages widened. From 1916 to 2006, Darfur's multiple communities struggled to attain inclusion in the political system dominated by Khartoum's elites.

In the postcolonial period, the traditional political parties such as the Umma, the DUP, and the Muslim Brotherhood pursued policies that negated the Afro-Islamic pillars of the Sudanese identity and highlighted their "Arab" roots. Darfur's various elites—formerly unified by their membership in the Islamic *umma*—found themselves treated as the *awlad al-gharb* (the children of the west), subordinated to the *awlad al-balad* in Khartoum. The peoples of Darfur suffered through the catastrophic drought and famines of the 1970s and 1980s, exacerbated by the irresponsible policies of decisionmakers in Khartoum.[17] Moreover, they bore the brunt of the proxy wars between Chad and Libya, in which Khartoum's policies demonstrated the government's priority to be that of consolidating a coercive policy of Arabization. In the late 1980s and 1990s, Darfur's communities found their Islamic credentials—as members of the *umma*—devalued by Khartoum's rulers, who supported groups that emphasized their "Arabness" over those who asserted their "African" roots. The center's intervention and support for Darfur's "Arab" communities plunged the region into bloody wars waged in ways that violated the traditional norms that had enabled the diverse Afro-Arab-Islamic communities to coexist peaceably, albeit unequally, for over two centuries.[18]

The permeability of Darfur to the political upheavals on its borderlands with Chad and Libya engendered transborder ethnic alliances that put the juridical identity of Sudan and Chad at risk. Subsequent cross-border invasions led to the involvement of not only regional players but also international powers. The activities of the Failaka al-Islamiyya, a precursor of the more global Al-Qaida—exacerbated by Khartoum's arming of "Arab" militias under the guise of jihadist campaigns—were countered with equal destructiveness by local militias brandishing their African identity. All these combined to create the conditions for the crimes against humanity that propelled the region into chaos at the end of the twentieth century. This nightmarish fusion of ill-fated policies, formulated and enacted by disparate local, national, and regional forces, could not be countered by the emergence of local advocates of equal citizenship rights, such as Daoud Bolad, whose belated efforts to redress the effects of past wrongs met with a tragic end.[19] The militarization of Darfur, from within and without, during the late 1980s until the early 2000s, resulted in the emergence of two political streams: (1) a secular, multiethnic movement espousing Sudanism and advocating a restructuring of the architecture of the Sudanese state to facilitate more equitable sharing of power and wealth; and (2) a neo-Islamist revival and redefinition of Darfur's role in a *sharia*-ruled, unified Sudanese state. The former movement associated with the SLA is linked to disparate anti-Khartoum forces in N'Djamena, Asmara, and Tripoli and their international allies, while the latter movement is articulated by the JEM, which is hampered by past failures of Islamist regimes to live up to their stated ideals.

The political conversion of Darfur's inhabitants from Khartoum's jihadist foot soldiers fighting against rebels in the south and east, into armed rivals jolted the legatees of the *awlad al-balad* out of their complacency and into violent action, targeting the rebels and their supporters. Fifty years after independence, Darfur's rebels find themselves enmeshed in the labyrinth of identity politics that had enabled the regime in Khartoum to play southern groups against each other until the signing of the 2005 peace agreement. How well the factional leaderships of the SLA and JEM learn the lessons on how to unify their constituencies and to craft viable power-sharing arrangements will determine whether there will be a radical restructuring of twenty-first-century Sudanese politics. If Darfur's leaders succeed in articulating the desiderata of equitable citizenship for the *awlad al-gharb* versus the hegemonic *awlad al-balad,* they may bridge the ideological, ethnic, and religious divide that has for too long delayed the emergence of a multinational democratic New Sudan.

Darfur: The Afro-Arabo-Islamic Sultanate in the Sudanic Heartland

Darfur constitutes a fusion of a centralized African kingship with the organizing ideologies of Islamization and Arabization that accompanied the Afro-Arab sultanate that emerged in the 1650s and lasted until 1916.[20] It epitomizes the quintessential hybrid character of Sudan with the promise of, on the one hand, bridging the Afro-Arab divide by building a multiethnic framework for coexistence while, on the other hand, generating new wars of identity fueled by memories of past injustices.

Its political landscape is littered with the remains of wars of conquest from both the pre-Islamic and Islamic eras, and its social map yields an interesting array of population units with seasonal migration patterns and kinship networks in widely dispersed communities. By the mid–seventeenth century, the Fur had emerged as the dominant power of the Kayra dynasty under the leadership of Sulayman Solongdungo, who ruled during the approximate period 1650–1680.[21] The Kunjura-Fur, who claimed kinship with the Musabbat Arabs and from whom the sultans of the Kayra descended, later claimed Hilali or Abassi lineage, thereby fusing the Afro-Arab heritage of the blended communities with membership in the Islamic *umma.*[22]

Darfur's geographic location made it a commercial hub for the trans-Saharan trade in slaves, ivory, and ostrich feathers with the Maghrib and beyond. In its heyday during the seventeenth and eighteenth centuries, the sultanate of Darfur thrived on wars of conquest and its commercial hegemony over the caravan routes to Cairo, Fezzan, and Mediterranean states straddling the African and European continents. Unlike the Funj dynasty, which was overtaken by both immigrant Arab tribes and Muhammed Ali's Ottoman armies, the Kayra dynasty emerged as a composite but nevertheless coherent political dynasty that combined indigenous Fur-based socioeconomic hierarchies and exogenous political structures adopted from the Daju and Tunjur kingships, which preceded its rise to power in the region.[23]

Contracting political marriages between warring groups expanded familial ties to embrace scattered communities and linked them to the ruling center dominated by the Fur, whose control of the arable areas enabled them to pursue a sedentary imperial lifestyle.[24] The Kayra sultans drew upon their pastoralist client communities of the north (such as the Zaghawa, Meidob, Northern Rezeigat, and Zayadiya) and of the south (the Habbaniya, Taisha, Southern Rezeigat, and Beni Helba) for their militaristic exploits.[25] Their armies reduced communities that refused to submit to servitude—such as those who have come to be known as Fertit, indicating peoples who preferred to move away rather than accept sultanic bondage, which also carried with it obligations to convert to the victors' imported religion of Islam.[26] In times of scarcity or war, some of the nomadic Zaghawa, Masalit, and Baggara "became Fur" through a system of assimilation into the host community providing refuge.[27] In time, with intermarriages and the institutionalization of patron-client relationships, the mainly Muslim inhabitants of Darfur developed layers of identities. These identities embraced familial origins and extended kinship ties and political alliances based on an amalgam of indigenized Islamic values introduced both by West African and by Arab *fugara,* all of which created a hybrid cultural framework that accommodated West African jihadism to local forms of Sufism.[28]

This borderland reflects the rise and fall of predatory indigenous kingdoms and Afro-Arab sultanates that shaped the socioeconomic functions and political identities of its diverse communities. The historical imprint of its militant pre-Islamic kingdoms of Daju, Tunjur, and Fur has left behind vivid memories of its fearsome *fursan* (horsemen/knights) who led the cattle and slave raids. The Kayra sultanate, which emerged as a hybrid between the ruling elite of the Fur, its northern Zaghawa tributaries, and Arab settlers, gradually extended its rule over the vast region from the edges of Bahr al-Ghazal to the arid desert areas straddling the Chad-Libyan borderlands. Unlike the Funj sultanate of Sennar in the east, which only highlighted its Arab identity, the Fur sultanate nurtured and maintained its Afro-Arabo-Islamic heritage without derogating its indigenous roots. The Furawi language, together with indigenous rituals and titles of both pre-Islamic and Islamic offices, continues to be used alongside Arabic—adopted as the language of the court and religion. Three centuries after its establishment, we can still find terms such as *shartay* (district chief) and *fashir* (royal camp) still in use in Darfur.

The sultanate followed a policy of assimilation by incorporating not only the smaller sedentary communities into its "inner circles" but also the West African religious *fakis* and traders, thereby creating a multiethnic hierarchy linked to the center.[29] Darfur's Afro-Arabo-Islamic dynastic rulers maintained their rule by incorporating selective polities and inflicting rapacious violence on recalcitrant communities seeking to preserve their autonomy or ancestral patrimony. Memories abound of the well-organized campaigns of the sultanate's *fursan,* who are remembered for their ferocity in battle.

By the early eighteenth century, Sulayman's successors, Sultans Musa and Abu Baker, had expanded beyond their original homelands in the Jebel Marrah and had moved their *fashirs* (royal camps) from the mountains to the plains, thereby subjugating both non-Arabs and Arabs and both cultivators and camel and cattle herders. Although these sultans extended their control over the camel-herding Aballa Arabs, the cattle-herding Baggara continued to elude full control by seeking refuge in the southeastern peripheries of Darfur and across the river to the Bahr al-Ghazal areas.[30] The Baggara Arabs avoided paying tribute to the rival sultanates of Darfur and Wadai by emigrating out of their domains and establishing new homesteads in the southeastern and central plains.[31]

The wars between the two sultanates raged from 1720 to 1750, a period in which Darfur's export of slaves provided steady revenue for even bigger wars. During the period 1785–1786, the Kayra sultans conquered the vast plains of Kordofan and the areas bordering on the Bahr al-Ghazal, thereby monopolizing the slave trade and the caravan routes along the infamous *darb al-arba'in* (forty days road). Fur hegemony within the sultanate remained unchallenged until the 1873–1874 invasion of the territory of Zubayr Rahma, who coveted their monopoly of the trade caravan to Cairo and beyond. Zubayr succeeded in scattering the army and killing the Fur sultan, Ibrahim Qarad, in 1874 at Manawashi, but his control of Darfur was short-lived, since the Ottoman viceroy arrived in Darfur, claimed the conquered territory, and placed the ruthless *zariba* merchant under house arrest in Cairo. Turco-Egyptian rule over Darfur, 1874–1881, with remnants of the ruling classes rebelling against the new rulers and former tribute-paying subjects breaking free from their obligations, prevented the "shadow" sultans from ousting the alien invaders from the east. Thus, the golden age of the Kayra sultanate was brought down by the bold military strategy of the slave merchant and his *bazingers* and the occupation by the khedive's troops, who collected slaves and tribute from the vanquished inhabitants. The seven years that followed the defeat of the Kayra sultans plunged the region into lawlessness, where roaming bandits and the Turkiyya armies preyed on vulnerable communities.[32]

The (1881–1898) Mahdist uprising, with its promise of righteous rule for all believers, found fertile ground in Darfur, which became the launching ground for the millenarian revolt. The western horsemen, led by the ardent disciple (and later successor) of the self-proclaimed Mahdi, Muhammad Ahmad Abdallah of the Taai'sha (a section of the Baggara of southern Darfur), spearheaded the revolutionary transformation of Sudan into an Islamic caliphate capable of ousting the rapacious rule of the Turkiyya associated with the European infidels. Refusal to join the Mahdi's eastward marches to wage jihad against the Anglo-Egyptian rulers led to wars, deportations, and, in some cases, slavery. Traditional rulers of Darfur—the young Ali Dinar ibn Zacharia among many others—were forced to join the *tahjir* and were taken to Omdurman. This led to the scattering of anti-Mahdist "westerners" throughout the Nile Valley and beyond, while the pro-Mahdist westerners marched to victory in 1885. Despite the impressive military victories of the *ansar,* they were met by overt and covert resistance from religious leaders who viewed the Dongolawi shaikh's bid for divinely inspired rule as suspect. Moreover, his accompanying western horsemen—considered unfit to rule over the *awlad al-balad*—did not inspire the legitimacy necessary to govern the Nile Valley. With the death of the Mahdi in June 1885, the Khalifa Abdullahi assumed control over the movement and for thirteen years ruthlessly put down the many insurrections against the Mahidiyya, including the efforts by Fur Mahdists to delink their sultanate from the power center at Omdurman.[33]

Darfur's diverse inhabitants—nomadic, sedentary, Arab, African, and Afro-Arab—who had given refuge and nurtured the millenarian insurrection in 1881, started to chafe under the iron rule of their kinsman Khalifa Abdullahi. Resentment brewed from all sections, with the remnants of the Kayra sultanate launching rebellions and mobilizing support for an end to their subordination to the Nile Valley–centered theocratic rule. The West African communities of pilgrims and traders who found their livelihoods threatened by the khalifa's prohibition against the pilgrimage to Mecca, along with the Baggara who trekked back to their territories, formed a wide anti-Mahdist constituency. Thus, the belated decision by His Majesty's government to oust the Mahdist government, ostensibly to avenge the death of General "China" Gordon, found a large number of allies united in their desire to throw off Mahdist rule. Lord Kitchener defeated the armies of Khalifa Abdullahi on September 2, 1898, on the plains of Karari, marking an end to the *awlad al-balad*'s subordination to the horsemen from Darfur. Ali Dinar b. Zakariya, a grandson of Sultan Muhammad al-Fadl who had been held hostage by the khalifa, returned to his homeland and restored the rule of the Kayra sultanate and ended Darfur's entanglement with the governance of the territories of the Nile Valley.[34]

The young sultan's experience at the hands of the zealous Mahdists led to the continuation of the politics of "pragmatism" that defined the majority of Sahelian Islamic polities.[35] Darfur's Kayra sultanate had accommodated Islam as a ruling ideology alongside its indigenous forms of beliefs and institutions, which allowed innovation as well as the preservation of pre-Islamic values and norms.[36] The restored sultanate under Ali Dinar demonstrated a remarkable pragmatism—a close approximation of secularism—during his eighteen-year reign, from 1898 to 1916. Although the shadow of alien rule of the Anglo-Egyptian Condominium loomed large during his reign, his pragmatic policies reflected an adherence to the Afro-Arabo-Islamic traditions more than the fundamentalist militancy of the Wahabbists imported from the Arabian Peninsula. Michael Gomez's definition of what is meant by pragmatism in the age of jihadism appears to be a driving force in the economic and foreign policies of the Fur sultan seeking to maintain his autonomy from the infringement of the Sanusiyya in the north, the Tijaniyya in the west, and the French and Anglo-Egyptians in the east.

> Pragmatism is a policy in which the pursuit of commercial and agricultural advantage supersedes all other considerations, to the extent that alliances and rivalries with both neighboring polities and European powers are determined by economic expediency, and are subject to rapid and frequent realignment. Foreign policy is not formulated on the basis of advancing the claims of Islam within the region.[37]

Ali Dinar provided a welcome respite from the rampant disorder and famine that had accompanied the reign of the Mahdiyya. Unfortunately, his refusal to submit to the tutelage of either the British or the French made him an unwelcome intrusion in the designs of the European empire builders. His efforts to widen his political networks through alliances with the Ottoman Porte and the Central European powers inimical to shared French and British interests in the region led to a tightening of the "bonds of silk" that had characterized the relationship between the sultanate and its Anglo-Egyptian overseers in Khartoum.[38] The sultan's refusal to accommodate French incursions on his western borders and submit to British injunctions to desist taking any action against the interlopers led first to diplomatic friction followed by open rebellion. The sultan's forces entrenched themselves in the Jebel Marrah and defied the British forces for six months until Ali Dinar and his two sons were ambushed and killed by British forces in November 1916. Ali Dinar's death marked the end of Darfur's autonomy and the transformation of the sultanate into the western periphery of the power center in Khartoum; but his legacy of pragmatism and de facto secularism, along with the inhabitants' traditions of holding communal dialogues and the shared experience of marginalization by the center, provide the cornerstone for a durable peace.

From Sultanate to Western Province:
Politics of Exclusion, 1956–2006

Darfur's boundaries in the twentieth century were determined by negotiations between British and French colonial officials, who limited the area to a total of 503,180 square kilometers, including some of Sudan's arable land—land that also sits atop rich reserves of petroleum.[39] In the twentieth century, after their incorporation into the administrative framework of "northern" Sudan, Darfur's inhabitants came to be known as the *awlad al-gharb* (children of the west), dependent on the largesse of their former rivals, the *awlad al-balad,* who had gradually emerged as the heirs of the "political kingdom" overseen by the Anglo-Egyptian Condominium. Postindependence regimes ruling from the power center in Khartoum regarded their "western" acquisition as little more than a source of cheap labor for its development schemes in the Nile Valley and of foot soldiers for its armies. The political subordination of Darfur to Khartoum was accompanied by a loss of its local markets to the control of the *jellaba* traders, whose arrival was followed by the exodus of the young and able-bodied men, who went to work in the plantations set up in the Gezira scheme or to serve in the army.

Darfur languished unnoticed by Nile Valley politicians for a quarter of a century until the belated announcement of electoral politics that temporarily increased the "constituency" value of the province. In October 1944, the Khatmiyya-led Unionist Party marched under the banner "Unity of the Nile Valley." In February 1945, the Umma Party, led by Sayid Abdel Rahman (the posthumous son of the Mahdi) and supported by the British, countered the Unionist Party's platform with a demand for Sudanese independence. In 1946, the secular Sudanese Communist Party and the Islamist Muslim Brotherhood were established. With British support, the Umma Party canvassed for support in Darfur. In the 1953 parliamentary elections, Darfur's vote went overwhelmingly to the Umma Party. This pattern of voting was repeated until the rise to power of the Muslim Brotherhood in the 1980s. The Islamists proved to be the most uncompromising opponents of the dynastic Mahdists, whose leaders were in the mold of the traditional *awlad al-balad.* The Communists, although strong in the northern and eastern peripheries, failed to establish a strong constituency in the less industrialized western regions.[40] The Sudanese Muslim Brotherhood, for their part, gradually built up support among Darfur's northeastern communities, which yielded one of their earliest victories. In the May 1965 elections, the Islamic Charter Front's candidate in the Zaghawa stronghold of Kutum won a seat. Forty years later, the avowedly Islamist JEM continues to draw its support from the same constituency that cast its lot for the lone candidate of 1965.

The Umma Party, which received the majority of votes in Darfur, consistently squandered its support by refusing to acknowledge the regional leaders as their equals in Khartoum.[41] Umma members in Darfur were authorized to operate only as agents of the party rather than as interlocutors between periphery and center. This pattern was also replicated by the DUP and the NIF vis-à-vis their members in Darfur. The failure of both the sectarian parties as well as the Islamists to embrace Darfur's populace as full citizens rather than as second-class occupants of the geopolitical frontier of the Sudanese state led the region's dissidents to forgo electoral alternatives and to join the plethora of armed groups that had been engaged in confrontation with Khartoum since the early decades of independence. Denied their rights as conationals and as equal members in the Islamic *umma*, Darfur's postcolonial citizens were forced to refashion their identity along ethnoterritorial lines, pitting, on the one hand, the *awlad al-gharb* against the *awlad al-balad* and, on the other hand, the claimants of singular identities, such as the Ifrigiya/Zurga/Black African, against the settler/Non-Black/Arab. Clearly, the casualty of these constructed identities was that the Islamic identity that had buttressed the blending of the African and Arab roots of Sudanic populations was deemphasized. Deprived of the sociopolitical cement that had joined the Afro-Arabo-Islamic polity for over two centuries, Darfur's communities became divided along ethnic lines. Economic marginalization of the province in the face of the relative prosperity of the center created a sense of grievance that evolved into a politics of resentment.

Ethnicization of Local Dissent and Center-Periphery Dynamics

Anti-"northern" sentiments flared up during the first decade of independence (1956–1965), followed by the activities of clandestine urban and rural political organizations. The earliest urban-based movement, Lahib al-Ahmar (Red Flame), limited its activities to publishing and disseminating pamphlets accusing *jellaba* communities of exploiting the local population. Its activities dwindled with the increase of scrutiny by local intelligence agents, but it was soon supplanted by a more broadly constructed organization known as Soony in 1963. Soony advocated political and economic reform for the entire region of Darfur. Its name denoted the highest summit of the Jebel Marrah, symbolic of the glories of the Kayra sultanate and in memory of the defiant stand of its last ruler, Ali Dinar, in 1916. Soony's multiethnic membership and the large number of its rank-and-file members who were in the Sudan Defence Force alarmed policymakers in Khartoum and precipitated swift responses. Local recruits into the army were dismissed en masse, and stringent restrictions were placed on the entry of "westerners" into the police academy and higher echelons of the Sudan Defence Force. Whereas the Red Flame's pamphleteers had been dismissed by the larger

society as the work of a few disaffected urbanites, Soony's advocacy of reform and articulation of resentment at Khartoum's policy of economic and
political exclusion ignited a regional debate centering on the need for socioeconomic development and political representation. The ineffectiveness of
both the Red Flame and Soony, which had operated clandestinely, led to a
regional consensus that new types of organizations should be formed that
would foster dialogue rather than be mere vehicles of dissent.

In 1963, the Darfur Development Forum (DDF) was established, joining the mushrooming number of ethnic-based organizations that addressed
economic and sociopolitical concerns of the peripheral peoples of the Nuba
Mountains and the eastern Beja. The DDF's membership was multiethnic,
although its founders were mainly ethnic Fur. Its emphasis on the region's
economic development inevitably touched on the unequal relationship
between the political appointees of the center—the *awlad al-balad* and their
jellaba clients—and the multiethnic elite of the western periphery inhabited
by the *awlad al-gharb*. The 1964 coup by Abboud quickly dismissed the
efforts of Darfur's intelligentsia to craft mechanisms of communication to
stem the tide of the politics of resentment that had surfaced with the activities of the Red Flame and Soony. Abboud's strong-arm tactics did not
encourage dialogue over the parceling out of lands for mechanized agricul-
ture, nor did they lessen the growing alienation of Darfur's population.

The May 1969 coup that brought Numeiri to power restructured center-
periphery relations and granted autonomous rule to local elites. Unfortunately, the impending famine of the 1970s and 1980s decimated the livelihoods of Darfur's rural majority— farmers and herders—and presented the
Fur-dominated regional government with challenges of equitable distribution
of resources among the famine-stricken communities. The patronage politics
that emerged during the governorship of Ahmed Diraige placed the Fur at the
pinnacle of the regional government, with the other groups forming multiethnic coalitions to respond to the demands of their constituencies. The large
influx of people fleeing their scorched *dars* and in urgent need of refuge for
their families and animals faced a maze of patronage networks from which
they were "ethnically" excluded. Conflicts over access to water and pasturage increased as farming communities began to feel threatened by the
increasing number of *naziheen* (displaced) who crowded into their villages.

The pastoralists, desperate to save remnants of their herds, drove their
cattle into farming areas, violating age-old seasonal restrictions that had been
the basis for centuries of coexistence. The rules that governed the traditional
interaction between the two symbiotic groups—farmers and herders—unraveled as the resources dwindled and the antagonists resorted to using force
rather than relying on the traditional mechanisms of conflict resolution for
which Darfur was renowned.[42] In tandem with the spiraling violence was the

entrenchment of an imported ideology of ethnic polarization that fed the infernal logic of communal fears of expansion of what Sharif Harir called the "African belt" versus the "Arab belt." Harir, in 1994, referred to the crisis in Darfur as an "erupting volcano" and defined the Fur-Arab conflict of 1987 and 1989 as a resource-driven conflict that developed into a "regional ethnic war of a quasi-international character." His prescient analysis has been validated with tragic consequences for the region and the nation as a whole and is worth quoting at length:

> Unlike many other ethnic conflicts that took place in Dar Fur, the destruction that came with this war was total. . . . Its brutality was sustained by both sides. The Arabs using mounted *razzias* called "knights" (*fursan*), cut the throats of their Fur victims and burned them alive when they survived their machine guns and rocket-propelled grenades. The Fur did likewise whenever they had a chance, using their combatants called "militias" (*malishait*). The Arabs violated Fur farms and burned their produce and uprooted orchards. The Fur counter-attacked by burning pasture and by denying their enemies access to water resources. The Arabs looked to Libya for the supply of armaments and as a source of ideological inspiration; the extension of the "Arab belt" (*al hizam al arabi*) in Africa and the liberation of the Arab world. The Fur looked at the model presented by the Sudan People's Liberation Army (SPLA) for inspiration, but towards Hissein Habre and, via him, to the anti-Libyan mosaic (USA and Egypt) as possible sources of armament. In between, their irrespective educated elites mobilized resources to guarantee supplies of arms and ammunition from the local market. The two parties also sought alliances with the political parties at the center in order to further their case within the government apparatus to their own advantage or the disadvantage of their opponents in the conflict; the Arabs were closely allied to the Umma party and the Fur were allied to the Democratic Unionist Party (DUP) who were coalition partners at that time.[43]

That the parties to the conflict were able to come to a common gathering called by mediators chosen by each side and present their respective "logic" bears testimony to the resilience of traditional mechanisms of conflict resolution of Darfur's communities. Nevertheless, it is interesting to note that although both the delegations were led by community leaders and seasoned politicians, the respective positions were each delivered by young schoolteachers who delivered the ideological justifications based on the "infernal logic" that fueled the violence. The words delivered by the two young interlocutors demonstrate the internationalization of the conflict through the use of symbolically laden terms such as "dirty war," "genocidal course," "holocaust," "complete annihilation," and "AK47 and G3 assault rifles." In contrast to the Fur and Arab positions, the government's position reflected a reconciliatory tone to the two parties but held that the conflict was one that was imposed on the Sudanese by "malignant external forces."[44]

The following excerpts from the tribal reconciliation conference, held in Al Fasher a quarter of a century before the escalation of the conflict into genocidal acts, may provide a better understanding.[45]

> [The Fur position:] The dirty war that has been imposed on us [i.e., the Fur] began as an economic war but it soon assumed a genocidal course aiming at driving us out of our ancestral land in order to achieve certain political goals. . . . At the present time we are witnessing yet another and yet more sinister phase of this dirty war: the aim is a total holocaust and no less than the complete annihilation of the Fur people and all things Fur. How are we to understand the brutal mutilation of Fur victims and the burning alive of residents of Fur villages? The message is quite clear: empty the land and do not allow any Fur survivors to come back and reestablish their villages. . . . The basic fuel of this war is racism. This conflict is about their attempt at dividing people of Dar Fur region into "Arabs" against "blacks" (*zurga*), with superiority attributed to the former.[46]
>
> [The Arab position:] Our Arab tribe . . . and Fur coexisted peacefully throughout the known history of Dar Fur. However, the situation was destabilized towards the end of the seventies when the Fur raised the slogan "Dar Fur is for Fur.". . . The Arabs were depicted as foreigners who should be evicted from this area to Dar Fur. To give substance to this slogan, the Fur "militia" forces were trained under the supervision of the Fur Governor of Dar Fur in the period between May 1986 and September 1986 replacing, thus the traditional throwing sticks, clubs, and spears with AK47 and G3 assault rifles and rocket-propelled grenades. Ours is a legitimate self-defense and we shall continue defending our right of access to water and pasture. However, let us not be in doubt about who began the war: it is the Fur who in their quest to extend the so-called "African belt" (*al Hizam al Zunji*) wanted to remove all the Arabs from this soil.[47]

It would appear that the discourse of genocide was planted in the 1980s and took root, fanned by both the adventurism of the foreign policies of Khartoum and the responses of its brutal external allies. With the addition of the combustible campaigns of jihadism and the resurfacing of the noxious spread of racism camouflaged as the spread of Arab civilization by force, the opportunity that had appeared with the reconciliation conference of 1989 was missed. In a tragic fulfillment of the infernal logic of the "wars of survival" construct within which the Fur and Arab camps operated, both sides pursued the "dirty war." The support given to the Arab side by Khartoum demonstrated that the formidable power of the state rejected the claims of those who considered themselves to be "Africans." The final years of the twentieth century, which witnessed the transformation of what had been a demand for political reform, economic development,[48] and social justice, had, through tragic policies and missed opportunities, created the conditions for the perpetration of crimes against humanity. Darfur inhabitants joined those of the Nuba Mountains and of south Sudan in facing the ire of a hegemonic center surrounded by multiple fronts.[49]

Flashpoint Darfur: Portraiture Politics

In 2003–2004, the world witnessed apocalyptic scenes, captured on television screens, of the Janjaweed—modern-day reincarnations of the *fursan* of the fearsome armies of the Fur sultanate of yesteryear—wreaking havoc on villages. Although violence had been a constant feature of this region, it had been contained by the different regimes by a combination of coercive and accommodative policies. The clandestinely organized unrest of the 1960s, indicative of ethnonationalist rumblings in the western periphery, simmered on until the 1980s when Sadiq al-Mahdi's government launched a policy of supporting Chadian rebels and arming their murahaleen kinsmen engaged in wars against their sedentary rivals. The genocidal wars against the Nuba of Kordofan and the rebels of the south spilled over into Darfur when Darfur's disillusioned elites sought external assistance from both the SPLM/A and the Chadian government. Garang's New Sudanism provided the ideological balm that initially unified the "westerners" and facilitated the rise of the Darfur Liberation Front, precursor of the SLM/A and JEM.

This realignment of "westerners," who had previously served as foot soldiers in the jihads against the "southerners" and in the genocidal wars waged against the Nuba, coincided with a number of critical events: (1) the collapse of the Addis Ababa Agreement in the south, (2) the drought and famine of the early 1980s that had ravaged the area and triggered resource-driven conflicts pitting farmers against pastoralists, (3) the rescission of the Fur-dominated regional government, (4) the transplantation and adaptation of the vision of a New Sudan into Darfur to counter the ethnocentric and polarized propaganda of the Zurga-Arabi camps, and (5) the "militarization" of the region due to the spillover of the Chad-Libyan war and the rise of Sudanese nationalism in the face of the increased presence of alien armed groups, which led to the reconciliation of the warring groups of sedentary farmers and pastoralists. The success of the conference of tribal reconciliation of July 1989 demonstrated that the imported ideologies of identity wars were not as deeply rooted as the historic, socioeconomic, and political ties that bound Darfur's Afro-Arabo-Islamic populace. This uneasy peace was shattered by the exclusionary and fundamentalist policies of the Islamist regime that replaced the Sadiq al-Mahdi government.

The rise to power of the NIF and its theocratic ideologue, Hassan al-Turabi, swiftly unraveled the fragile peace by openly pursuing a policy of coercive rule and the adoption of jihadism in lieu of dialogue with aggrieved communities throughout the country. The multiethnic coalition of Fur, Zaghawa, and Masalit elites that had governed the region since 1986 shattered. Some of its political personalities went into exile; others joined the NIF and were soon disillusioned by their exclusion from the reinvented *umma* dominated by the *awlad al-balad*, who snubbed their avowedly

Islamist coreligionists—the *awlad al-gharb*—from the "west" while embracing distant "Arab" kin from neighboring Chad and Libya who sowed destruction in the western periphery. This led to a slow but gradual exodus from the racialized *umma* to the rainbow coalition promised by Colonel John Garang of the SPLM/A, whose espousal of an all-embracing African identity and a secular ideology had won over Nuba nationalists, recalcitrant Beja rebels, and some stalwart members of the DUP and Umma Party.

An alliance of the western, eastern, and southern peripheries in the 1990s threatened the *awlad al-balad*'s three-century-old hegemonic rule from Khartoum. Although Khartoum politicians had succeeded in delaying the inevitable coming together of the aggrieved parties through astute exploitation of ethnic differences as well as promises of righteous Islamic rule, the minority ruling elite could no longer prevent the maturation of the opposing political elite, who formed a multiethnic armed coalition demanding citizenship and power sharing. The mobilization of Darfur in the 1990s and the alignment of its ethnonationalist groupings with those of the other dissident groups arrayed against the center in Khartoum presented the regime with the unthinkable—the loss of the hegemony of the *awlad al-balad*—on the eve of its worldwide recognition as an Arabo-Islamic petrostate.

The failure to institute a more inclusive form of government had driven leaders of marginalized areas, such as Abel Alier, John Garang, Yusuf Khuwa, and Daud Bolad, to launch armed insurrections, which were met with the central government's systematic campaigns of annihilation. The minority regime's wars, against its opponents in the peripheries, were accompanied by episodic peace agreements that were violated before the ink dried on the documents, leaving a legacy of bitterness and distrust.[50] The unwillingness of the *awlad al-balad* to grant actual citizenship rights to its aggrieved peripheral subjects led to what René Lemarchand has aptly termed "a logic . . . of an 'infernal machine,' of a situation in which challenge provokes repression, terrorism, counter-terrorism, until there is no longer the possibility of compromise with the adversary."[51] The pursuit of "admonitory massacre(s)" by Khartoum and its marauding Janjaweed resuscitated the vestigial racism that reemerged in some of the virulent distortions of the traditional recitation of *hakkama*.[52] Although its origins are entrenched in the relations of inequality between its multiethnic inhabitants, the flashpoint of Darfur that shocked the world in 2003 needs to be understood as the denouement of a series of struggles of the inhabitants of a formerly autonomous political entity reduced to a periphery of the riverain elites of Khartoum and their clients. Khartoum's response—usually a neglected dimension—also needs to be examined as extremely violent preemptive efforts to reestablish control over the nation's most arable lands adjacent to areas of proven oil resources located in "northern" Sudan.

Darfur's intercommunal violence is more than an ethnic intifada. Failure to comprehend the complex interplay of economic, geopolitical, and historical factors will result in the formulation of ill-fitting solutions that do not facilitate the prospects for a just and durable peace. Leo Kuper provides useful insights that may provide a deeper understanding of the pace of the logic of the particular "infernal machine," which, if understood in its totality, may be halted before it reaches a point of no return—a point where

> there is no longer the possibility of understanding, of dialogue, of adjustment of interests . . . [where] evolutionary programs of reform have broken down, and there has been an elimination of the middle ground which might have offered a social basis for policies of reconciliation. Relationships across racial or ethnic divisions become tenuous, guarded, suspect, and dangerous. There are no longer effective interracial or interethnic political associations. The *interlocutors valuables,* the influential mediators, have disappeared from the scene. The society is now divided into two mutually exclusive hostile camps. There is a superimposition of cleavages and an accumulation of issues of conflict. Associated ideologies proclaim the irreconcilability of goals, the illusory nature of reforms, and the necessity and justice of violence.[53]

As Khartoum's "infernal machine" of professional army troops and marauding militias wreaked havoc on the fields and hamlets of Darfur, regional mediators led by the African Union shuttled from capital to capital in search of consensus between rebel factions and government spokespersons. Peace continued to elude the Republic of Sudan as it celebrated its fiftieth anniversary of independence in 2006, which also marked five decades of war with its peripheries and remained bound to the center through ruthless policies of coercion and terror. Recognizing the role of past wars, broken promises, and the distrust between the government and rebels is critical to understanding why peace continues to elude modern Sudan. The UN General Assembly's and the African Union's refusal to support the European Union's efforts to sanction Sudan's violations of human rights also attests to the gulf between the official discourse of African heads of state to protect civilians, and the unofficial consensus to pursue the old norm of nonintervention in the internal affairs of a "fraternal" country. The "new spirit of 'owning' more of Africa's problems" appears to have been corrupted into yet another creative way of maintaining the "old boys club" spirit, which had characterized the now defunct Organization of African Unity. What remains tragically clear is that despite the recent lessons of Rwanda and the Balkans, the victims of war and crimes against humanity continue to be powerless to defend themselves against the power of those wielding sovereignty. The only lesson learned is that the very regimes perpetrating the crimes against humanity have refined their discourse of the indefensible and utilized diplomacy and oil wealth, as well as their access to regional and international institutions, to evade international accountability.[54] Unfettered by sanctions or threats of political ostracism, the regime perpetrating atrocities engages in endless dialogues intended to wear out their opponents on the ground, which stymie the well-intentioned and well-funded peace process. Failure to understand the corrosive effects of the unwillingness and/or inability to acknowledge the inhumane suffering of a distant community can only lead to the "routinisation of atrocity . . . escalation of violence . . . with a genocidal touch characteristically expressed in the slaughter of non-combatants, the aged, women, and children."[55] What needs to be remembered is that the final objective is not just that the conflict is resolved but how it is resolved and with what consequences for both the victims and the perpetrators of violence.

The Quest for Conflict Resolution

Conflict resolution in Darfur is occurring within a national, regional, and international environment replete with both opportunities and challenges. Efforts to resolve this conflict in the short-to-medium term rely on how all the parties seize these glaring opportunities while minimizing the debilitating challenges. The Comprehensive Peace Agreement presents an institutional model for reconciliation in Sudan, particularly among minorities contesting a variety of citizenship claims. At the same time, the settlement may embolden radicals in Khartoum who may perceive self-determination as a source of further fragmentation of the postcolonial state. The inauguration of the Government of National Unity (GNU) has the potential to bring more voices to the debate about Darfur, furnishing a larger national consensus that may facilitate an agreement. But conflicts within the amorphous structures of the GNU could also potentially invite the institutional paralysis and political procrastination reminiscent of Khartoum's approach to the south in the 1970s and 1980s.

Regionally, IGAD's participation in the north-south peace process had already established an indispensable presence of neighbors that was fundamental to the search for negotiated settlements in Sudan. In Darfur, however, the geographical center of conflict has shifted to non-IGAD players in Central Africa, where the core actors—Chad and Libya—have different stakes and roles in the conflict. In addition, while the IGAD intervention focused primarily on achieving a peaceful settlement before external military intervention, the Darfur conflict has forced the military engagement of the African Union, under circumstances of a constrained mandate and a dearth of resources. Internationally, there were opportunities for collective action on Darfur stemming from the existing international attention focused on Sudan, but this presence was constrained by the need to engage the government for a successful outcome in the south. US leadership, in particular, was hampered by competing claims arising from the war on terrorism that forced close collaboration with the Khartoum government, the war in Iraq, and international demands for a forceful action in light of widespread abuses that amounted to genocide.

Initial Confrontation and Reactions, February 2003–January 2004

The SLM/A led the first attacks against government forces and targets in February 2003, coinciding with the breakthrough in the north-south dialogue following the signing of the Machakos Protocol. Its leadership subsequently released a Political Declaration accusing the government in Khartoum of systematic marginalization, racial discrimination, and economic exclusion; and in language reminiscent of Garang's SPLA, it described its objectives to be

> a united democratic Sudan . . . predicated on full acknowledgment of Sudan's ethnic, cultural, social, and political diversity. Viable unity must be therefore ultimately based on the right of self-determination. . . . The fundamental imperatives of a viable unity are an economy and political system that address the uneven development and marginalization that have plagued the country since independence. . . . Religion and politics . . . must be kept in their respective domains, with religion belonging to the personal domain and the state in the public domain. . . . SLM/A firmly opposes . . . the Khartoum Government's policies of using some Arab tribes . . . to achieve its hegemonic devices that are detrimental both to Arabs and non-Arabs.[56]

Unprepared for a full-scale insurgency in the west, the local authorities in western Darfur tried to negotiate with the SLM, but the talks stalled after the Janjaweed assassinated a popular Massalit leader. In retaliation, the SLA seized a strategic town on the Chad border and captured arms and equipment from its garrison. In April 2003, the fighting spread into North Darfur state with a combined SLA/JEM attack on the airport outside El Fasher, the provincial capital.[57]

The coordinated attacks by the two movements revealed the inadequacy of the government military, hence the decision to rely primarily on the Janjaweed, reinforced by helicopter gunships and bombers from the national air force. In Khartoum's calculation, the stakes in Darfur were higher not just because of the high number of soldiers serving in the national army from the region, but also because of the potential implications of the rebellion for the stability of the central government.[58] Throughout the summer and fall of 2003, the attacks by the Janjaweed and government forces led to death or displacement among the Fur, Massalit, and Zaghawa. With close to 200,000 refugees in Chad, the government of President Idriss Deby, a close ally of Khartoum but with ethnic links to the Zaghawa, faced a delicate humanitarian and political problem.[59] President Deby interceded between the government and the SLM, mediating a cease-fire in N'Djamena in September 2003. But the cease-fire did not last, as both sides resumed fighting and the humanitarian crisis worsened. The Chadian leadership initially regarded Darfur as a local conflict amenable to resolution given the existing pattern of cross-border ethnic alliances and historical ties, but the crisis soon overwhelmed their capacity.

International actors responded slowly at first, but pressure from leading nongovernmental organizations (NGOs) and international humanitarian agencies was important in directing attention to the enormity of the disaster and the need for relief assistance. The obstruction of humanitarian efforts by the government in the face of the looming food crisis deepened the crescendo of condemnations that were to grow into accusations of genocide in Darfur. In February 2004, a Swiss NGO, the Center for Humanitarian Dialogue, sought to broker an agreement for humanitarian access, but Khartoum refused, claiming that such access would help the military effort of the rebels. As a compromise, Bashir turned to President Deby for a new mediation initiative in March 2004 to address humanitarian and political issues.[60]

The N'Djamena talks gathered a wide range of international observers from the United States, the European Union, the Center for Humanitarian Dialogue, and the AU. Organized as a single delegation, the SLM and JEM sought a larger role for Western observers that neither the Chadians nor the Khartoum government would countenance. Politically naïve and inexperienced, the SLM and JEM saw Western observers as helping their cause at the negotiating table. There were also disagreements among the international observers about specific roles and mandates. To reduce these differences, the Chadian mediators opted to allow Western observers to participate only in sessions dealing with humanitarian concerns and excluded them from the political talks.[61] In early April 2004, the Chadian team presented a draft cease-fire agreement that was more favorable to the government than to the rebel positions. Outmaneuvered by both the government and the mediator, on April 8, 2004, the rebel movements joined the government in signing the N'Djamena cease-fire agreement that pledged to suspend hostilities for forty-five days, exchange prisoners, and facilitate humanitarian access to victims of the war. The Sudanese government also committed itself to "neutralize armed militias." More decisively, the parties agreed to establish a cease-fire commission, staffed by the signatories and external observers, to implement the agreement.

In subsequent talks on political concerns at the end of April 2004, the parties signed an agreement that stipulated a conference of "all representatives of

Darfur" to seek a comprehensive solution to the conflict. Although the agreement referred to the ultimate establishment in Darfur of a "democratic political culture to guarantee to the population of the region their political, economic, and social requirements," it stressed that "the government of the Sudan must assure that the armed militias are neutralized and disarmed according to a program to be decided upon."[62] Both rebel movements quickly disavowed the political agreement, insisting on direct talks with the government for a comprehensive settlement instead of the proposed all-inclusive conference. At the same time, internal differences occurred in both the SLM and the JEM, presaging the start of the fragmentation of Darfur's rebel movements.[63]

Despite claims by both sides to respect the humanitarian cease-fire agreement, widespread violence continued relentlessly. With the emergence of internal tensions in the rebel movements, Khartoum and its allied militias regained the political and military initiative after the negotiations at N'Djamena. As the AU began to take a leading role in the entire crisis, President Deby's mediation became marginal. This was because, as Hugo Slim has pointed out,

> President Deby's political relationship with the Sudanese government is complicated. Khartoum had supported his invasion of Chad from his exile in Darfur. At the same time, Deby is also a member of the Zaghawa people who spread across the Sudanese-Chadian border. This group is suffering a major part of Khartoum's violence, and much of the SLA leadership is Zaghawa. While Deby made a creative and acceptable mediator, his own loyalties were deeply split and the Chadian process lacked the political leverage necessary to give the talks credibility and weight.[64]

As part of the shifting locus of mediation, the parties signed an agreement in Addis Ababa, at the end of May 2004, on the implementation modalities of the N'Djamena cease-fire agreement that acknowledged the AU as the core international body and the operational arm of the cease-fire agreement.

International Engagement and the Abuja Negotiations, August 2004–May 2006

By the summer of 2004, as the crisis deteriorated, the UN established the Joint Implementation Mechanism (JIM) to monitor events in Darfur, but major powers in the Security Council resisted demands for a robust military action to protect civilians and guarantee the unimpeded supply of humanitarian relief. Needing government cooperation to reach an agreement in Naivasha, Western countries were reluctant to push for more forceful measures that they did not have the political will to muster. With their armed forces ensnared in Afghanistan and Iraq, the United States and Great Britain were reluctant to be perceived as threatening to invade another Muslim country.[65]

The international community resolved the intervention dilemma by designating the AU to intervene in the name of African solutions, with promises of logistical support and financial backing. In this division of labor, the UN Security Council would boost diplomatic pressure on Khartoum to facilitate delivery of humanitarian aid. Dovetailing with the AU's efforts to enhance its conflict management capacity, this sharing of responsibilities underestimated the scale of the humanitarian and security conundrum in Darfur. In the early phase of protracted negotiations on the size and mandate of the African Union Mission in Sudan (AMIS), the government conceded to a team of sixty monitors supported by 305 troops from Rwanda and Nigeria, under Brigadier General Okonkwo of Nigeria. The AMIS mandate was limited to protecting the monitors and providing security to internally displaced persons (IDPs) receiving humanitarian assistance. In July 2004, with the situation worsening in Darfur, the AU proposed a plan for the conversion of AMIS into a full-fledged peacekeeping force that would protect civilians, neutralize the Janjaweed, and facilitate the delivery of humanitarian assistance, but Khartoum adamantly opposed such a large force and such a strong mandate.[66]

On the political front, Nigerian president Olusegun Obasanjo, in his capacity as AU chairman, organized direct negotiations between the government and representatives of the SLM and the JEM in Abuja starting in August 2004. On the eve of the Abuja talks, the United States lobbied for UN Security Council Resolution 1556, which demanded that the government cease all offensive military operations, disarm the Janjaweed, and arrest its leaders. Threats of sanctions were tagged to the resolution in the case of failure to comply, and the UN secretary-general was authorized to report progress in thirty days. The former prime minister of Niger, Hamid Elgabid, led the mediation team at Abuja, assisted by the AU secretariat. Although the mediators proposed a broad agenda focusing on humanitarian, security, political, and economic issues, the parties insisted on according priority to humanitarian and security concerns. This strategy worked well for the government side, but for the rebels, it contained the danger of distracting from the political dimensions of the conflict. As Alex De Waal aptly noted, "By focusing on issues that are secondary to the outbreak of the war, the rebels are failing to develop a political agenda that can be the basis for a settlement."[67] The government's negotiating strategy was to revisit the terms of the April 2004 cease-fire agreement that provided for the disarmament of both the rebels and Janjaweed. For the rebels, however, the priority was on security, humanitarian access, and the government's unilateral disarmament of the Janjaweed. These contrasting positions led to a deadlock in Abuja, necessitating the postponement of the talks.

At the end of August 2004, in the face of the collapse of the Abuja talks, UN secretary-general Kofi Annan submitted a report mandated by UN Security Council Resolution 1556 in which he concluded that the government had "not met its obligations" to stop "attacks against civilians and ensure their protection" and urged the rapid expansion of AMIS.[68] But even after US secretary of state Colin Powell conceded in September 2004 that the government and its allies were committing genocide, the most that the divided UN Security Council could do was to establish a UN commission to investigate the atrocities in Darfur. The United States also strongly advocated for the expansion of the AU force to 3,000 troops and 1,000 police officers.[69] In a revised deployment framework approved in October 2004, the AU settled on expanding the AMIS to 3,320 police and soldiers to monitor IDP camps, militia attacks against civilians, government disarmament of militias, and cessation of hostilities by all parties. At Khartoum's insistence, AMIS increased its numbers without changing its mandate.

In a resumption of the Abuja talks in early November 2004, the AU mediators obtained a modest agreement between the belligerents. On November 9, 2004, Khartoum agreed to expeditiously implement its stated commitment to neutralize and disarm the Janjaweed and armed militias; strictly abide by the provisions of the N'Djamena April 8, 2004, agreement; take all steps required to prevent all attacks, threats, intimidation, and other forms of violence against civilians; and protect the rights of IDPs.[70] In a major concession, the government yielded to rebel demands on the banning of military flights over Darfur. But despite the celebratory mood in Abuja, the November 9 agreements were, with the exception of the restriction on military flights by Khartoum, simply a reiteration of the previous provisions contained in the original N'Djamena cease-fire agreement. To underscore the limits of concession making at Abuja, within hours of signing the agreement that was supposed to bring peace to the region, Sudanese government forces stormed the El Geer refugee camp near Nyala, in southern Darfur, attacking men, women, and children.[71] Furthermore, in a major offensive in December 2004, the government mounted an offensive that seriously weakened rebel positions on the ground. These attacks demonstrated that in the absence of a political process to deal with the escalating problems, the negotiations at Abuja were not breaking new ground.

Overshadowed by the triumphs of Naivasha, Darfur resurfaced in the international conscience in early March 2005 in the context of deep divisions between the United States and its Western allies over a proposal for the International Criminal Court (ICC) to probe alleged war crimes in Darfur. The UN Commission on Darfur "strongly" recommended referring the proposal to the ICC in The Hague, which is mandated to try cases involving war crimes and genocide, but the United States, which has remained opposed to the creation of the ICC, instead proposed a separate UN war crimes tribunal in Tanzania to handle the crimes in Darfur. In a compromise, the United States abstained from a Security Council resolution that referred fifty-one names to the ICC for formal investigation of allegations of atrocities against unarmed civilians in Darfur. At the same time, the Security Council adopted a resolution that strengthened the existing arms embargo on the parties and imposed an asset freeze and travel ban on those deemed responsible for atrocities or who were thought to be violating the cease-fire agreement.[72]

At the end of May 2005, the AU's Peace and Security Council proposed to boost the strength of AMIS from 3,320 to 7,731. But efforts to restart the Abuja negotiations, which had collapsed in December 2004, were fruitless. In his report to the Security Council in February 2005, the UN secretary-general's special representative to Sudan, Jan Pronk, had presented a gloomy picture of the peace prospects. Although he acknowledged that the government had shown a "willingness to negotiate, toughly, but seriously," he blamed the rebels for stalling: "Darfur rebels have become less cooperative in talks, and their attacks on police increased, while some groups directly impeded humanitarian work by looting cars and trucks, and even abducting the national staff of humanitarian agencies, severely reducing the delivery of assistance."[73] In the spring of 2005, the SLM refused to return to the negotiations unless the AU came up with more solid protection mechanisms for civilians in Darfur, and the United Nations took over the mediation of the talks.[74]

Similarly, efforts to restart the talks were hampered by the emergence of competing mediation initiatives from Egypt and Libya reminiscent of the North African initiatives in southern Sudan.[75] In May 2005, Libya brought together representatives of the SLM and JEM, who agreed that the two groups should resume negotiations with the government without preconditions. As part of this initiative, Libya also organized a summit meeting of heads of state from Chad, Gabon, Nigeria, Libya, Egypt, Eritrea, and Sudan, who agreed to include the North Africans in the peace process without shifting the venue from Abuja.[76] In May 2005, amid criticisms that the AU had failed to establish a credible negotiating process, the AU secretariat appointed Salim A. Salim, former OAU secretary-general, to chair the mediation team.

Under Salim's leadership, the Abuja talks resumed in June 2005, but the talks hit an early impasse over the observer status of representatives from Chad and Eritrea. The JEM accused Chad of supporting Khartoum, while the Sudanese government delegation alleged that Eritrea was the main backer of the rebels. Unlike the previous negotiations, which had focused on security and humanitarian issues, the mediators forced discussions on political issues, underscoring the urgency of a political settlement that would underwrite the previous security and humanitarian protocols. Toward this end, the mediators prepared a draft Declaration of Principles that embraced the equitable distribution of power and national wealth and respect for ethnic, cultural, and religious rights. The major impediment to the negotiations was the upsurge of infighting within the two rebel groups. The split in the SLM occurred when some members declared allegiance to President Abdel Wahed Mohamed al-Nur, a Fur, and others rallied around Secretary-General Minni Minnawi, a Zaghawa. At Abuja, Minnawi's supporters, claiming to command the larger fighting force, denounced Nur, head of the SLM negotiating team in Abuja, declaring that he no longer represented them. Similarly, an internal rift beset the JEM between groups claiming to represent field commanders who had rejected the JEM's political leadership. On July 5, 2005, the mediators achieved agreement on the DOP, in which the central government pledged to grant Darfur regional autonomy under a reformed federal constitution respecting the traditional land ownership rights of indigenous minorities. More important, both sides agreed to find ways to pay reparations to those who had suffered in the civil war and to guarantee the right of IDPs to return to their homes and places of origin. The weight of this achievement, however, was, undercut by the internecine conflicts within the rebel movements.[77]

Beyond the conference table, the split within the SLM had the most significance, as rival factions battled for control in Darfur. In October 2005, human rights organizations and the UN accused the SLM of complicity in the death of hundreds of civilians, three AU peacekeepers, and two civilian contractors, and the kidnapping of AU personnel. The SLM was also blamed for engaging in banditry and impeding humanitarian operations, thereby threatening an international engagement that was already inadequate in resources and mandates. Moreover, the infighting in the SLM started to weaken its internal support and international sympathy. As one observer remarked, "The rebels, Lord knows, have legitimate grievances and legitimate aspirations, but their lack of discipline on the ground is making it too easy for the other side—whether they are Janjaweed or government-supported Janjaweed—to do things and stop the international community from crying out as clearly as we would if we could be absolutely of the point of view that the rebels are not at fault in any of the [attacks]."[78] As the ethnic strife in the SLM started to overshadow the conflict between the government and rebels, Libya organized a reconciliation summit of its feuding leaders in Tripoli in July 2005, but the meeting did not lessen the animosities.

A new round of Abuja talks in mid-September 2005 equally failed to discuss the substance of the Declaration of Principles; instead, the AU mediators organized workshops where the rival delegations tried to achieve some initial consensus on the key issues of power and wealth sharing and security arrangements. Although the mediators subsequently designated commissions to study these three issues, most of the negotiations were devoted to procedural rather than substantive issues. The AU mediators acknowledged the disarray in Abuja, caused by the divisions in the rebel leadership and the deteriorating relations between Sudan and the AU. This deterioration was due to the renewed government collaboration with the Janjaweed against unarmed civilians in Darfur. With the talks set to restart in late November 2005, UN Secretary-General Annan gave the parties until December 31, 2005, to secure a final settlement in the conflict.[79]

At the end of October 2005, the two critical pillars of external engagement in Darfur—AMIS and the Abuja process—were proving inadequate in making a difference in a war that, according to UN estimates, had affected some 3.3 million people: 1.8 million IDPs; 200,000 refugees in Chad; and 300,000 deaths. The inadequacy of AMIS, in turn, spurred renewed calls for the United States, NATO, and the UN to urgently provide more support to the African force and to strengthen its mandate to effectively defend innocent civilians against the violence. As a Refugees International report noted,

> With the recent upsurge in violence over the past two months, AMIS shortcomings have come into full focus. AMIS does not have the ability or the resources to carry out its job of monitoring a ceasefire that is widely violated by all sides in an escalating two and half years of conflict. . . . If the U.S. is serious about preventing civilian casualties in Darfur, it and its NATO allies, in partnership with the AU, need to move quickly to strengthen the mandate of AMIS, provide more troops, greatly increase logistical and organizational assistance to AMIS, and bring pressure to bear on the Government of Sudan to disarm the Janjaweed and allow AMIS to perform its job.[80]

On the negotiating front, the Abuja talks established a negotiating framework, but without yielding significant breakthroughs. Even as the SPLM, as part of the Government of National Unity, prepared to join the negotiations in Abuja, there were widespread criticisms about the lack of professionalism in the negotiations since their inception. The ICG report notes:

> The AU did not have an established mediation capacity when the negotiations began. It sought to draw expertise from within its own Conflict Management Center but it made a crucial mistake in failing to consult and engage the experienced mediation team from the IGAD process between Khartoum and the SPLM. Donor support to the negotiations has been limited, in terms of both political and financial support.[81]

Amid Khartoum's determined efforts to assume the chairmanship of the AU in January 2006, a seven-country committee devised a compromise that led to the selection of President Denis Sassou-Nguessou of Congo-Brazzaville. With no solution in sight on the Darfur crisis, the AU would have faced a credibility

crisis if President Bashir took charge of the organization. As part of the compromise, Sudan is expected to succeed Congo in the AU chairmanship in
2007.[82] Although the AU renewed the mandate of the 7,000-strong AMIS force,
most of the debates continued to revolve around its incapacity to fulfill its objectives to protect civilians. As a result, there were wide-ranging international
diplomatic efforts to find alternatives, ranging from proposals to authorize
20,000 UN peacekeeping troops to the use of NATO forces in support of
AMIS. Most of these initiatives faced strong opposition from Sudan and its
core supporters in the UN Security Council, China and Russia.

Sudan's insistence that it would not allow any UN forces in Darfur without a peace agreement galvanized attempts by the AU to reinvigorate the
Abuja peace negotiations. Throughout March and April 2006, negotiations
revolved around an AU draft proposal; the mediators also established April
30 as the deadline for the conclusion of the talks.[83] In a sign of growing seri-
ousness on Khartoum's part, the government delegation included the SPLM
and Vice-President Ali Osman Taha. In addition to proposals for a cease-fire,
disarmament, and reintegration of rebel forces into the national army, the
draft proposals included new components: reversion of western Sudan to the
borders established at independence in 1956; the creation of a Transitional
Darfur Regional Authority (TDRA), to be headed by a senior special assistant
to the president with the participation of the SLM, the JEM, and the governors of the three states; the permanent status of Darfur would be determined
through a referendum held simultaneously in the three states by 2010; and
an immediate transfer of $300 million to Darfur, with $200 million a year
thereafter.[84]

AU mediator Salim described the draft agreement as "just an honorable
for all the parties."[85] Nevertheless, the rebels immediately rejected it, complaining that it did not meet many of their key demands in the three main
areas of security, power sharing, and wealth sharing. The government, however, quickly jumped on the agreement, revealing its readiness to sign
despite some misgivings about the text.[86] It was not until the joint intervention of US deputy secretary of state Zoellick, UK development secretary
Hilary Benn, AU chairman Sassou-Nguesso, and Nigerian president
Obasanjo that the leading movement, the SLM, conceded to the proposals,
leading to the signing of the Darfur Peace Agreement on May 5, 2006. But
the JEM and the SLM's splinter group refused to sign the agreement, reiterating demands for the post of vice-president in the Khartoum government
and for Darfur to have a greater share of national wealth. One of the key
points to breaking the deadlock was a US amendment to the peace plan that
called for the integration of 4,000 rebels into Sudan's armed forces, 1,000
into the police force, and training of an additional 3,000 rebels at military
colleges.[87]

High-level Western and African involvement in the Abuja process reflected last-ditch efforts to allay the worsening humanitarian situation and

force Khartoum's acceptance of the deployment of UN forces to assist the AU implement of the peace plan. Equally important, with key parties signing the agreement, the previously recalcitrant international community can no longer prevaricate and procrastinate on a robust engagement that would save Darfur from further misery. Although the smaller rebel groups refused to sign the agreement, genuine and spirited efforts toward implementation may ultimately encourage them to join the peace process. In welcoming the peace deal, UN Secretary-General Annan urged the protagonists to "seize this historic moment and sign the agreement, which will bring this tragic chapter in the history of Sudan to an end."[88]

Depite the signing of a peace agreement, questions remain about how the demands of Darfurians will be addressed by the former-guerrillas-turned-statesmen, who have yet to build an institutional basis in the newly formed government of national reconciliation in Sudan. Will Salva Kiir, Reik Machar, and their local, national, regional, and international partners "associate,"[89] for the collective good of the nation, and take steps to halt the atrocities and provide a real instead of virtual forum for addressing grievances? Will the AU, the UN, the EU, and the United States coordinate their efforts to implement the peace agreement? What guarantees can regional and international actors secure to ensure that the Khartoum government abides by the agreement? Will the demands of the Darfur rebels and their conationals in the east, central, and north be lost in yet more empty verbiage of summitry, or can the outcomes of the Abuja process address the root causes of the conflict with the urgency and dignity it deserves? The answers to all these questions lie in the political will of all the parties involved to acknowledge grievances and to heal wounds, which is the only approach to achieving a just and equitable peace.

Conclusion

Darfur's conflict shares characteristics with others that have driven Sudanese politics in the past decades: economic marginalization of the region and centralization of power in Khartoum. But the conflict also captures three overlapping dimensions: a traditional conflict over scarce resources; the polarization of Sudanic communities—inextricably linked through ties of history, kinship, and culture; and the demands of political inclusion and economic integration by marginalized regions. The emergence of open defiance and militant opposition to the central government by the rebels is a concrete manifestation of the resentment over the denial of citizenship rights for half a century. The upsurge of violence in Darfur was a reminder that Sudan's conflict was never entirely a north-south or a Muslim-Christian struggle. The rebels seized the historic moment of the conclusion of IGAD talks in

Kenya to force their unmet grievances onto the international table, capturing the increasing discontent among the various parties that were not included in the IGAD process.

As it has evolved into a serious humanitarian crisis, the conflict reflects not only the perils of selective peace in Sudan, but also the unwillingness (rather than the inability) of international actors to marshal the resources required to reverse it. The coalescence around a weak AMIS exemplifies the dilemma of international efforts, which lack the institutional consensus of regional actors that had facilitated the painfully slow resolution of the GOS-SPLM/A . Unlike the southern Sudanese conflict, which had found an institutional home in IGAD, the crisis in Darfur is bereft of a political space within which the grievances of its protagonists can be ironed out.

In light of the crimes committed by all parties and the plight of the peoples of Darfur, it is imperative that national, regional, and international actors ensure that they are not parties to the accommodation of policies of genocide by any other name. Regardless of the labels given to the atrocities committed by all parties in Darfur, it is imperative that the moral outrage over the killing fields of Darfur be expressed in order to prevent the onset of the callousness of national, regional, and public opinion that to date constitutes the major obstacle to peace. As the world has learned in the decade since Rwanda, political will is crucial to giving life to the protestations of "never again." To avoid the costs of continued war, both the government and rebels should gradually find common ground around a core set of objectives: the rebels winning a larger share of the national resources, as well as cultural recognition and equitable representation; and the government in Khartoum securing an agreement that guarantees the end of any challenges from its western periphery. But reaching such a mutual settlement depends on the confluence of internal coherence of the Darfur parties, a responsive national government, and multiple pressures and incentives from regional and international actors.

Notes

1. Mahmood Mamdani, "How Can We Name the Darfur Crisis: Some Preliminary Thoughts," *Pambazuka News,* October 7, 2004, available at www.pambazuka.org/index.php?id=24982.

2. Leo Kuper, *The Pity of It All: Polarisation of Racial and Ethnic Relations* (Minneapolis: University of Minnesota Press, 1977), p. 254.

3. Norman O'Neill, "Class and Politics in the Modern History of the Sudan," in Norman O'Neil and Jay O'Brien (eds.), *Economy and Class in Sudan* (Brookfield, VT: Avebury), p. 56.

4. *Report of the International Commission of Inquiry on Darfur to the UN Secretary-General, Pursuant to Security Council Resolution 1564 of 18 September 2004* (Geneva: United Nations, January 25, 2005).

5. For details on the historic references of the term, see Abdullahi Ibrahim, "*Janjaweed:* What's in a Name?" *Sudan Studies Association Newsletter* 24, no. 2 (2004): 15–16.

6. Amnesty International. *Darfur: Rape as a Weapon of War: Sexual Violence and Its Consequences,* AFR54/076/2004, July 2004, pp. 9–18.

7. Sharif Harir, "'The Arab Belt' and the 'African Belt,'" in Sharif Harir and Terje Tvedt (eds.), *Shortcut to Decay: The Case of the Sudan* (Uppsala: Scandinavian Institute of African Studies, 1994), p. 146.

8. Darfur's autonomous existence and the demonstrated military capability of its kings and sultans resulted in a centralized rule of the diverse populations from the seventeenth to the nineteenth centuries. Khartoum's neglect of Darfur during the period 1916–2006 has also provided a basis for the emergence of a regional consensus over its lack of representation. See R. S. O'Fahey and M. I. Abu Salim, *Land in Dar Fur: Charters and Related Documents from the Dar Fur Sultana* (Cambridge: Cambridge University Press), 1983.

9. The testimonies of both the "African" and the "Arab" groups of Darfur presented to the mediators at the conference of tribal reconciliation during 1987–1989 acknowledged that each side had been wronged. The rich documentation of that period provides a useful source of information that can still be drawn on to reach a consensus on mutual accommodation of citizenship rights and power sharing. See O'Fahey and Abu Salim, *Land in Dar Fur.*

10. Merveyn Hiskett, *The Course of Islam in Africa* (Edinburgh: Edinburgh University Press, 1994), p. 70.

11. In informal conversations outside the country with people from Darfur, only those who claimed Fur identity or had kinship ties through marriage appeared to be at ease with these terms.

12. Alex de Waal narrates that, as late as 1971, Sultan Bahr el-Din of Dar Masalit did not recognize his membership in "Dar Fur" if it implied that the entire territory was of the "domain of Fur." For details, see de Waal, *A Famine That Kills: Darfur, Sudan, 1984–1985* (Oxford: Clarendon Press, 1989), p. 230.

13. The *haakura* is the land tenure system based on the granting of estates by the sultans of Dar Fur. For details, see O'Fahey and Abu Salim, *Land in Dar Fur,* pp. 13–21.

14. For detailed discussions of the fragmentation of Darfur's rebel groups and external perspectives, see International Crisis Group, "Unifying Darfur's Rebels: A Prerequisite for Peace," Africa Briefing No. 32, Nairobi/Brussels, October 6, 2005; "The EU/AU Partnership in Darfur: Not Yet a Winning Combination," Africa Report No. 99, October 25, 2005. The case of the establishment of Oromia as a federal unit of post-1991 Ethiopia indicates the importance of territorial identity and the dignity that comes with acknowledging ownership.

15. See Douglas H. Johnson's land analysis of the factionalism of southerners' dissidence, *The Root Causes of Sudan's Civil Wars,* 2nd ed. (Bloomington: Indiana University Press, 2004), pp. 93–200.

16. Darfur's rebels do not have the advantages of the IGAD forum, which, under the leadership of the Kenyan mediators in partnership with the United States and European countries, was able to ensure an alternative to failed peace talks in Abuja.

17. de Waal, *A Famine That Kills.*

18. For a well-documented analysis of the interplay between domestic, regional, and international violence, see Sam C. Nolutshungu, *Limits of Anarchy: Intervention and State Formation in Chad* (Charlottesville: University Press of Virginia, 1996).

19. Daoud Bolad's defection from the NIF to the SPLM/A and his death at the hands of his former colleagues validate Edmund Burke's wise warning for those who seek to bring about change. For details on this brief but important act of rebellion that heralded the larger crisis, see Alex de Waal (ed.), *Islamism and Its Enemies in the Horn of Africa* (Bloomington: Indiana University Press, 2004), pp. 98–99.

20. R. S. O'Fahey provides an excellent background for the emergence of the Kayra dynasty of Darfur. The Fur are "a negroid people of unknown origin, who may be related to some of the tribes of western Bahr al-Ghazal, such as the Feroge. . . . They say that Firat, from whom came many of the western Bahr al-Ghazal tribes, was the brother of Fir, the eponymous founder of the Fur. . . . The Kayra Sultanate of Dar Fur grew out of what was probably in origin a Fur tribal chiefdom. The impetus to change from tribal chiefdom to a supra-tribal sultanate probably came from long-distance caravan trade; the agent, an Arab or Arabized Muslim, who intermarried with the chiefly family. The Kayra dynasty of the Fur seems to have been established sometime in the first half of the seventeenth century by Sulayman Solongdungo . . . the son or descendant of an Arab father and a Fur mother, who drove out the Tunjur and whose rule is associated with the establishment of Islam as the court cult." See R. S. O'Fahey, "Religion and Trade in the Kayra Sultanate of Dar Fur," in Yusuf Fadl Hasan (ed.), *Sudan in Africa* (Khartoum: Khartoum University Press, 1971), pp. 87–88.

21. It is interesting to note that few comparisons have been made between the Fur dynasty, which emerged in the west, and the Funj dynasty, which rose in the Nile Valley, despite the similarities between the folklore that surrounds the founding stories of the rise to power of "Arabized" or "Arab" chiefs such as Abdallah Jamma of the Funj and Sulayman Solngdungo of the Fur.

22. Yusuf Fadl Hasan, "External Islamic Influences and the Progress of Islamization in the Eastern Sudan Between the Fifteenth and Nineteenth Centuries," in Hasan, *Sudan in Africa*, p. 84.

23. For one of the earliest "reconstructions" of Arab immigrants, compiled during the Anglo-Egyptian period, see H. A. MacMichael, *A History of the Arabs in the Sudan and Some of the People Who Preceded Them and the Tribes Inhabiting Darfur*, vol. 2 (New York: Barnes & Noble, 1967).

24. The Zaghawa and Meidob were linked to the Fur aristocracy through marriages. The smaller sedentary groups such as the Berti, Birgid, Daju, Didanga, Marareet, Mima, and Fulani were integrated into what can be considered the "inner circles" of the sultanate. See Harir and Tvedt, *Shortcut to Decay,* p. 153.

25. Ibid. In contrast to the social and political integration of the smaller sedentary communities, relations with the northern and southern Rezeigat, Zayadiyya, Beni Helba, and Habbaniya remained confrontational until the twentieth century.

26. See R. S. O'Fahey, "Fur and Fartit: The History of a Frontier," in John Mack and Peter Robertshaw (eds.), *Culture History in the Southern Sudan Archaeology, Linguistics and Ethnohistory* (Nairobi: British Institute in Eastern Africa, 1982).

27. O'Fahey, "Fur and Fartit," pp. 87–88.

28. See Muhammad Mahmoud, "Sufism and Islamism in the Sudan," in David Westerlund and Eva Evers Rosander (eds.), *African Island and Islam in Africa: Encounters Between Sufis and Islamists* (London: Hurst, 1997), pp. 169–172.

29. For an illuminating historical background to the Fur sultanate, see Harir, "'Arab Belt' vs. 'African Belt,'" pp. 151–154.

30. The different Baggara Arabs—the Messiriya, Humur, Hawazma, and Rezeigat—who migrated to Kordofan and established new homelands to form a block called Ataya, linked through their forced migrations. See Ian Cunnison, *Baggara*

Arabs: Power and Lineage in a Sudanese Nomad Tribe (London: Oxford University Press, 1966), pp. 6–7.

31. Cunnison, *Baggara Arabs.*

32. Gérard Prunier, *Darfur: The Ambiguous Genocide* (London: Hurst, 2005), p. 15.

33. For details on the reign of Khalifa Abdullahii and his opponents, see P .M. Holt, *A History of the Sudan: From the Coming of Islam to the Present Day* (London: Longman, 1988), pp. 99–108.

34. Jay Spaulding and Lidwien Kapteijns (eds.), *An Islamic Alliance: 'Ali Dinar and the Sanusiyya, 1906–1916* (Evanston, IL: Northwestern University Press, 1994), p. 4.

35. Michael A. Gomez, *Pragmatism in the Age of Jihad: The Pre-colonial State of Bundu* (Cambridge: Cambridge University Press, 1992).

36. Yusuf Ibrahim, the Fur governor appointed by the khalifa, had joined the Mahdist camp but later organized an unsuccessful rebellion to free Dar Fur from the Mahdi's rule. His bid to restore the sultanate failed, and the khalifa's supporters beheaded him.

37. Gomez, *Pragmatism in the Age of Jihad,* p. 2.

38. For insights into the nature of the relationship between the sultanate and the Sudan Political Service, see Francis M. Deng and M. W. Daly, *Bonds of Silk: The Human Factor in the British Administration of the Sudan* (East Lansing: University of Michigan Press, 1989). See also Prunier, *Darfur: The Ambiguous Genocide.*

39. North Darfur (*Shamal Darfur*) occupies the largest area, 296,420 sq. kms; South Darfur (*Janub Darfur*) is next in size covering an area of 127,300 sq. kms; and West Darfur (*Ghrab Darfur*), which straddles the porous border with Chad, covers an area of 79,460 sq. kms.

40. The Nubians of the north and the Beja of eastern Sudan had been displaced from their ancestral homelands and been transformed into the proletariat of the large-scale state-owned enterprises and smaller private enterprises. See Tim Niblock, *Class and Power in Sudan: The Dynamics of Sudanese Politics, 1898–1985* (Albany: State University of New York Press), pp. 8–48; Ahmad Sikainga, *City of Steel and Fire: A Social History of Atbara, Sudan's Railway Town, 1966–1984* (Portsmouth, NH: Heinemann, 2002), pp. 123–173.

41. This tokenism was a pattern established as early as the inclusion of the Rezeigat shaikh Ibrahim Musa Madibo and the sultan of Dar Masalit in the 1944 Advisory Council of Northern Sudan. The same could be said for the cooptation of Ahmed Diraige, founder of the DDF, into the Umma Party, as well as the NIF's marginalization of Daoud Bolad, whose defection to the SPLM/A signaled a watershed event that rejected the pattern. See Prunier, *Dafur: The Ambiguous Genocide,* p. 39.

42. Mohammad Suliman, "Ethnicity from Perception to Cause of Violent Conflict: The Case of the Fur and Nuba Conflicts in Western Sudan," paper presented at the CONTICI International Workshop, Bern, Switzerland, July 8–11, 1999, p. 3.

43. Harir, "'Arab' vs. 'African Belt,'" p. 145.

44. Ibid., pp. 147–148.

45. The tribal reconciliation conference of Dar Fur was held at Al Fasher on the eve of the military coup that brought the NIF to power. The mediators, delegates, and government representatives, meeting on May 29–July 8, made recommendations that brought a brief peace.

46. Harir, "'Arab Belt'" vs. 'African Belt,'" p. 146.

47. Ibid., p. 147.

48. These demands were publicized with the publication and dissemination of the *al-Kitab al-Aswad* (Black Book) in 2000. For the English-language version, see Speakers of Truth and Justice, *The Black Book: Imbalance of Power and Wealth in Sudan.* It is available online at www.sudanjem/english/books/blackbook_part 1/20040422_bbone .htm. For a comprehensive review of the book, see Abdalla Osman El Tom and M. A. Salih, "The Black Book of Sudan,"*Review of African Political Economy* 30, no. 97 (September 2003): 511–514.

49. For details on the dynamics in Sudanese politics of the different 'fronts" that have challenged the regime in Khartoum since the 1990s, see Leenco Lata, *The Horn of Africa as Common Homeland: The State and Self-Determination in the Era of Heightened Globalization* (Waterloo, ON: Wilfred Laurier University Press, 2005), pp. 143–153.

50. Abel Alier, *Southern Sudan: Too Many Agreements Dishonoured,* 2nd ed. (Reading, UK: Ithaca Press, 1992).

51. Leo Kuper attributes this phrase to René Lemarchand in the introductory chapter, "The Logic of an Infernal Machine." For details, see Leo Kuper, *The Pity of It All: Polarisation of Racial and Ethnic Relations* (Minneapolis: University of Minnesota Press, 1977), p. 1.

52. *Hakkama* is traditionally a form of poetry that extols bravery and stigmatizes cowardice in times of war and peace. See Adan Azain, "Sudan: Women and Conflict in Darfur," *Review of African Political Economy* 30, no. 97 (September 2003): 479-510.

53. Kuper, *The Pity of It All,* p. 9.

54. Gill Lusk aptly captured the tragic irony when she said that Khartoum had learned to "calibrate finely what it can get away with." See *The Economist,* December 3–9, 2005, p. 26.

55. For a better understanding of this process, which is eloquently addressed by René Lemarchand, see Kuper, *The Pity of It All,* pp. 194–195.

56. The Sudan Liberation Movement and Sudan Liberation Army (SLM/SLA) Political Declaration.

57. Hugo Slim, "Dithering Over Darfur? A Preliminary Review of the International Response," *International Affairs* 80, no. 5 (2004): 813–817.

58. "International Focus on Darfur," *Africa Confidential,* August 27, 2004, pp. 2–3.

59. Emeric Rogier, *No More Hills Ahead: The Sudan's Tortuous Ascent to the Heights of Peace,* Clingendael Security Paper No. 1 (The Hague: Netherlands Institute of International Relations, August 2005), p. 96; Ulrich Mans, "Briefing: Sudan: The New War in Darfur," *African Affairs* 103 (2004): 291–294.

60. Slim, "Dithering Over Darfur," pp. 814–816.

61. Robert O. Collins, "Disaster in Darfur," *Africa Geopolitics,* nos. 15–16 (summer–fall 2004); Slim, "Dithering Over Darfur," p. 817.

62. "Agreement between the government of Sudan and the Sudan Liberation Movement/Justice and Equality Movement, under the auspices of H. E. Idriss Deby, president of the Republic of Chad, chief of state, assisted by the African Union and the United Nations," N'Djamena, April 25, 2004.

63. Collins, "Disaster in Darfur."

64. Slim, "Dithering Over Darfur," p. 814.

65. Alex De Waal, "Briefing: Darfur, Sudan: Prospects for Peace," *African Affairs* 104 (2005): 133.

66. International Crisis Group, *The EU/AU Partnership in Darfur: Not Yet a Winning Combination,* ICG Africa Report No. 99 (Nairobi: ICG, October 25, 2005).

67. De Waal, "Briefing," p. 130.

68. Report of the Secretary-General Pursuant to Paragraph 6 and 13 to 16 of Security Council Resolution 1556 (2004).

69. "Mr. Powell and Darfur," *Washington Post,* September 9, 2004, p. A26.

70. "Protocol on the Improvement of the Humanitarian Situation in Darfur," Abuja, November 9, 2004.

71. "Government Allies Attack Refugee Camps," Integrated Regional Information Networks (IRIN), November 10, 2004.

72. US Department of State, "U.S. Offers Three Resolutions to Speed End of Crisis in Darfur,"Washington, DC, March 23, 2005.

73. Report of the UN Secretary General's Special Representative to Sudan, Jan Pronk, February 2005.

74. "Darfur Rebels Want UN to Supervise the Talks with Sudan Government," Inter Press Service, February 8, 2005. In May 2005, Darfur rebels imposed a new precondition, that the war crimes suspects must be arraigned before an international court before the resumption of talks with the government.

75. "African Leaders Work on New Summit for Darfur Crisis," IRIN, February 28, 2005.

76. Ibid.; "Sudan/Darfur/Libya-Declaration," Qatar News Agency, May 17, 2005.

77. "Nigeria: Darfur Peace Talks Back on Track in Abuja," UN Integrated Regional Information Networks, June 10, 2005; "Annan Welcomes Promising Developments Related to Sudan's Troubled Darfur Region," UN News Service (New York), June 10, 2005; "Nigeria-Sudan: Back to the Table: Darfur Talks Resume After Initial Delays," IRIN, June 13, 2005.

78. "Opportunity to Jump-Start Sudan May Be Lost Over Darfur—U.S. Negotiator, Charles Snyder," AllAfrica.com, April 11, 2005.

79. "Sudan: Annan Calls for International Action Over Darfur Conflict," IRIN October 21, 2005.

80. Refugee International, *No Power to Protect: The African Union Mission in Sudan,* IRIN, November 2005. See also International Crisis Group, *The EU/AU Partnership in Darfur.*

81. International Crisis Group, *The EU/AU Partnership in Darfur,* p. 9.

82. Adam Mynott, "African Union Defers Darfur Issue," BBC News, January 24, 2006.

83. "Darfur Peace Deal Tabled," UN Integrated Regional Informational Networks, April 26, 2006.

84. "Mediators Say Darfur Peace Deal Is Up in the Air," Reuters, April 30, 2006.

85. "AU Extends Darfur Peace Deadline by 48 Hours After Rebels Refuse to Sign," UN Integrated Regional Information Networks, May 1, 2006.

86. "Rebels Still Split on Darfuf Peace," UN Integrated Regional Information Networks, May 5, 2006.

87. "Annan Presses Khartoum on Peace Force," BBC News, May 6, 2006.

88. "Despite Ongoing Peace Talks, Violence Worsens in Darfur," UN News Service (New York), May 2, 2006; "Darfur Relief Efforts Near Collapse due to Fading International Support—UN Official," UN News Service (New York), April 20, 2006.

89. Edmund Burke, *Thoughts on the Cause of the Present Discontents,* vol. 1.

7

The Quest for Peace: Negotiating Between "Old" and "New" Sudan

Our major problem is that the Sudan . . . is still looking for its soul, for its true identity.[1]

All the glowing and glamorous chorus chanting "Peace has come to Sudan" is not true. It has not come. We have to bring it, it has not actually entered the lives of the people.[2]

If we wish to move beyond apparent consent and to grasp potential acts, intentions as yet blocked, and possible futures that a shift in the balance of power or a crisis might bring to view, we have little choice but to explore the realm of the hidden transcript.[3]

Half a century after Sudan's independence, the past continues to haunt the present as violent efforts to seek redress for past injustices cast dark shadows on what otherwise would have been Sudan's hour of glory as an emergent petrostate in the twenty-first century. No longer dwarfed by Egypt's past glory or the claims to hegemony by Ethiopian chroniclers, Sudan's fiftieth anniversary celebrations of independence (and the approaching centennial of Darfur's incorporation) were envisioned by the country's ruling elite as occasions on which they could demonstrate their defiance of those who dared to disapprove of the cruel and effective ways in which they have historically dealt with any resistance to their hegemonic objectives. President Bashir and his diplomats have, for the time being, deftly sidestepped international efforts to hold them accountable on charges of having committed crimes against humanity while gaining access to lucrative international markets (with the notable exception of the United States). Clearly, twenty-first-century Sudan has emerged from the shadows of Egypt[4] (its northern neighbor and former occupier) and supplanted Ethiopia (its eastern neighbor and rival throughout the nineteenth and twentieth centuries) as the regional hegemon[5] of the Horn.

Sudan's emergence as the newest petrostate was made possible mainly because of the ruling regime's monopoly of oil-rich areas (south Sudan,

Kordofan, and Darfur) and its control of pipelines (Port Sudan). Khartoum's post-1989 hegemonic elite pursued policies that led to an alliance of the numerous opponents from the center and from the peripheries—opponents that experienced different degrees of repression, ranging from political marginalization to large-scale killings. Policies of systematic removals and displacements, ostensibly fought as jihads, fueled the resource wars in the south, west, and east and led to increasing alienation of the majority of Sudanese from their leaders. The atrocities and extrajudicial killings of political opponents ushered in an era where the Sudanese norm of accommodation had no place, thereby leading more and more citizens to contemplate waging war in order to be heard.

The Islamists' misconstruction of the moral geography of *dar al-Islam,* and *dar al-harb* to wage wars on coreligionists (in Darfur and the Nuba Mountains) also shattered the myth that membership in the *umma* guaranteed the security of all Sudanese Muslims. In the end, the manipulation of southern aspirations to the sharing of power and wealth, through the signing of so many peace accords with faction leaders, reduced southern federalists to tribute-paying inhabitants of a modern-day *dar al-ahd.* The Turabi-led project of placing Sudan at the forefront of a global Islamic revivalist movement—which included the insertion of Wahhabist elements contemptuous of Sudan's Sufi *tariqahs* and traditional leaders of the Umma Party and the DUP—led to the fracturing of members of the *awlad al-balad* and the cementing of alliances with opposition leaders from the south, east, and, west. The exile of Khatmiyya and Mahdist leaders from the power center led to the loss of support from the heartland of the *awlad al-balad* in the northern and eastern regions. Contemporary Sudan thus finds itself at a crossroads between maintaining the hegemony of the "Old Sudan," predicated on rule by conquest, and facing the demands of the the advocates of a "New Sudan"—demands based on the inalienable right of all Sudanese to a life of dignity, security, and equality under the law.

Sudan's anniversary celebrations were marred by the AU's refusal to allow President Bashir—accused of genocide—to chair the summit, although it was held in Khartoum. The violence in Darfur continued to cast shadows on the prospects for peace in the south, where discontented voices began to be heard questioning whether the CPA could bring peace and prosperity to the long-suffering peoples of the south. While Darfur's armed groups, the SLM and JEM, were convened by the AU and UN to discuss "peace" with the GOS, the Eastern Front vanguard blasted oil pipelines to protest their exclusion from ongoing dialogues. Without John Garang, with his diplomatic savoir faire, at the helm of the promised New Sudan, waging war reemerged as the only path for opponents seeking to win peace. The paradox of peace in the Sudan is how to end the vicious cycle where the avenue to peace is traversed by those strong enough to wage war. For those Sudanese excluded from the CPA, the lessons of the SPLM/A and the success of Darfurian groups in getting a place at the peace table clearly provide precedents.

During the period 2002–2005, Garang, the seasoned veteran of many wars and failed peace agreements, had held out hope that with the debunking of the old racial and geographic divides that had been inherited from the Old Sudan of the first millennium, a New Sudan with the promise of equality could be built. Six months after the signing of the CPA, the architect of the vision of a multinational Sudan—an Afro-Arab Sudan at peace with itself—had met his death in a helicopter crash. Garang's death robbed Sudan of an invaluable interlocutor who may have been able to prevent the spiraling violence in Darfur and the possible unraveling of the fragile peace in the south.

The CPA: Peace Agreement or Initiative for War?

One year after its signing, the CPA did not live up to its claim to being a "comprehensive" peace agreement and reflected an absence of clout in the negotiations with Darfur's quarreling rebels and the Eastern Front. The exclusion of the SPLM/A's allies in Darfur, the north, and the east—whom Garang had cajoled into joining a loose alliance against the post-1989 regime in Khartoum—transformed the CPA into a potential template for more bilateral agreements between the GOS and its armed opponents. A fact little noted in 2005 was that the impetus for peace had been the steady pressure on the regime by rebels waging war from multiple fronts, all seeking a place at the peace table. The SPLM/A, the oldest and largest of all of Sudan's rebel organizations, had by the end of the twentieth century obtained the moral and financial backing of major Western powers. This veteran organization had also learned numerous survival lessons during its half century of existence. Under the leadership of Garang, who drew lessons from the examples of his erstwhile allies and neighbors, the SPLM/A waged a campaign to convince all Sudanese "to put an end to racism," which "various regimes in Khartoum have found . . . a useful thing to institutionalize,"[6] while externally pursuing military and diplomatic linkages to unite all dissidents against the hegemonic center. Garang, who was both celebrated as a comrade-in-arms and expelled as a threat from his bases in exile by his Eritrean and Ethiopian hosts, had taken the lessons of the successes of their guerrilla leaders,[7] who had ousted their respective regimes by pursuing a public rapprochement with their factional rivals. Garang's success in establishing links with the guerrilla armies of Darfur in the west and the NDA and their allies in the east is a notable achievement that has led to numerous conferences, dialogues, and pacts among the opponents of the NIF regime. While the public transcripts were couched in terms of the shared objectives and solidarity of all members, the constant factionalism

and splintering of the alliance provides insights into the off-stage discourses—ethnic, religious, and ideological—that resulted in the inclusion
of the Nuba, Ingessana, and Abyei, while the Darfuri groups, the Beja, and
the NDA were excluded from the "comprehensive" peace agreement signed
in 2005.

Garang, a former member of Anyanya, galvanized Christian activists to
lobby against Islamist atrocities in the south. Presenting himself as a pan-
Sudanist, he played a major role in converting members of Darfur's political and military elite to join the opposition, along with the traditional leaders of the Umma Party and the Khatimiyya blocs, in working together to
overthrow their former allies and mentors of the Islamist regime that came
to power in 1989. The colonel also waged ruthless campaigns against
southern Sudanese who pointed out his disregard for democratic dialogue,
despite his constant invocation of the term. Those who survived his wars of
extermination did so by signing agreements with the GOS and later negotiating their inclusion in the CPA. In an ironic twist of fate, some of Garang's
most critical opponents have outlived the man whom southerners regard as
the architect of the CPA. Garang's Darfuri allies, especially the SLM/A,
have paid the highest price for their affirmation of the vision of the New
Sudan and are now bereft of his political guidance in the intricacies of
peacemaking. The factionalism and lack of experience of Darfur's rebels
have also led to a sharpening of regional rivalries among the leaders of
Chad, Libya, Egypt, Eritrea, and Ethiopia. As the various faction leaders of
Darfur shuttle from Asmara to Tripoli, from Cairo to N'Djamena, to Khartoum and Addis Ababa, a closer scrutiny of their public discourses and
encoded messages will become necessary in order to unravel the obstacles
to a viable peace in the country.[8]

Within the Sudanese arena, what appears to be a Bashir-Turabi rapprochement may provide indicators of new developments in the fractured
peace talks between the two secular factions of the SLM/A and the JEM,
whose links to Turabi's Islamist constituency are becoming more visible.
Examination of the processes of making and breaking alliances within the
opposition arena would yield invaluable insights into discourses that remain
hidden from public view. The conduct of former SPLM/A members in the
GNU and their relations with the SLM/A (regarded as Garang's acolytes)
and the JEM, said to be supported by Turabi, provides a different reading of
possible alliances. The traditional blocs of supporters of Sadiq al-Mahdi and
the Mirghani-led Khatmiyya present another layer of interaction that will
determine whether the Eastern Front will remain united or will fragment
over policy options vis-à-vis the Bashir regime in Khartoum. The unfolding
conflict in eastern Sudan, which has united the rural-based Beja and
Rashaida nomads with the urban-based resistance of Port Sudan and Atbara,
also has the potential for bridging the west-east gap and for presenting Khar-

toum with a unified political and military resistance that would require a refocusing of attention on the shared objectives of the inhabitants of the western and eastern peripheries.

The Discourse of "Genocide"
Versus "Crimes Against Humanity"

The untimely death of Garang in July 2005, a mere three weeks after his accession to the vice-presidency of the GNU, blunted the negotiating edge held by this shrewd veteran of opposition politics. The vice-presidency and his experience as the spokesperson for the SPLM/A had invested him with legitimacy that may have enabled the CPA to expand its purview to include the demands of the SLM/A, JEM, NDA, and Eastern Front into his expansive vision of the "New Sudan." His death removed the focus from his vision of the New Sudan, which had been instrumental in establishing a consensus that the Old Sudan—based on the hegemony of the *awlad al-balad*—needed to be discarded for peace to prevail in the nation. Garang's absence from the helm of the GNU and the inability (or unwillingness) of his successors to check the military excesses of Khartoum's armed forces and militias against the rebels in Darfur and eastern Sudan, emboldened the recalcitrant hegemonic elite to begin eroding the spirit and letter of the CPA's guarantees for wealth and power sharing. Khartoum's officials, having received international accolades as major peace partners in the 2005 CPA, utilized their newfound pedigree to counter global accusations of genocidal acts in Darfur. Despite the United States' unilateral declaration of the Khartoum's leaders as *génocidaires* and statements by the UN and EU accusing them of perpetrating crimes against humanity, Sudan has managed to retain enough support from its regional allies in Africa and the Middle East to avoid a costly ostracism. Sudanese diplomats proved their mettle as formidable foes when they linked US unilateral acts in Iraq with the lone superpower's unilateral statement accusing them of genocide, resulting in a frenzy of anti-American support. While reaping the benefits of US support for the CPA, they deftly resorted to reaching out to African, Arab, and Muslim allies, casting themselves as the next possible target of US aggression after Iraq.[9]

A multilateral UN response to the ethnic-cleansing campaigns of the apocalyptic horsemen of Darfur and the escalation of the rebel counterattacks that victimized thousands of civilians was deflected by Khartoum's timely appropriation of the slogan "African Solutions for African Problems." This freed UN Security Council members from having to make decisions to halt the violence to avert a tragedy similar to what had taken place in Rwanda a decade earlier. It also ensured that Khartoum's actions would be scrutinized by friendly peers at the newly reconstituted African Union. This particular spin even found its way into popular African discourse, portraying the tragedy of Darfur as an "opportunity . . . to build on the global concern . . . [and a] test . . . to defend African sovereignty in the face of America's global 'war on terror.'"[10] What is notable is that the coming together of the public transcripts (of the need for punitive actions for acts of genocide) and the hidden transcripts (of the majority's distrust of US intentions in launching "the war on terror" and of the antiwar sentiments in Iraq) created an ambience of permissiveness that allowed Khartoum to prosecute its brutal war in Darfur using the same strategy and tactics that had proved effective in the South for many decades. Thus, rather than address the painful question of whether Africans and their international counterparts have been remiss in their duties to fellow human beings in southern Sudan subjected to inhumane onslaughts, the immediate reaction of the majority of Africans was to be suspicious of US motives in accusing Sudan of genocide. The African American response was markedly different, and consistently and unflinchingly expressed empathy and acknowledged the suffering of the victims of war in the south as well as in the west.

The deafening silence of 700 African intellectuals gathered at the AU's impressive First Conference of Intellectuals from Africa and the Diaspora, held in Dakar, Senegal, in October 2004, is testimony to the existence of public discourses[11] that berate "Westerners and Americans" and private expressions of dismay at the killings of "Black Africans." The participants disbanded without an "open" discussion of the crisis in Darfur, although there was no shortage of informal expressions of fears of a second Rwanda in the making. It is notable that the euphemism "second Rwanda" was used to describe the atrocities in Darfur. The UN and EU's choice was "crimes against humanity," while US officials appeared undeterred by the suspicions regarding its motives in taking the moral high ground on Darfur, while its troops were embroiled in human rights violations in Iraq. Unfortunately, the United States' "naming" of the GOS and its associates as *génocidaires* was not accompanied by the necessary actions to halt the killings. Paradoxically, the only power in the world that unambiguously stated that genocide was taking place in Darfur was also the same one that insisted on the signing of a peace agreement that excluded the demands of the SLM/A and JEM.

Old Myths and New Metaphors: Whose Responsibility to Protect Whom?

In light of the racially charged coverage of Darfur and its eclipse of the long-awaited agreement to end the "Southern Problem," one cannot help but note that Khartoum has emerged with its ego slightly dented and its reputation tarnished but without suffering any punitive sanctions. Although vociferous objections by neighboring Chad and numerous NGOs—and the disapproval of the EU, the UN, and the United States—resulted in Khartoum's being denied the status of serving as chair of the AU in January 2006, President Bashir and cohorts were spared a public dressing down by their peers. Escaping such censure was a considerable achievement for Sudan's leaders and diplomats in light of the enormous amount of time and resources expended to ascertain that the regime in Khartoum had indeed committed crimes against humanity, as well as the UN's high-level policy formulations exhorting member states of their "responsibility to protect" citizens. As Sudan looks to the future, it is unclear what role Sudanese society will play in owning the peace in the south as well as the multiple wars that simmer in other peripheries. For Khartoum and its periphery, the CPA and Darfur are contrasting stories about the crisis of state and nation building, but they are also paradigmatic illustrations of the problems and possibilities of managing these challenges.

In recent times, Sudan's political contestations and confessional conflicts have been addressed by creative leadership, broad-based coalition formation, and an ideological fealty to the inchoate, but promising, vision of a New Sudan. These qualities propelled momentous events such as the creation of the NDA and the negotiations leading to the CPA. The NDA broke the historical divide that had impeded coalition building across the north and south around concrete and positive-sum national concerns. Yet despite being poised to undergo radical ideological and institutional transformations, neither the multinational character of the NDA nor the long-awaited imprimatur of Khartoum and the SPLM/A on the drawn-out Machakos Protocol and the Naivasha agreements resulted in concrete steps to guarantee the promise of equal membership for *all* Sudanese. Although the vision of a New Sudan provided the blueprint for power- and wealth-sharing agreements between the SPLM/A and the GOS, the 2005 peace agreement was a contradiction rather than an affirmation of a multinational state premised on equality and reciprocity. If the CPA remains captive to the past historical precedents of "broken promises" that characterize south Sudan politics, what are the chances that the vision of a New Sudan will survive its champion?

Although the death of Garang constituted a severe loss for the SPLM/A at a historical moment of triumph, the smooth transition to his deputy, Salva Kiir Mayardit, held high hopes for the realization of the shared dream. Although Kiir once accused Garang of treating the movement as "his own property,"[12] the challenge is whether he will transcend some of Garang's alleged flaws. As a southern Sudanese observer counseled, "He must resist all factors inimical to internal political stability such as the allure of personalized power, bad governance, and the centralized authoritarian command and control structures that served them well in the war."[13] Can the prospect for peace reemerge if the SPLM/A, under Kiir, honors Garang's commitment to old allies and "reassure[s] Easterners and others in the North that it is not abandoning plans to be a national party . . . [and] . . . take the lead in political talks in the East."[14] If SPLM/A troops are forced or choose to evacuate their posts in eastern Sudan, leaving their old allies exposed to Khartoum's ire, will the old myths of solidarity still hold? In the absence of charismatic personalities such as Garang and the poetic Yusuf Khuwa, one wonders if Kiir and his cohorts in the GNU will have the capability and the oratorical panache to demand and attain the respect of the populace they are supposed to protect. The late Khuwa, who lived in eastern Sudan as well as in Darfur, highlighted the importance of respect and dignity in the pursuit of the common objective of constructing a New Sudan.[15] Such candor in bringing out the hidden transcript on the not-so-cordial relations between opposition groups is not only refreshing but also useful in identifying unnamed obstacles that may hinder the pursuit of officially stated objectives of the southern-eastern alliances that may be held hostage to the corrosive effect of engrained racism between different regional representatives. Understanding the realm of such hidden transcripts may also shed light on why there may exist a reluctance within the rank and file of the SPLM/A as well as among southern members of the GNU to confront the Khartoum elite's efforts to eliminate opposition in the wars raging in the east and west. Nevertheless, the willingness of Sudanese nationalists to openly air their views against such collusion with the Khartoum regime and their urging of Salva Kiir to uphold the alliance leaves room for hope that aggrieved sentiments emanating from the stigma of racism may remain "hidden from public view and never 'enacted.'"[16] Should the SPLM/A's alliance with the NDA, the SLM/A, JEM, and the Eastern Front continue to hold, there is hope that pragmatism will transcend the pettiness of the racism of unenlightened conationals and avoid being ensnared into the hegemonic trap of inducements into piecemeal pacts of members of the loose alliance against Khartoum. The UN, the EU, and the United States could enhance the prospects of successful peace talks if their envoys would be sensitized to the hidden presence of landmines such as those that threaten dialogue with the SLM/A, JEM, and the Eastern Front.[17]

Institutional questions loom large in the newly created structures of the GNU. The CPA defined the following power-sharing arrangement in the GNU: the NCP of President Bashir has 52 percent of all executive and legislative posts; the SPLM has 28 percent; the northern political parties have 14 percent; and the southern parties have 6 percent. While this arrangement allows the GNU to forge a consensus on rebuilding a more stable Sudan, expanding the basis for inclusiveness, and democratizing the previously authoritarian structures around Khartoum, the acrimony surrounding the drafting of the interim constitution underscored the GNU's democratic deficit, leading to charges of a narrow elite pact between the NCP and the SPLM.[18]

Although the composition of the sixty-member Constitutional Review Commission (CRC) mirrored the power-sharing formula outlined in the CPA, many political groups in the north, west, and east felt excluded by the CPA and voiced their discontent, claiming that a new constitutional dispensation demands wider representation and a meaningful form of democratic mandate. A hastily constituted CRC established to meet the CPA's tight timetable could hardly have been the most representative institution to furnish legitimate and long-term solutions to Sudan's enormous problems. In general, the transitional institutions are going to be the venues for contests over the management of power at the center, with significant implications for the periphery. Whether transitional institutions will avoid political and organizational paralysis will determine the subsequent negotiations on the future of Sudan. How the GNU deals with governance strains produced by the centrifugal forces in the periphery and the centripetal ones at the center will test the emergence of a new culture of participation without intolerance in Sudan.[19]

The problem of finding inclusive institutions is not one that is confined to the north. In the south, the importance of a south-south dialogue has revolved around the search for approaches to tame ethnicity, especially the tensions between the Nuer and Dinka. In an initiative led by former president Daniel arap Moi in the spring and summer of 2005, the SPLM/A entered into negotiations with the armed militia groups together with their political wing, the South Sudan Defense Forces (SSDF), about modalities of their integration into the SPLM/A. These negotiations yielded agreements on the equitable sharing of leadership positions and the need for promoting dialogue and reconciliation among various ethnic groups. But there are lingering suspicions among a minority of the militia forces formerly allied to the Sudanese military about the terms of participation in programs such as demobilization, disarmament, and rehabilitation (DDR) and integration in the SPLA.[20]

The transition from a culture of violence to a culture of peace is, at heart, an economic phenomenon mediated by resource availability and use. Despite the publicity surrounding the wealth-sharing components of the peace agreement, it will take a long time for the resources to filter to communities traumatized by war and the lack of economic opportunities. Both the north and south confront socioeconomic problems that are natural outcomes of decades of war and conflict. For the south, in particular, the anticipated oil revenues and donor pledges pale in comparison with the scale of reconstruction challenges. This is more difficult because the south lacks basic physical infrastructure and is deficient in administrative and human capacity.

The UN Security Council's unanimous vote to deploy a 10,000-strong peace force to southern Sudan to monitor the CPA in July 2005 symbolized the continued international engagement in the peace process. From previous experiences of peacekeeping forces in Africa, however, the vote did not necessarily translate into speedy deployment. The UN resolution allowed for a time frame of 240 days for the troop deployment, raising fears of delays in starting the critical components of DDR and the formation of new armed forces. Yet the expectations are that the Sudanese have learned from the examples of Rwanda and the Democratic Republic of Congo (DRC) that implementing peace agreements depends much more on political willingness generated by parties on the ground than on reliance on the unrealistic bureaucratic timetables of deployment established in New York. To a large extent, sturdy peace agreements require an element of internal policing by the parties themselves as they wait for external commitments.

Darfur overshadowed the UN deployment vote, underscoring the dangers of selective peace in Sudan. The agonizing debates over boosting the capacity of the AU forces in the Darfur conflict are reminiscent of the limits of international engagement and the absence of political will to confront acts of impunity judged as crimes against humanity. Halfhearted international engagement in Darfur is reminiscent of the debates of the 1990s, but it is also framed by changes in Khartoum's relations with the major players in the Security Council that have denuded the international consensus on military intervention.

By default, therefore, the weakly mandated and underresourced AU peacekeeping force in Darfur symbolizes the institutionalization of international tokenism that now marks approaches to African conflicts in the twenty-first century. Viewed as a test case for the growing pains of AU peacekeeping abilities, the deployment of AMIS has provided the illusion of movement on an enormous humanitarian crisis for which, perhaps, international action has no ready-made solutions. Since the 1960s, regional actors have made meaningful engagements in Sudan as interlocutors between Khartoum and its southern periphery. This is the practice that produced the Addis Ababa Agreement and the CPA, and it is the involvement that provides the most realistic option for reconciling national and regional responsibilities against the backdrop of perennial resource constraints. In the end, Africa's contribution to a peace agreement in Darfur will need to go beyond providing troops whose mandate is restricted to monitoring atrocities visited upon civilians.

The victory of the vision of a New Sudan now faces the test as both southerners and northerners engage in daily interaction as equal members of Sudanese society. The visions of the Old Sudan—based on coercive measures and denigration of the disenfranchised—may not be buried in the proverbial dustbins of history if the conflict in Darfur persists. Peace cannot reign in the south if destruction, looting, and pillage persist in the west, east, or center. This is the challenge that faces the quest for peace in Sudan.

Whither Pax Sudanica?

An equitable and just peace must acknowledge the many ties that bind the peoples of Sudan. Some aspects of this shared history bear the scars of past crimes against humanity, such as slavery, while others, such as the socio-economic and political ascendancy of the descendants of the indigenous/Africans/Arabs, are a living testimony to the positive attributes of cosmopolitanism. The peoples of the Sudan have been mired in wars and the aftermath of many an act of wanton destruction because they have yet to acknowledge the different strands of their body politic. It may not be too late to heed the words of Garang, who said, "Talking is good, it can produce more talks and more talks can produce peace."[21] The assumption is that in the process of sharing ideas and airing grievances, the issues that render peace a fugitive can be addressed. More than any other society of the Horn of Africa, the peoples of this vast nation have retained a healthy respect for dialogue and the importance of intra-Sudanese communication in the resolution of feuds, hostilities, and wars—as demonstrated by the numerous peace conferences that resulted in the cessation of hostilities. The tradition for seeking peace through dialogue exists, but what is required to ensure that talks lead to peace rather than to broken promises is a framework for reconciling the public transcripts, produced by the hegemonic elites and subordinated groups, with the hidden transcripts.

Such a shift will render irrelevant the geographic and ideological divides of communities into *kafirs* and *mu'iminin,* into abodes of war and of peace. And such a shift will render irrelevant the imposition of barriers and enclosures—justified as ancestral *dars*—to prevent the mobility and integration of Sudanese citizens.[22] If Sudan is to prosper as a nation in the new century, its leaders must cease to interpret bona fide peace agreements as modern versions of the millennial *dar al-ahd,* denoting pacts subject to unilateral abrogation by the sultan.[23] Willingness to recognize the past without remaining its prisoner may be a first step toward correcting the injustices of the past and constructing a shared future built on mutual respect and accommodation.

The history of piecemeal peace has failed to honor the memory of the immense human and material costs of the centuries of conflict that preceded the emergence of the modern state of Sudan in 1956. Peace cannot be realized without an acknowledgment of the violence that has ripped the fabric of Sudan's communities. Pragmatic policymaking and a spirit of reconciliation will be necessary to overcome the horrors suffered under the Old Sudan's alliance of *amirs, zariba* mercantilists, and militias, and to begin the construction of a New Sudan.

Notes

1. John Garang, *John Garang Speaks,* edited and introduced by Mansour Khalid (London: Kegan Paul International, 1987), p. 128.

2. Bishop Caesar Mazzolari, quoted in Emily Wax, "Peace Force in Darfur Faces Major Challenges," *Washington Post,* November 21, 2005.

3. James S. Scott, *Domination and the Arts of Resistance: Hidden Transcript* (New Haven: Yale University Press, 1990), p. 16.

4. For an illuminating discussion of the "hidden transcripts" of Egyptian-Sudanese relations, see Eve M. Trout Powell, *A Different Shade of Colonialism: Egypt, Great Britain and the Mastery of the Sudan* (Berkeley: University of California Press, 2003), pp. 156–167.

5. For a brief discussion of the demise of Ethiopia's hegemonic elite, faced by a concerted opposition from the peripheries, see Ruth Iyob, *The Eritrean Struggle for Independence: Domination, Resistance, Nationalism, 1941–1993* (Cambridge; Cambridge University Press, 1993), pp. 136–138.

6. Garang, *John Garang Speaks*, p. 126.

7. See Alex de Waal, "The Politics of Destabilisation in the Horn, 1989–2002," in de Waal (ed.), *Islamism and Its Enemies in the Horn of Africa* (Bloomington: Indiana University Press, 2004), pp. 202–204.

8. Julie Flint and Alex De Waal, *Darfur: A Short History of a Long War* (London and New York: Zed Books, 2005), pp. 86–96.

9. Barry Rubin captures this jarring contradiction in what can be construed as the "public" and "hidden" transcripts of Sudanese diplomatic discourse when, "Sudan . . . requested U.S. help in resolving its civil war one day, and a week later bemoaned the fact that the Arabs do not fight the United States in Iraq." See Rubin, *The Long War for Freedom: The Arab Struggle for Democracy in the Middle East* (Hoboken, NJ: John Wiley, 2005), p. 146.

10. Mahmood Mamdani, "How Can We Name the Darfur Crises?" *Pambazuka News,* October 2004.

11. Ruth Iyob attended this meeting and was the sole voice at the plenary to ask the question "What About Darfur?" to which the public answer was silence. Following the end of the conference, a number of people privately expressed support for the "voicing" of concern over Darfur.

12. "Garang Foes May Lose in Salva Kiir's Regime," *The East African,* August 23, 2005. See also "Exclusive: The Meeting That Nearly Split SPLM," *The East African,* August 23, 2005; John Young, "John Garang's Legacy to Peace Process, SPLM/A and the South," *Review of African Political Economy* 32, no. 106 (December 2005): 535–548.

13. Okiya Omtatah, "What the New Southern Sudan Leaders Must Do," *The Nation,* August 8, 2005.

14. International Crisis Group, *Saving Peace in the East,* Africa Report No. 102 (Washington, DC: ICG, January 5, 2006), p. 19.

15. Yousif Kuwa Mekki's anecdotes of routinely encountered forms of racism include one in which he said, "Our friends the Hadendowa, if you are black with this curly hair they call you *keeshiab,* which means *abid,* slave in English." See "Things Were No Longer the Same," in Suleiman Musa Rahhal (ed.), *The Right to Be Nuba: The Story of a Sudanese People's Struggle for Survival* (Lawrenceville, NJ: Red Sea Press, 2001), p. 27.

16. James C. Scott, *Domination and the Art of Resistance* (New Haven, CT: Yale University Press, 1990).

17. For a better understanding of the challenges and prospects for peace, see International Crisis Group, *Sudan: Saving Peace in the East,* Africa Report No. 102 (Washington, DC: ICG, January 5, 2006).

18. See, in particular, John Young, "Sudan: A Flawed Peace Process Leading to a Flawed Peace," *Review of African Political Economy* 32, no. 103 (March 2005): 99–113.

19. See Oystein H. Rolandsen, *Guerrilla Government: Political Changes in the Southern Sudan in the 1990s* (Sweden: Nordiska Afrikainstitutet, 2005), pp. 143–155.

20. International Crisis Group, *The Khartoum-SPLM Agreement: Sudan's Uncertain Peace,* Africa Report No. 96 (Washington, DC: ICG, July 25, 2005).

21. Garang, *John Garang Speaks,* p. 121.

22. For a detailed discussion of the barriers to full citizenship in contemporary Sudan, see Amir H. Idris, *Conflict and Politics of Identity in Sudan* (New York: Palgrave MacMillan, 2005), pp. 95–108.

23. For a detailed discussion of the classical interpretations of the terms *'ahd, 'sulh,* and *baqt,* see Bernard Lewis, *The Political Language of Islam* (Chicago: University of Chicago Press, 1991), pp. 80–81.

Chronology

100 B.C.E.	Introduction of the camel to North Africa.
640 C.E.	Arrival of Arabs and beginning of Islamization of Africa.
652	*Baqt* treaty concluded between Abdallah bin Sa'ad and Nubians.
711	Arab conquest of North Africa.
969–1169	Fatimids rule over North Africa.
1250	Mameluk take-over of Egypt.
1400s	Funj migrations northward from the Blue Nile.
1504–1821	Eastward and northward expansion of the Funj kingdom.
1517–1574	Ottoman conquest of North Africa, with the exception of Morocco.
1650–1750	Emergence of the sultanate of Dar Fur.
1820	Invasion of Sudan by forces of Muhammad Ali Pasha of Egypt.
1820–1881	Turco-Egyptian rule, also known as the Turkiyya.
1841	Opening up of the marshlands of the *sudd* to large-scale incursions by merchants from the Nile Valley, Ottoman and Egyptian troops, and Europeans.
1863–1867	Sudanese troops dispatched to Mexico to assist French troops in Mexico.
1869	Opening of Suez Canal. Establishment of Italian settlements on Eritrean coast.
1873–1874	Conquest of the sultanate of Darfur by the forces of Zubayr al-Rahma.
1881	Muhammad Ahmad announced that he is the "Mahdi" chosen to reform the land.
1882–1898	Defeat of the Turkiyya and the establishment of a theocratic Mahdist state.
1897	Italy retroceded Kassala to the Anglo-Egyptian govern-

ment in December 1897 after its defeat at the hands of Menlik's army in the Battle of Adowa in March 1896.

1898–1916	Restoration of the sultanate of Darfur by Ali Dinar.
1899	Signing of the Condominium Agreement between Britain and Ottoman Egypt.
1899–1955	Anglo-Egyptian Condominium and the reinstatement of the Second Turkiyya.
1916	Anglo-Egyptian annexation of the sultanate of Darfur.
1929	Anglo-Egyptian Agreement on use of the Nile waters.
1945	Founding of the Arab League.
1947	Juba Independence Conference.
1953	Anglo-Egyptian Agreement providing for Sudanese self-government.
1955	Torit mutiny and the onset of the first civil war.
1956	Sudan's accession to independence.
1958	Military takeover of elected government.
1960s	Construction of the Aswan Dam by Gamal Abdel Nasser; dam causes flooding of ancestral lands of the Nubians and produces a decade of displacement.
1965	Round Table Conference.
1969	Military coup d'état bringing Ja'far Numeiri to power. A military-led coup led by Muammar Qaddafi, deposes King Idris of Libya.
1972	Addis Ababa North-South Agreement. Sudan Socialist Union established.
1976	Mutiny of former Anyanya members in Wau.
1979	Oil discovered in Upper Nile and southern Kordofan.
1980	Southern Regional Assembly dissolved. Southern boundaries redrawn to enable government to transfer oilfields into the north.
1981	Influx of Chadian refugees into Darfur. Diraige appointed Fur governor; *kasha* instituted in the "Three Towns" of Khartoum targeting "westerners" and "southerners."
1982	Government announces 500 southern Sudanese volunteers to support Iraq against Iran.
1983	Formation of the southern Sudan People's Liberation Movement/Army (SPLM/A).
1985	Pacifist leader of the Republican Brothers, Mahmaud Muhammad Taha, executed for apostasy. Ja'far Numeiri is deposed by a military coup. Escalation of famine and drought.
1986	Election of Sadiq al-Mahdi as the prime minister. Official support given to tribal militias, the murahaleen, who led the government's campaigns against armed dissidents in

the south, in Darfur, in the southern Blue Nile Hills, and in the Nuba Mountains.

1987   State of emergency declared and systematic attacks waged on Nuba Mountains. Escalation of Zaghawa-Fur clashes in Darfur.

1989   Military coup d'état brings to power Omar al-Bashir and NIF. NDA established. Popular Defence Forces Act promulgated.

1990   SPLM/A Agreement with National Democratic Alliance (NDA). Chadian forces enter Darfur.

1991   First NDA summit in Addis Ababa after fall of Mengistu regime. SPLM/A forced to leave their camps. Split occurs in the SPLA leading to emergence of Nasir faction. SPLA-Torit forces led by Daoud Bolad launch attacks inside Darfur.

1992   Jihad is declared against dissidents in Nuba Mountains and the south. Daoud Bolad captured and executed. Abuja negotiations between SPLM/A and GOS.

1993   Start of IGAD negotiations. SPLA-United formed by Lam Akol and other opponents of John Garang. Government offensives around Heglig oilfield.

1994   First national convention held in Chukudum attended by multi-ethnic representatives. Attacks by Uganda's Lord's Resistance Army (LRA) on Sudanese refugees increase. Libyan-Chad conflict ends over demarcation of Aouzou Strip. IGAD unveils Declaration of Principles (DOP).

1995   Sudan Alliance Forces (SAF) and Beja Congress admitted into NDA at its Asmara meeting in 1995. Failed assassination attempt of Egyptian president Hosni Mubarak in Addis Ababa.

1996   Omar al-Bashir elected as president of the Sudan. Osama bin Laden leaves Sudan. Southern factions sign agreement with GOS. Sadiq al-Mahdi escapes from Sudan into Eritrea.

1997   NDA captures Karora. SAF overrun Osama bin Laden's training camps in Hamish Koraib and capture equipment. SPLA forces in Nuba Mountains repulse government attacks.

1998   Ali Osman Taha, former NIF foreign minister, becomes first vice-president. GOS offers to hold referendum on future of southern Sudan. Increased clashes between Rezeigat and Masalit in Darfur. Southern Sudanese factionalism rife, leading to many betrayed agreements.

1999   President Bashir dismisses the National Assembly and southern state assemblies. National Congress (former NIF) emerges as only legitimate political party. Fighting escalates in northern and western Darfur. Wunlit peace agreement signed between the Dinka of Bahr al-Ghazal and the Nuer of western Upper Nile. Ugandan-Sudanese diplomatic relations resume. NDA successfully blows up oil pipes near Atbara. Turabi proposes constitutional amendments to curtail President Bashir's powers.

2000   President Bashir reelected despite general boycott. Sudanese-Eritrean diplomatic relations resumed. Beja Congress and NDA increase attacks on oil installations. *Black Book* published in Khartoum attributed to Khalil Ibrahim, exposing the hegemony of the *awlad al-balad* and discrimination against peripheral communities. Turabi's PNC sponsors demonstrations from El Fasher to Atbara. NDA conference held in Massawa, Eritrea. Umma Party withdraws from NDA and Sadiq al-Mahdi returns to Khartoum.

2001   SPLA and Turabi's PNC sign MOU in Geneva leading to Turabi's arrest. US Senate passes Sudan Peace Act. Senator John Danforth appointed special envoy to Sudan. GOS begins cooperation with US intelligence agencies to identify terrorist networks. UN Security Council lifts diplomatic sanctions against Sudan. US sanctions remain in place. Resumption of IGAD negotiations.

2002   Nairobi Declaration signed between Garang's SPLM/A and Machar's Sudan People's Defence Force (SPDF). Abyei Declaration signed between Messirya and Ngok Dinka. SPLM/A and SPDF attacks lead to suspension of oil-drilling operations. Sudanese National Alliance and Sudan Alliance Forces merge. SPLM–Umma Party talks begin. Signing of Machakos Protocol (June), GOS-SPLA agreement for cessation of hostilities (October), and MOU (November). Government paramilitary raid at Shoba in Northern Darfur; more clashes and arrests in Golu, including SLM leader, Abdelwahab Mohamed Nur.

2003   Darfur Liberation Front (DLF) captures Golu in northern Darfur. DLF renamed Sudan Liberation Movement/Army (SLM/A). The existence of Justice and Equality Movement (JEM) announced from abroad. SLA-JEM attacks on Nyala and El-Fasher, Kutum, and Tine lead to unleashing of GOS-armed and paid Janjawwed militias, whose destructive missions of burning, looting, and branding victims was facilitated by aerial bombing. SLM demands for inclusion in ongoing peace process between GOS and SPLM/A rejected. Atrocities continue to be witnessed by international media and international nongovernmental organizations (INGOs).

2004   GOS launches systematic offensive in Darfur using both Janjaweed and its regular armed forces. SLM/A admitted into membership of NDA leading GOS to suspend ties with NDA. Africa bloc in UN Human Rights Commission rejects international criticism of GOS atrocities in Darfur. Turabi arrested on charges of conspiring to launch coup. United States declares crisis to be genocide; EU and UN skirt naming dilemma. SLA-JEM fighting breaks out, exposing absence of unity among rebel ranks. UN Security Council holds special meeting in Nairobi and passes Resolution 1574 demanding an immediate cessation of violence.

2005 Signing of the Comprehensive Peace Agreement (CPA) on January 9. UN Commission of Inquiry reports that "crimes against humanity" had been committed by all actors: GOS, Janjaweed, and armed guerrillas of Darfur. African Union (AU) observers arrive in Sudan. UN Resolution 1556 passes demanding disarming of Janjaweed. Formation of Government of National Unity (GNU). Death of John Garang in helicopter (July); Garang replaced by his deputy, Salva Kiir Mayardit. UN Security Council authorizes deployment of the United Nations Mission in Sudan (UNMIS).

2006 Abuja peace talks on Darfur inconclusive. AU role comes under increasing criticism as new peace initiatives (e.g., Slovenian) are floated; violence is unabated. Bashir-Turabi rapprochement on horizon as dissatisfaction at slow pace of CPA implementation is expressed by GNU members such as Salva Kiir, Rebecca Garang, and civilians in southern Sudan. Dissension among rebel leaders splits the SLM and JEM into numerous factions and delays the signing of a final and binding peace agreement and end to hostilities.

Acronyms

ACP-EU	Africa Caribbean Pacific–European Union
AMIS	African Union Mission in Sudan
AU	African Union
BC	Beja Congress
CPA	Comprehensive Peace Agreement
CPMT	Civilian Protection Monitoring Team
CRC	Constitutional Review Commission
DDF	Darfur Development Front
DDR	demobilization, disarmament, and rehabilitation
DOP	Declaration of Principles
DUP	Democratic Unionist Party
EPLF	Eritrean People's Liberation Front
EPRDF	Ethiopian People's Revolutionary Democratic Front
EU	European Union
GNU	Government of National Unity
GOS	government of Sudan
GUNM	General Union of the Nuba Mountains
HEC	High Executive Council
ICC	International Criminal Court
ICF	Islamic Charter Front
ICG	International Crisis Group
IDP	internally displaced person
IGAD	Intergovernmental Authority on Development
IGADD	Intergovernmental Authority on Drought and Development
IMF	International Monetary Fund
INEC	Interim National Executive Council
IPF	IGAD Partners Forum
JEM	Justice and Equality Movement

188

JIM	Joint Implementation Mechanism
MOU	Memorandum of Understanding
NANS	National Alliance for National Salvation
NCP	National Congress Party
NCSD	National Council for the Salvation of Dar Fur
NDA	National Democratic Alliance
NGO	nongovernmental organization
NIF	National Islamic Front
NUP	National Unionist Party
OAU	Organization of African Unity
OLS	Operation Lifeline Sudan
PDF	Popular Defence Forces
RCC	Revolutionary Command Council
RNS	Revolution of National Salvation
SAF	Sudan Alliance Forces
SANU	Sudan African National Union
SLM	Sudan Liberation Movement
SLM/A	Sudan Liberation Movement/Army
SPDF	Sudan People's Defence Force
SPLM/A	Sudan People's Liberation Movement/Army
SPLM/A–Nasir	Sudan People's Liberation Movement/Army–Nasir
SPLM/A–United	Sudan People's Liberation Movement/Army–United
SSDF	South Sudan Defence Force
SSIA	South Sudan Independence Army
SSIM	South Sudan Independence Movement
SSLM	South Sudan Liberation Movement
SSPG	Southern Sudan Provisional Government
TMC	Transitional Military Council
UN	United Nations
UNHCR	United Nations High Commissioner for Refugees
UNMIS	United Nations Mission in Sudan
UP	Umma Party
VMT	Verification and Monitoring Team
WFP	World Food Programme

Glossary

Aballa: camel nomads.

'abdiyya: estate slavery or "slave settlements" established during heyday of the sultanate of Dar Fur based on a type of serf-lord relationship requiring exchange of labor and goods for patronage and protection.

ahl: people; used at times to indicate indigenous roots or clan ties.

amir al-mu'minin: commander of the faithful.

ansar: followers of the Mahdi (guided one or messiah).

Arabic: a Semitic language related to Hebrew and to Ethiopic languages.

Arabism: belief system that privileges those who identify as Arabs and that presumes the superiority of Arab values and norms over others.

Arabization: gradual process of transmission of norms, values, belief systems, and institutions of governance associated with the peoples of the Arabian Peninsula; process includes adoption of the Arabic language as well as the intermingling of Arab populations with indigenous societies of Africa.

awlad al-balad: "children of the land," a term that has come to denote the riverain peoples of the Nile Valley claiming descent from a fusion of indigenous and Arab communities. Its use in social discourse serves as a social marker to differentiate nonhegemonic Sudanese communities, identified by region or ethnic origin—such as Garaba/Fallata/Takarna—and referred to as "westerners"; Janubiyyin (southerners); and Nubawi "Nuba" and Hadendowa (indiscriminately used to embrace all Beja).

awlad al-garb: "children of the west," term used to refer to the indigenous and settled communities of the western regions of Sudan.

Baggara: cattle nomads.

baqt: specifically refers to a pact concluded between the governor of Egypt and the rulers of Nubia in the seventh century to provide Egypt with an annual tribute of approximately 360 slaves in exchange for commodities.

baraka: blessing received from religious leaders, or shaikhs, believed to possess special powers enabling them to perform *karamas* (miracles) due to their closeness with the Creator.

Bazinger: slave soldiers of the *zariba* owners and trading communities (not synonymous with Jihaddiyya, who were troops that underwent professional training).

Bedouin: nomadic pastoralists whose livelihood is herding sheep, goats, and camels, mostly found in and around the Sahara Desert.

Beja: one of the most ancient communities of northeastern Sudan and Eritrea, located in the region between the Nile and the Red Sea. Their indigenous language, *To-Badewi,* is in current use among some Ababda and Hadendowa and some branches of the Eritrean Beni Amir. The Beja Confederacy includes larger and smaller groups that have, throughout the ages, sought to ensure the survival of their communities and protect their patrimony.

bilad as-Sudan: "land of the blacks," a term coined by medieval Muslim geographers in Sahelian Africa to denote the areas from present-day Dakar to Djibouti. In the nineteenth century, due to the rivalry between French and British colonial powers, the western half, reaching to Lake Chad, came to be known as the French Soudan while the eastern territories fell under the British sphere of control and came to constitute the present-day Republic of Sudan.

dar: abode; domain; territory of; homeland.

dar al-ahd: "domain of the covenant/treaties," in which territories and inhabitants conclude agreements that enable them to retain conditional proprietorship of their areas and jurisdiction over their constituencies. *Dar al-ahd* refers to the existence of an intermediate theological/ideological geography that takes into account the existence of domains that were not subjugated by force. In C.E. 652 (A.H. 31), the governor of Egypt, Abdallah b'Sa'ad, faced with the Nubians' refusal to submit to the invasion of their homeland, concluded a treaty, *ahd,* with his opponents ending the wars. The treaty came to be known as the *baqt* or *pactum* by which the Nubians would provide an annual tribute of slaves in exchange for provisions from Egypt.

dar al-harb: "domain/abode of war," inhabited by unbelievers or *kuffar*—unwilling to submit to Islam—upon whom Muslims could wage war for their refusal to "submit." Although the Quran does not advocate forced conversion to Islam, the theological/geographical/ideological divide between "unbelievers" and "believers" has been used to justify slave raids, plunder, and wars of conquest.

dar al-Islam: "domain/abode of Islam," referring to the territories inhabited by adherents of Islam—members of the *umma,* community of believers. Some exceptions are made for adherents of Judaism and Christianity, regarded in Islam as the "people of the book," who may be accorded tributary status.

dar al-sulh: "domain of truce/armistice," referring to territories that were not conquered by Muslim armies but were negotiated by belligerents for (temporary) cessation of war. *Dar al-sulh* presents an even more ambiguous analytical construct in the discourse of early Islamic wars of conquest and is at times used interchangeably with *dar al-ahd*, although it can be inferred that truces may be regarded as temporary obstacles to the incorporation of these autonomous lands into the *dar al-Islam*.

darb al-arba'in: "forty days road," trade route from Darfur to Asyut through which slaves and goods were dispatched to Egypt and beyond.

dhimmis: protected status.

faki/faqih/fugara: religious teachers, holy men, jurists who settled throughout Sudan. As local leaders of the Sufi brotherhoods or *tariqas*, they played a major role in the gradual Islamization of the inhabitants of Sudan.

Falig al-Islami: Islamic Legion, a multinational armed force made up of Sudanese and Chadian political dissidents and migrants, sponsored by Libya's Muammar Qaddafi in the 1980s in his quest for unification/expansion of the Jumaharriya.

fiqh: jurisprudence.

Funj/Fung: the powerful indigenous kingdom that emerged in the region between the Blue and White Niles in the sixteenth century, with its capital in Sennar and with trade routes linking it to the Lake Chad area in the west and to Suakin and the Red Sea coast in the east.

Fur: community in western Sudan that gave rise to the sultanate of Fur during the seventeenth through nineteenth centuries and controlled the caravan trade and land route used by West African pilgrims to Mecca.

fursan: horsemen/knights of the sultanate of Dar Fur.

ghazwa/salatiyya: slave raids, or *razzias*, conducted with the permission of the sultan.

hakura/hawakir: estate grants awarded by the sultan.

Ingessana/Gamk: multiethnic and religious communities currently inhabiting the Ingessana Hills in the region of the southern Blue Nile. They refer to themselves as *gamk* (people of the hills).

intifada: uprising.

Islamism: social and political movement advocating reform of Muslim societies based on different (re)interpretations of *sharia*, the legitimacy of *itjihad*, as well as redefinitions of state-society relations in modernizing and postmodern societies.

Islamization: conversion to Islam and the adoption of sociocultural legal and political institutions associated with membership in the *umma*.

itjihad: renewal; the intellectual effort of Muslim jurists to reach autonomous religio-legal decisions.

Ja'aliyyin/Ja'ali: cluster of communities with shared indigenous/Nubian/ Arab ancestry claiming descent from a north Arabian ancestor, Ibrahim Ja'al, said to be related to the prophet Muhammad's uncle, al'Abbas.

jahiliyya: ignorance about Islam.

Janjaweed: composite term of *jinn* (spirit/ghost) and *jawad* (horse) to refer to outlaws or bandits wreaking havoc over communities.

jebel: hills, mountains.

jellaba: nineteenth-century small-scale merchants from the riverain areas who established the earliest trade networks, which were later integrated into the large-scale trade in slaves and ivory by powerful merchants such as al-Zubayr Rahma and Rabah, who not only established armed companies, *kubanniya,* protected by *bazingers,* but also carved out large territories that they claimed as rulers.

jihad: Muslim holy war or spiritual struggle against infidels; a crusade or struggle.

Jihadiyya: slave troops who underwent professional military training for the purpose of ensuring Muhammad Ali Pasha's rule in Egypt and Sudan with minimum reliance on the troops of the Ottoman Porte.

Juhayna: cluster of communities that claim descent from the South Arabian Peninsula and include the Baggara of southern Kordofan and Darfur.

kafir: infidel, pagan.

kasha: The central government's policy of rounding up IDPs and refugees and deporting them to camps.

Kush: ancient kingdom of Central Nile Valley whose rulers conquered most of Egypt in the eighth century B.C.E. and ruled its inhabitants for over fifty years.

Mahdi: the guided one, messiah—terms used to indicate an individual chosen by God to bring about the salvation of the community that has strayed from the "true" path.

Mahdism: a fusion of Sufism and Islamism that led to the construction of a reformist movement launched by the messianic Muhammad Ahmad in nineteenth-century Sudan.

makks: indigenous rulers.

malishat: Fur paramilitary forces established in response to the marauding irregulars destabilizing settled communities.

mujahidin: tribal militias recruited to lead the NIF regimes into the official government-sponsored militias.

murahaleen: traditional scouts of seasonally migrating communities recruited as irregular troops by officials of the post-Numeiri regime's campaigns against the guerrilla armies of southern Sudan and the Nuba Mountains.

muwalid: "born in the country," used historically to denote Sudanese descendants of West African origin, or migrants and refugees, and to justify the government's denial of citizenship until 1989.

naziheen: displaced.

Nuba: multiethnic and multireligious communities currently inhabiting the Nuba Mountains in Kordofan. Although the term *Nuba* has come to denote a shared political identity, the Nuba peoples speak over fifty languages related to the Niger-Kordofanian language family.

Nubians: one of the most ancient communities found in northern Sudan and southern Egypt and the first to confront the first waves of Arab invaders in the seventh century.

shaikhs: religious leaders and spiritual teachers of Islam.

sharaf: tribal nobility, a status usually acquired by constructing a geneology linking an individual (and his household) to the prophet Muhammad, his companions, or his kin.

sharia: Islamic holy laws.

Sudanism: the view or belief system that fosters a sense of nationalism based on shared membership in the multinational state of Sudan, without discrimination on the basis of region, ethnicity, or creed. Sudanism as an ideological construct was championed by John Garang as the unifying foundation for the vision of the New Sudan.

sudd: barrier; indicating the natural obstacles presented by the marshy swamps of the land, beyond the Kiir River (later known as Bahr al Arab).

Sufism: a form of Islam that highlights a personal and direct relationship with God attained through renunciation of material goods and constant affirmation of humility and love of faith. Rituals of affirmation include *dhkr,* aimed at enabling its dedicated disciples to serve as interlocutors between the divine and earthly worlds in guiding their followers to the right path.

Sufi orders: religious orders or brotherhoods characterized by a reverence of a Sufi master or shaikh recognized for his knowledge of Islam and the goodness, beauty, and beneficence of the Creator, and his disciplined pursuit of the true path or *tariqah.* Among the many *tariqahs* established in Sudan are the Quadriyyah, Shadhiliyya, Hindiyya, Majdhubiyya, Sammaniyya, Islamiyya, Mahidiyya, and Khatmiyya.

tahjir: reenactment of the prophet's exile *hejra.*

tajdid: renewal.

tariqah: see Sufi orders.

tariq al-Sudan: land route used by West African pilgrims to Mecca.

Turkiyya: "rule by the Turks," indicating two periods in Sudanese history: (1) 1821–1885, which ushered in the forces of Muhammad Ali Pasha, the Ottoman viceroy and governor of Egypt, interrupted by the Mahidiyya in

1885; and (2) 1898–1956 when Sudan was placed under the "joint" rule of the Anglo-Egyptian Condominium.

umma: community of believers.

unsuriya: Arabic term used to denote racism as a a negative aspect of tribalism, mainly to criticize the establishment of ethnoregional associations such as the Darfur Development Front (DDF), the General Union of the Nuba Mountains (GUNM), the Black Block (BB), and the Beja Congress during the first decade of Sudanese independence.

zariba/zaraib: enclosures used to deposit slaves before their sale, under guard by well-armed slave merchants and their *bazingers.*

zariba al-hawa: enclosures that shut out the nomadic pastoralists of Darfur and Kordofan from grazing areas, hence depriving them of their capacity to survive.

zurga: pejorative term for "blacks," implying inferior status or a slave past.

Bibliography

Achieng', Judith. "Politics-Sudan: Government, Rebels Agree to Revive Peace Talks," Inter Press Service, January 18, 2000.
———. "Politics-Sudan: Rebels Blame Khartoum for Failed Peace Talks," Inter Press Service, August 7, 1998.
Africa Confidential. "International Focus on Darfur," August 27, 2004.
———. "Sudan: Cairo Competes," December 19, 1997.
———. "Friends of IGADD," March 31, 1995.
———. "Unconvincing Transition?" October 22, 1993.
Africa News. "Sudan: Khartoum Accepts Libyan-Egyptian Peace Initiative," July 7, 2001.
———. "Sudan: Opposition Groups Meet to Coordinate Peace Proposals," June 28, 2001.
———. "North Africa; Sudan, Egypt, Libya Issue Joint Communiqué After Talks in Khartoum," January 13, 2000.
Africa Report. "The EU/AU Partnership in Darfur: Not Yet a Winning Combination," October 25, 2005.
Africa Research Bulletin. "Sudan Isolation Deepens," January 1996.
———. "Sudan: Peace Talks," May 1994.
———. "Sudan: U.S. Warning," April 1994.
———. "Anti-government Demonstrations," October 1993.
Agence France-Presse. "Sudan Peace Talks Begin," January 14, 2002.
———. "US Envoy Starts Sudan Mission," November 14, 2001.
———. "Libya's Gadaffi Arrives in Sudan for Talks on Arab Peace Plan," July 17, 2001.
———. "Sudanese Opposition Backs Arab Peace Plan But Asks for More," June 29, 2001.
———. "Egypt, Libya Hand Government, Opposition Peace Bid Proposals," June 26, 2001.
———. "Sudan Peace Talks End in Deadlock," January 2000.
———. "Egypt and Libya Sign Accord on Sudan," November 12, 1999.
———. "Egypt, Libya Set Ball Rolling for Sudan Peace Conference," August 10, 1999.
———. "Sudan: Hope for 'New Momentum' at IGAD Talks," April 15, 1999.
———. "Sudanese Rebels Begin Ceasefire to Help Famine Victims," July 15, 1998.

———. "Kenyan Foreign Minister Says 'Significant Progress' Made in Talks May 8, 1998," May 9, 1998.

———. "Sudanese Minister in Cairo to Discuss Ties," January 12, 1998.

———. "Sudan Against Peace Talks Summit: Report," May 14, 1993.

Agnew, John, and Stuart Cordridge. *Mastering Space: Hegemony, Territory and International Political Economy.* London: Routledge, 1995.

"Agreement Between the Government of Sudan on One Part, the Sudan Liberation Movement and the Justice and Equality Movement on the Other Under the Auspices of H. E. Idriss Deby, President of the Republic of Chad, Chief of State, Assisted by the African Union and the United Nations," N'Djamena, April 25, 2004.

Albino, Oliver. *The Sudan: A Southern Viewpoint.* London: Oxford University Press, 1970.

Ali, M. Taisir, and Robert O. Matthews (eds.). *Durable Peace: Challenges for Peace-building in Africa.* Toronto: University of Toronto Press, 2004.

Alier, K. Abel. *Southern Sudan: Too Many Agreements Dishonoured,* 2nd ed. Reading, UK: Ithaca Press, 1992.

AllAfrica.com. "Opportunity to Jump-Start Sudan May Be Lost Over Darfur-U.S. Negotiator, Charles Snyder," April 11, 2005.

Amnesty International UK. "Darfur: Rape as a Weapon of War: Sexual Violence and Its Consequences," July 2004. www.amnestyusa.org/countries/sudan/document .do?dz23FE42969B6C168A80256EC900529EDO.

Anderson, Benedict. *Imagined Communities: Reflections on the Origin and Spread of Nationalism.* London: Verso, 1991.

Andrews, George Reid. *The Afro-Argentines of Buenos Aires, 1800–1900.* Madison: University of Wisconsin Press, 1980.

ANP English News Bulletin. "Pronk Attempts to Re-open Sudanese Peace Negotiations," May 28, 1996.

Arab Press Service Organization. "Sudan: Government, Rebels Agree on 'Multicultural, Multi-religious' Solution," June 6, 1992.

Asher, Michael. *A Desert Dies.* New York: St. Martin's Press, 1986.

Assefa, Hizkhias. *Mediation of Civil Wars: Approaches and Strategies—The Sudan Conflict.* Boulder, CO: Westview Press, 1987.

Associated Press. "State of Emergency Declared in Sudan," December 12, 1999.

Awori, Horace. "Sudan-Peace: Regional-Sponsored Talks Collapse," Inter Press Service, September 8, 1994.

———. "Sudan-Politics: Peace Talks in Danger," Inter Press Service, August 25, 1994.

———. "Sudan-Politics: Still Talking About Peace," Inter Press Service, May 23, 1994.

———. "Sudan: SPLA Factions Agree on Common Agenda for Peace Talks," Inter Press Service, January 7, 1994.

———. "Sudan: Council of Churches Asks U.N. to Intervene in Civil Strife," Inter Press Service, August 17, 1993.

———. "Sudan: SPLA Faces Toughest Test Yet," Inter Press Service, August 13, 1993.

———. "Rebel In-fighting Fuels Government Offensive," *Africa Research Bulletin,* August 1993.

Azain, Adan. "Sudan: Women and Conflict in Darfur," *Review of African Political Economy* 30, no. 97 (September 2003): 470–510.

Azevedo, J. Mario. *Roots of Violence: A History of War in Chad.* The Hague: Gordon & Breach, 1988.

Badal, Raphael K. "Political Cleavages Within Southern Sudan: An Empirical Analysis of the Redivision Debate." In Sharif Harir and Terje Tvedt (eds.), *Shortcut to Decay: The Case of the Sudan.* Uppsala: Scandinavian Institute of African Studies, 1994.
BBC Monitoring Service. "Kenyan President Says Sudanese to Have a Final Say on Peace," June 2, 2001.
———. "Regional Summit on Sudan Issues Joint Communiqué," June 2, 2001.
BBC News. "Fighting Erupts in Eastern Sudan," June 21, 2005. http://news.bbc.co .uk/go/pr/fr/-1/hi/world/africa/4114374.stm.
BBC Summary of World Broadcasts. "Libya-Egyptian Initiative Achieves Progress in Sudanese Conflict," January 11, 2001.
———. "Garang Said Not to Favor Partition from North," May 19, 2000.
———. "Garang Wants Northern Opposition included in Regional Peace Initiative," May 17, 2000.
———. "Opposition Leader Mahdi Commends Egyptian-Libyan Peace Initiative," April 13, 2000.
———. "Opposition Ummah Army Withdraws Confidence in Garang's Leadership," March 24, 2000.
———. "Peace Talks in Kenya Reportedly End in Deadlock," March 1, 2000.
———. "Government Delegation Arrives in Nairobi for Peace Talks with Rebels," February 23, 2000.
———. "Egypt Says Its Sudan Plan Is Viable," October 23, 1999.
———. "Sudanese Rebels Reject Peace Plan," August 30, 1999.
———. "Envoy in Cairo Discusses Peace Efforts, Relations with Egypt," August 17, 1999.
———. "SPLM Leader John Garang Tells Kenyan TV: Khartoum Authorities 'Evil,'" August 14, 1999.
———. "Foreign Minister Says 'Ball Is in the Opposition's Court,'" August 10, 1999.
———. "Opposition Calls for National Dialogue Conference After Libyan Mediation," August 5, 1999.
———. "Sudan Peace Talks Deadlocked," August 6, 1998.
———. "Government, SPLA Agree to Referendum on Self-determination, More Talks," May 8, 1998.
———. "Government and Southern Rebel Movement Agree to Continue Cease-fire," March 13, 1996.
———. "Sudanese Rebel Movement Declares Cease-fire," March 3, 1996.
———. "Official Accuses Egypt of Involvement in Latest 'Ugandan Attack,'" November 29, 1995.
———. "Bashir Unhappy at IGADD's Partiality, Says Talks at Dead End," September 22, 1994.
———. "IGADD Summit in Addis Ababa," September 8, 1993.
———. "Sudan: Bashir's Army Day Speech: Claims Victory over SPLA Leader Garang," August 17, 1993.
———. "Sudan: Foreign Minister Looks Forward to OAU Summit," June 10, 1993.
———. "Sudanese Peace Talks: Report on Delegations' Joint Communiqué," June 8, 1992.
———. "Sudanese Leader Stresses Achievement of National Peace, August 19, 1991.
Bechtold, Peter K. "Military Rule in the Sudan: The First Five Years of Jafar Numayri," *Middle East Journal* 29, no. 1 (winter 1975).
Bender, Gerald. *Angola Under the Portuguese: The Myth and Reality.* Berkeley: University of California Press, 1978.

Besteman, Catherine. *Unraveling Somalia: Race, Violence and the Legacy of Slavery.* Philadelphia: University of Pennsylvania Press, 1999.

Bigg, Mathew. "Agencies Skeptical About Sudan Ceasefire," Reuters, July 15, 1998.

Black, Jeremy. "Geographies of War: The Recent Historical Background." In Colin Flint (ed.), *The Geography of War and Peace: From Death Camps to Diplomats.* New York: Oxford University Press, 2005.

Bol, Nhial. "Africa-Politics: Sudan Blames Neighbors as Rebel Offensive Rages," Inter Press Service, November 1, 1995.

———. "Sudan-Politics: Khartoum Rejects Eritrea's Mediation Role," Inter Press Service, January 10, 1995.

———. "Sudan-Eritrea: Diplomatic Row Erupts over Destabilization Claims," Inter Press Service, November 29, 1994.

———. "Sudan-Peace: Kenyan Envoy Visits War-torn South," Inter Press Service, November 1, 1994.

———. "Sudan-Refugees: Eritreans Prepare to Go Home," Inter Press Service, October 31, 1994.

———. "Sudan-Politics: Muslim Leader Declares War on Secularism," Inter Press Service, October 10, 1994.

———. "Sudan-Politics: Any Prospect for Peace?" Inter Press Service, August 29, 1994.

Bol, Nhial, and Charles Wachira. "Sudan-Eritrea: Khartoum Appeals to Asmara Not to Close Embassy," Inter Press Service, December 6, 1994.

Borzello, Anna. "Uganda-Sudan-Politics: Your Enemy, My Friend," Inter Press Service, November 10, 1995.

Brody, Jennifer D. *Impossible Purities: Blackness, Femininity, and Victorian Culture.* Durham, NC: Duke University Press, 1998.

Bryant, Lisa. "Sudan Opposition Talks," Voice of America, Correspondent Report No. 2-237210, August 17, 1998.

Burke, Edmund. *Thoughts on the Cause of the Present Discontents,* vol. 1. London: G. Routledge, 1913.

Buzan, Barry. *People, States, and Fear: An Agenda for International Security Studies in the Post–Cold War Era,* 2nd ed. Boulder, CO: Lynne Rienner Publishers, 1991.

Camões, Luiz Vaz de. *The Lusiads.* Translated by William C. Atkinson. Middlesex, UK: Penguin Books, 1952.

Caputo, Philip. *Acts of Faith.* New York: Alfred A. Knopf, 2005.

Cohen, Herman. *Intervening in Africa: Superpower Peace-making in a Troubled Continent.* New York: Macmillan, 2000.

Collins, Robert O. "Disaster in Darfur," *Africa Geopolitics,* nos. 15–16 (summer–fall 2004).

———. "Africans, Arabs, and Islamists: From the Conference Tables to the Battlefields in the Sudan," *African Studies Review* 42, no. 2 (September 1999).

———. *The Waters of the Nile: Hydro-politics and the Jonglei Canal, 1900–1988.* Oxford: Oxford University Press, 1990.

———. *Land Beyond the Rivers: The Southern Sudan, 1898–1918.* New Haven: Yale University Press, 1971.

———. "Sudanese Factors in the History of the Congo and Central West Africa in the Nineteenth Century." In Yusuf Fadl Hasan (ed.), *Sudan in Africa.* Khartoum: Khartoum University Press, 1971.

———. *The Southern Sudan, 1883–1898: A Struggle for Control.* New Haven: Yale University Press, 1962.

Communiqué issued at the adjournment of talks between SPLA and government, Nairobi, May 1993.

Comprehensive Peace Agreement. *Machakos Protocol,* July 20, 2002. *Framework Agreement on Security Arrangements During the Interim Period Between the Government of Sudan (GOS) and the Sudan People's Liberation Movement/ Army (SPLM/A),* Naivasha, Kenya, September 25, 2003; *Framework Agreement on Wealth Sharing During the Pre-interim and Interim Periods Between the Government of Sudan (GOS) and the Sudan People's Liberation Movement/Army (SPLM/A),* Naivasha, Kenya, January 7, 2004; *Protocol Between the Government of Sudan (GOS) and the Sudan People's Liberation Movement (SPLM) on the Resolution of the Conflict in Abyei,* Naivasha, Kenya, May 26, 2004; *Protocol Between the Government of Sudan (GOS) and the Sudan People's Liberation Movement (SPLM) on Power Sharing,* Naivasha, Kenya, May 26, 2004; *Agreement on Permanent Ceasefire and Security Arrangements, Implementation of Modalities During the Pre-interim and Interim Periods Between the Government of Sudan (GOS) and the Sudan People's Liberation Movement/Army (SPLM/A),* Naivasha, Kenya, December 31, 2004; *Agreement on Implementation Modalities Between the Government of Sudan (GOS) and the Sudan People's Liberation Movement/Army (SPLM/A),* Naivasha, Kenya, December 31, 2004.

Crone, Patricia. *Slaves on Horses: The Evolution of the Islamic Polity.* Cambridge: Cambridge University Press, 1980.

Cunnison, Ian. *Baggara Arabs: Power and Lineage in a Sudanese Nomad Tribe.* London: Oxford University Press, 1966.

Daily Nation. "Nairobi and "President Receives Report on the Sudan," September 8, 1994.

———. "Sudanese Peace Open," May 21, 1994.

———. "'Warring Faction Refuses to Sign Treaty as Scheduled," April 12, 1994.

Daly, M. W. *Imperial Sudan: The Anglo-Egyptian Condominium, 1934–1956.* Cambridge: Cambridge University Press, 1991.

Daly, M. W., and Ahmad Alawad Sikainga (eds.). *Civil War in the Sudan.* London: British Academy Press, 1993.

D'Aybaury, Hugo. *The Right to Be Nuba.* New York: Filmmakers Library, 1994.

DeCosson, E. A., *Fighting the Fuzzy-Wuzzy: Days and Nights of Service with Sir Gerald Graham's Field Force at Suakin.* London: Greenhill Books, 1990.

Deng, Francis M. "Sudan's Turbulent Road to Nationhood." In Ricardo R. Laremont (ed.), *Borders, Nationalism, and the African State.* Boulder, CO: Lynne Rienner Publishers, 2005.

———. "Abyei: A Bridge or a Gulf? The Ngok Dinka on Sudan's North-South Border." In Jay Spaulding and Stephanie Beswick (eds.), *White Nile, Black Blood.* Asmara, Eritrea: Red Sea Press, 2000.

———. *War of Visions: Conflict of Identities in the Sudan.* Washington, DC: Brookings Institution, 1995.

———. "Mediating the Sudanese Conflict: A Challenge for the IGADD," *CSIS Africa Notes,* No. 169, February 1995.

Deng, Francis M., and J. Stephen Morrison. *U.S. Policy to End Sudan's War: Report of the CSIS Task Force on U.S.-Sudan Policy.* Washington, DC: CSIS, February 2001.

Deng, Francis, and M. W. Daly. *Bonds of Silk: The Human Factor in the British Administration of the Sudan.* East Lansing: Michigan University Press, 1989.

de Waal, Alex. "Briefing: Darfur, Sudan—Prospects for Peace." *African Affairs* 104, no. 414 (January 2005).

———. *Islamism and Its Enemies in the Horn of Africa.* Bloomington: University of Indiana Press, 2004.

———. "The Right to Be Nuba." In Suleiman Musa Rahhal (ed.), *The Right to Be Nuba: The Story of a Sudanese People's Struggle for Survival.* Lawrenceville, NJ: Red Sea Press, 2001.

———. *A Famine That Kills: Darfur, Sudan, 1984–1985.* Oxford: Clarendon Press, 1989.

De Waal, Alex, and Abdel A. H. Salam. "Islamism, State Power and *Jihad* in Sudan." In de Waal (ed.), *Islamism and Its Enemies in the Horn of Africa.* Bloomington: Indiana University Press, 2004.

Do Nascimento, Abdias. *Mixture or Massacre? Essays in the Genocide of a Black People.* Buffalo, NY: Afrodiaspora, State University of New York at Buffalo, Puerto Rican Studies and Research Center, 1979.

"Draft Declaration of Principles," Nairobi, May 24, 1994.

Duffield, Mark. "The Fallata: Ideology and the National Economy in Sudan." In Norman O'Neill and Jay O'Brien (eds.), *Economy and Class in Sudan.* Aldershot, UK: Avebury, 1988.

———. *Maiurno: Capitalism and Rural Life in Sudan.* London: Ithaca Press, 1981.

Echenberg, Myron. *Colonial Conscripts: The Tirailleurs Sénégalais in French West Africa, 1857–1960.* Portsmouth, NH: Heinemann, 1991.

Economist, The, December 3–9, 2005, p. 25.

El-Affendi, Abdelwahab. "The Impasse in the IGAD Peace Process for Sudan: The Limits of Regional Peacemaking?" *African Affairs* 100, no. 401 (December 2001).

———. *Turabi's Revolution: Islam and Power in Sudan.* London: Grey Seal Books, 1991.

Electronic Mail and Guardian. "New US Sanctions Announced," November 7, 1997.

El-Gaili, Ahmed, T. "Federalism and the Tyranny of Religious Minorities: Challenges to Islamic Federalism in Sudan," *Harvard International Law Journal* 45, no. 2 (summer 2004).

El Hassan, Yahya. "Sudanese Leader Accuses U.S. of Sabotaging Talks," Pan-African News Agency, November 19, 1997.

Esipisu, Manoah. "U.N. Launches Food Airlifts to Southern Sudan," Reuters, June 12, 1993.

Ewald, Janet J. *Soldiers, Traders, and Slaves: State-Formation and Economic Transformation in the Greater Nile Valley, 1700–1885.* Madison: University of Wisconsin Press, 1990.

Fisher-Thompson, Jim. "Eritrean President Makes Big Impression in Washington: Moose Comments on Isaias Visit," US Information Agency (USIA), February 15, 1995.

Flint, Colin. *The Geography of War and Peace: From Death Camps to Diplomats.* Oxford: Oxford University Press, 2005.

Fint, Julie, and Alex De Waal. *Darfur: A Short History of a Long War.* London and New York: Zed Books, 2005.

Foreign Broadcast Information Service (FBIS). "Sudan Oppositionists Object to Meeting in Washington," December 14, 1999.

———. "Sudanese Government Says Emergency Not Coup d'État," December 13, 1999.

———. "Albright's African Tour, US Policy Viewed," November 1999.

———. "Sudan Rebels Said to Be in 'State of Conflict,'" October 23, 1999.

———. "Sudanese Opposition Alliance Issues Statement in Cairo," October 22, 1999.

———. "Sudan: Rebel Leader Garang Says No Plans to Meet Bashir," September 15, 1999.

———. "Meeting to Prepare Sudanese Peace Talks Set for October," September 12, 1999.

———. "Sudanese Minister Thanks Egypt, Libya for Initiative," September 12, 1999.

———. "Sudan Government, Rebels Meet Behind Closed Doors," July 20, 1999.

———. "Gaddaffi Accuses U.S. of 'Terrorism' Over Al-Shifa," June 19, 1999.

———. "Sudanese Opposition Leaders to Meet Egyptian and Libyan Officials," June 15, 1999.

———. "Sudan's Al-Mahdi on Rapprochement Prospect," June 15, 1999.

———. "Eritrea Tells Sudanese Opposition to Evacuate Embassy," May 16, 1999.

———. "Sudanese Opposition Welcomes al-Turabi–al-Mahdi Meeting," May 13, 1999.

———. "Sudanese Oppositionist Praises Al-Turabi–Al-Mahdi Meeting," May 4, 1999.

———. "Sudan: Secret Government, Opposition Talks Reported," April 30, 1999.

———. "Ethiopia–Sudanese Leader Sees Improved Ties in Future," March 31, 1999.

———. "Sudan Says Ready for 'Serious, Frank' Dialogue with US," March 17, 1999.

———. "President Omar al-Bashir on Dialogue with the West," January 1, 1999.

———. "Egypt: Sudan's Opposition NDA Issues Statement," August 18, 1998.

———. "Sudan: Sudan's NDA Issues Cairo Declaration," August 18, 1998.

———. "Sudanese Opposition Leaders Open Meetings in Cairo," August 15, 1998.

———. "Sudan: Italian Delegation Wraps Up Visit to Sudan," April 6, 1998.

———. "Italy: Official Previews Sudan Peace Mediation Talks in Nairobi," March 30, 1998.

———. "Sudan's al-Hindi on Results of Initiative," February 27, 1998.

———. "Sudanese Umma Party Adopts 'Action Plan,'" February 5, 1998.

———. "Sudan: Al-Mahdi on Sudanese Opposition Goals," January 7, 1998.

———. "Eritrea: Afewerki on Relations with U.S., Sudan," January 31, 1995.

———. "Kenyan Envoy Pays Visit, Meets with Officials," November 10, 1994.

———. "Relations Between Sudan, Uganda Said to Be Worsening," October 5, 1994.

———. "U.S Reportedly Seeking to Partition Sudan," September 12, 1994.

———. "Sudanese Peace Talks Reach Stalemate in Nairobi," September 8, 1994.

———. "Spokesman Suggests New Mechanism for Negotiations," August 31, 1994.

———. "Wells Meets Southern Assembly Members," June 17, 1994.

———. "U.S. Envoy Arrives with Clinton Letter," June 13, 1994.

———. "Sudanese President Calls Talks with Uganda 'Successful,'" June 1, 1994.

———. "Uganda, Sudanese Leaders Hold Talks in Austria," and "Talk Termed 'Tough, Productive,'" May 31, 1994.

———. "Government Delegation Issues Statement," April 15, 1994.

———. "IGADD Meeting on Aid Suspended," April 15, 1994.

———. "Al-Bashir, U.S. Envoy Meet: Foreign Minister Comments," April 4, 1994.

———. "Government Affirms Willingness to Meet Rebels," January 10, 1994.

———. "Minister on Garang Talks, U.S. Involvement," January 4, 1994.

———. "Regional Politics: IGADD Summit," September 21, 1993.

———. "Garang Views Formula for Two Confederal States," July 1, 1993.

———. "Foreign Minister on U.S. Relations," June 21, 1994.

Garang, John. *The Call for Democracy in Sudan.* London: Kegan Paul International, 1992.

———. *John Garang Speaks.* Edited and introduced by Mansour Khalid. London: Kegan Paul International, 1987.

Garrestson, Peter P. "Vicious Cycles: Ivory, Slaves, and Arms on the New Maji Frontier." In Donald Donham and Wendy James (eds.), *The Southern Marches of Imperial Ethiopia: Essays in History and Social Anthropology.* Cambridge: Cambridge University Press, 1986.

Gessi, Romolo Pasha. *Seven Years in the Sudan—Being a Record of Explorations, Adventures, and Compaigns Against the Arab Slave Hunters.* Collected and edited by Felix Gessi. London: Sampson Low, Marston, 1892.

Gomez, Michael. *Pragmatism in the Age of Jihad: The Pre-colonial State of Bundu.* Cambridge: Cambridge University Press, 1992.

Gordon-Reed, Annette. *Thomas Jefferson and Sally Hemings: An American Controversy.* Charlottesville: University Press of Virginia, 1997.

Hagos, Ghion. "Delegations Clash at Peace Talks," Pan-African News Agency, August 5, 1998.

Harir, Sharif. "'The Arab Belt' and the 'African Belt.'" In Sharif Harir and Terje Tvedt (eds.), *Shortcut to Decay: The Case of the Sudan.* Uppsala: Scandinavian Institute of African Studies, 1994.

Hasan, Yusuf Fadl. "External Influences and the Progress of Islamization in Eastern Sudan Between the Fifteenth and Sixteenth Centuries." In Hasan (ed.) *Sudan in Africa: Studies Presented to the First International Conference Sponsored by the Sudan Research Unit, 7–12 February 1968.* Khartoum: Khartoum University Press, 1971.

Hills, Richard L., and Peter C. Hogg. *A Black Corps d'Élite: An Egyptian Sudanese Conscript Battalion with the French Army in Mexico, 1863–1867, and Its Survivors in Subsequent African History.* East Lansing: Michigan State University Press, 1995.

Hirst, David. "Mubarak Risks Taking Sides in Sudan," *The Guardian,* August 17, 1998.

Hiskett, Mervyn. *The Course of Islam in Africa.* Edinburgh: Edinburgh University Press, 1994.

Hodgkins, Thomas. "Mahdism, Messianism and Marxism in the African Setting." In Yusuf Fadl Hasan (ed.), *Sudan in Africa.* Khartoum: University of Khartoum Press. 1971.

Holgersson-Shorter, Helena. "Authority's Shadowy Double: Thomas Jefferson and the Architecture of Illegitimacy." In Alexandra Isfahani-Hammond (ed.), *The Masters and the Slaves: Plantation Relations and Mestizaje in American Imaginaries.* New York: Palgrave Macmillan, 2005.

Holt, P. M. "The Islamization of Nilotic Sudan." In Brett Michael (ed.), *Northern Africa: Islam and Modernization.* London: Frank Cass, 1973.

Holt, P. M., and M. W. Daly. *A History of the Sudan: From the Coming of Islam to the Present Day.* London: Longman Group, 1988.

Holt, Thomas. "Explaining Racism in American History." In Anthony Molho and Gordon S. Wood (eds.), *Imagined Histories: American Historians Interpret the Past.* Princeton: Princeton University Press, 1998.

Huband, Mark C. "Thousands Flee New Fighting in Famine-racked Southern Sudan," *Washington Post,* August 18, 1993.

Human Rights Watch. *Sudan: Oil and Human Rights.* New York: Human Rights Watch, 2003.

Hunwick, John, and Eve Troutt Powell. *The African Diaspora in the Mediterranean Lands of Islam.* Princeton: Markus Wiener Publishers, 2002.

Hutchinson, Sharon. *Nuer Dilemmas: Coping with Money, War, and the State.* Berkeley: University of California Press, 1996.

Ibn Khaldun, *The Muqaddimah: An Introduction to History.* Translated from the Arabic by Franz Rosenthal. Princeton: Princeton University Press, 1969.

Ibrahim, Abdullahi. "Janjaweed: What's in a Name?" *Sudan Association Newsletter,* May 2004.

Idris, Amir H. *Conflict and Politics of Identity in Sudan.* New York: Palgrave MacMillan, 2005.

———. *Sudan's Civil War: Slavery, Race and Formational Identities.* Lampeter, ON: Edwin Mellen Press, 2001.

Independent (London). "Sudan Peace Plan Welcomed," July 5, 2001.

InterAfrica Group. *IGADD Mediation of the Sudanese Conflict.* Addis Ababa: Inter-Africa Group, July 1994.

Intergovernmental Authority on Development (IGAD). "IGAD Secretariat on Peace in the Sudan, The Machakos Protocol, July 2002." Nairobi: IGAD, 2002.

Integrated Regional Information Networks. "Sudan: Annan Calls for International Action Over Darfur Conflict," October 21, 2005.

———. "Nigeria-Sudan: Back to the Table: Darfur Talks Resume After Initial Delays," June 13, 2005.

———. "Nigeria: Darfur Peace Talks Back on Track in Abuja," June 10, 2005.

———. "African Leaders Work on New Summit for Darfur Crisis," February 28, 2005.

———. "Government Allies Attack Refugee Camps," November 10, 2004.

———. "Sudan: Little Progress Achieved at Peace Talks," July 26, 1999.

———. "Sudan-Eritrea: Reconciliation Agreement Signed," May 3, 1999.

International Crisis Group (ICG), *The EU/AU Partnership in Darfur: Not Yet a Winning Combination,* ICG Africa Report No. 99. Washington DC: ICG, October 25, 2005.

———. "Unifying Darfur's Rebels: A Prerequisite for Peace," Africa Briefing No. 32. Nairobi/Brussels: ICG, October 6, 2005.

———. *The Khartoum-SPLM Agreement: Sudan's Uncertain Peace,* Africa Report No. 96. Washington DC: ICG, July 25, 2005.

———. "God, Oil, and Country: Changing Logic of War in Sudan." Washington, DC: ICG, 2002.

Inter Press Service. "Darfur Rebels Want UN to Supervise the Talks with Sudan Government," February 8, 2005.

———. "East Africa: Leaders Set Up Mediation Committee on Sudan," September 7, 1993.

Iyob, Ruth. "The Foreign Policies of the Horn: The Clash Between the Old and the New." In Gilbert Khadiagala and Terrence Lyons (eds.), *African Foreign Policies: Power and Process.* Boulder, CO: Lynne Rienner Publishers, 2001.

James, Wendy R. "Social Assimilation and Changing Identity in the Southern Funj." In Yusuf Fadl Hasan (ed.), *Sudan in Africa: Studies Presented to the First International Conference Sponsored by the Sudan Research Unit, 7–12 February 1968.* Khartoum: Khartoum University Press, 1971.

Jelinek, Pauline. "Civil War in Southern Sudan Destroys Life for the People," *Calgary Herald,* June 15, 1993; "Sudan: Pressure on Garang," *Middle East International,* June 11, 1993.

Johnson, Douglas H. *Land Analysis of the Factionalism of Southerners' Dissidence: The Root Causes of Sudan's Civil Wars,* 2nd ed. Oxford: Indiana University Press, 2004.

———. *The Root Causes of Sudan's Civil War.* Bloomington: Indiana University Press, 2003.

————. "The Sudan People's Liberation Army and the Problem of Factionalism." In Christopher Clapham,(ed.), *African Guerrillas*. London: James Currey, 1998.

————. (ed.) *The Upper Nile Province Handbook: A Report on Peoples and Government in the Southern Sudan, 1931*. Compiled by C. A. Willis, published for the British Academy. Oxford: Oxford University Press, 1995.

————. *Nuer Prophets: A History of Prophecy from the Upper Nile in the Ninteenth and Twentieth Centuries*. Oxford: Clarendon Press, 1994.

Johnson, Harry. "The Crisis in Sudan: The North-South Conflict." *Mediterranean* 7, no. 3 (spring 1996).

Jok, Jok Madut. *War and Slavery in Sudan*. Philadelphia: University of Pennsylvania Press, 2001.

Kapila, Mukesh. "Mass Rape Atrocity in Sudan," BBC, March 19, 2004.

Keesing's Record of World Events. "Sudan: Peace Agreement with Southern Rebel Factions," April 1996.

————. "Sudan: Deteriorating Relations with Ethiopia," January 1996.

————. "Sudan: Call for Jihad," January 1995.

————. "Sudan: Economy," January 1994.

————. "Intensification of War in South," and "Fall of Southern Towns to Government Forces," March 1992.

Kempster, Norman. "Terrorism Case Puts Focus on Secretive Sudan," *Los Angeles Times,* June 26, 1993.

Kessler, Glenn. "Sudan, Southern Rebels Sign Accord to End Decades of War," *Washington Post,* January 10, 2005.

Khuwa, Yusuf. "Things Were No Longer the Same." In Suleiman Musa Rahhal (ed.), *The Right to Be Nuba*. Lawrenceville, NJ: Red Sea Press, 2001.

Kirwan, L. P. "Greek and Roman Expeditions to the Southern Sudan." In John Mack and Peter Robertshaw (eds.), *Culture History in the Southern Sudan: Archaeology, Linguistics and Ethnohistory*. Nairobi: British Institute in Eastern Africa, 1982.

Kizito, Edmond. "Uganda-Sudan Dispute Worsens," Reuters, April 23, 1995.

Kok, Peter. "Sudan: Between Radical Restructuring and Deconstruction of State Systems." *Review of African Political Economy* 23, no. 70 (December 1996).

Kuper, Leo. *The Pity of It All: Polarisation of Racial and Ethnic Relations*. Minneapolis: University of Minnesota Press, 1977.

Lacey, Marc. "Sudan and Southern Rebels Sign Deal Ending Civil War," *New York Times,* January 10, 2005.

Lane, Jill. *Blackface Cub, 1840–1895*. Philadelphia: University of Pennsylvania Press, 2005.

Lata, Leenco. *The Horn of Africa as Common Homeland: The State and Self-Determination in the Era of Heightened Globalization*. Waterloo, ON: Wilfred Laurier University Press, 2005.

Letzion, Nehemia, and Randall L. Powells. "The Eastern Sudan, 1822 to the Present." In Letzion and Powells (eds.), *The History of Islam in Africa*. Athens: Ohio University Press, 2000.

Le Vine, Victor T. *Politics of Francophone Africa*. Boulder, CO: Lynne Rienner Publishers, 2004.

Lieberman, Robert C. *Shaping Race Policy: The United States in Comparative Perspective*. Princeton: Princeton University Press, 2005.

Lobban, Carolyn F., and Kharyssa Rhodes (eds.). *Race and Identity in the Nile Valley: Ancient and Modern Perspectives*. Lawrenceville, NJ: Red Sea Press, 2004.

Lockwood, Christopher. "Food Aid Follows Ceasefire," *Telegraph,* July 16, 1998.

Los Angeles Times. "Sudan: Government Rejects Proposal to End War Analysis: What Hopes for Peace in Sudan?" November 13, 1997.

Lusk, Gill, "Sudan: War in Slow Motion," *Middle East International,* June 27, 1997.

———. "Sudan: Heavy Fighting," *Middle East International,* April 4, 1997.

———. "Sudan: Lull Before the Storm," *Middle East International,* February 7, 1997.

———. "Sudan: Opposition Offensive," *Middle East International,* January 24, 1997.

———. "Abuja Fails Again," *Middle East International,* May 28, 1993.

———. "SPLA Reconciliation," *Middle East International,* November 5, 1993.

MacMichael, H. A. *A History of the Arabs in the Sudan: And Some of the People Who Preceded Them and the Tribes Inhabiting Darfur,* vol. 2. New York: Barnes & Noble, 1967.

Macquet, Jacques. *The Premise of Inequality in Ruanda: A Study of Political Relations in a Central African Kingdom.* London: Oxford University Press, 1961.

Mahmoud, Fatima Babiker. *The Sudanese Bourgeoisie: Vanguard of Development?* Khartoum: Khartoum University Press, 1984.

Mahmoud, Muhammad. "Sufism and Islamism in the Sudan." In David Westerlund and Eva Evers Rosander (eds.), *African Island and Islam in Africa: Encounters Between Sufis and Islamists.* London: Hurst, 1997.

Mail and Guardian, "Sudan Scoffs at New US Sanctions," November 7, 1997.

Makris, G. P. *Changing Masters: Spirit Possession and Identity Construction Among Slave Descendants and Other Subordinates in the Sudan.* Evanston, IL: Northwestern University Press, 2000.

Malwal, Bona. "The Jimmy Carter Initiative," *Sudan Democratic Gazette,* March 1995.

———. "Sudan's Political and Economic Future: A Southern Perspective." In Charles Gurdon (ed.), *The Horn of Africa.* New York: St. Martin's Press, 1994.

———. "The Roots of the Current Contention." In Francis M. Deng and Prosser Giffords (eds.), *The Search for Peace and Unity in the Sudan.* Washington, DC: Woodrow Wilson Center, 1987.

Mamdani Mahmood. "How Can We Name the Dafur Crisis: Some Preliminary Thoughts," *Pambazuka News,* October 7, 2004. www.pambazuka.org/index .php?id=24982.

———. "When Does a Settler Become Native? Reflections on the Colonial Roots of Citizenship in Equatorial and South Africa." University of Cape Town Inaugural Lecture, New Series 208, May 13, 1998.

———. *Citizen and Subject: Contemporary Africa and The Legacy of Late Colonialism.* Princeton: Princeton University Press, 1996.

Mans, Ulrich. "Briefing: Sudan: The New War in Darfur," *African Affairs* 103, no. 17 (2004).

Maquet, Jacques. *Africanity: The Cultural Unity of Black Africa.* New York: Oxford University Press, 1972.

Markakis, John. *Resource Conflict in the Horn of Africa.* London: Sage Publications, 1998.

Marx, Anthony. *Making Race, Making Nations: A Comparison of South Africa, the United States, and Brazil.* New York: Cambridge University Press, 1998.

Matloff, Judith. "Sudan's Civil War Looking Less Civil War," *Christian Science Monitor,* January 31, 1997.

Mbitiru, Chege. "Rebels Say Sudan Bombed Town as Peace Talks Resume," Associated Press, January 16, 2000.

McClintock, David M. "The Southern Sudan Problem," *Middle East Journal* 24, no. 4 (autumn 1970).

Mendy, Peter Karibe. *Colonialismo Português em Africa: A Tradição de Resistência na Guiné-Bissau.* Lisbon: Instituto Nacional de Estudos e Pesquisas, 1994.

Mideast Mirror. "Garang: 'We Are Going to Activate the SPLA in Khartoum Proper,'" 14, no. 96 (May 22, 2000).

———. "The Solution for Sudan—by John Garang," May 17, 2000.

Monga, Celestin. *The Anthropology of Anger: Civil Society and Democracy in Africa.* Boulder, CO: Lynne Rienner Publishers, 1996.

Mukhtar, Al-Baqr al-Affif. "The Crisis of Identity in Northern Sudan: The Dilemma of a Black People with a White Culture." In Carolyn Fluehr-Lobban and Kharyssa Rhodes (eds.), *Race and Identity in the Nile Valle.* Lawrenceville, NJ: Red Sea Press, 2004.

Murphy, Kim. "Sudan's Road to Social Justice Paved with Fear," *Los Angeles Times,* August 16, 1993.

———. "Sudan Criticizes IMF for Suspending Its Membership," Xinhua News Agency, August 10, 1993.

Musa, Omar el-Hag. "Reconciliation, Rehabilitation, and Development Efforts in Southern Sudan," *Middle East Journal* 27, no. 1 (winter 1973).

Nadel, S. F. *The Nuba: An Anthropological Study of the Hill Tribes in Kordofan.* London: Oxford University Press, 1947.

Nation. "Moi Meets US Special Envoy to Sudan," January 14, 2002.

Naty, Alexander. "Memory and the Humiliation of Men." In James Wendy, Donald L. Donham, Eisei Kurimoto, and Alesssandro Triulzi (eds.), *Remapping Ethiopia: Socialism and After.* Oxford: James Currey Publishers, 2002.

Nduru, Moyiga. "Sudan-Politics: Khartoum Canvasses African Support Against Rebels," Inter Press Service, May 15, 1995.

New Vision (Kampala). "Albright and Museveni Hold Joint Press Conference," December 11, 1997.

New York Times. "A Cease-Fire Is Set in Sudan War," January 20, 2002.

Niblock, Tim. *Class and Power in Sudan: The Dynamics of Sudanese Politics, 1898–1985.* Albany: State University of New York Press, 1987.

Njuguna, Osman. "Sudan: IGAD Endorsed as Suitable Forum for Peace Process," All Africa News Agency, August 6, 1999.

Nolutshungu, Sam C. *Limits of Anarchy: Intervention and State Formation in Chad.* Charlottesville: University Press of Virginia, 1996.

Nyaba, P. A. *The Politics of Liberation in South Sudan: An Insider's View.* Kampala: Fountain Publishers, 1997.

Nyang. Sulayman, and Douglas Johnston, "Conflict Resolution as a Normative Value in Islamic Law: Application to the Republic of Sudan." In Douglas Johnston (ed.), *Faith-Based Diplomacy: Trumping Realpolitik.* Oxford: Oxford University Press, 2003.

Oduho, Joseph, and William Deng. *The Problem of the Southern Sudan.* London: Oxford University Press, 1963.

O'Fahey, R. S. "Fur and Fartit: The History of a Frontier." In John Mack and Peter Robertshaw (eds.), *Culture History in the Southern Sudan Archaeology, Linguistics and Ethno-History.* Nairobi: British Institute in Eastern Africa, 1982.

———. "Religion and Trade in the Kayra Sultanate of Dar Fur." In Yusuf Fadl Hasan (ed.), *Sudan in Africa.* Khartoum: Khartoum University Press, 1971.

O'Fahey, R. S., and M. I. Abu Salim. *Land in Dar Fur: Charters and Related Documents from the Dar Fur Sultanate.* Cambridge: Cambridge University Press, 1983.

Oluoch, Fred. "Sumbeiywo: The Unsung Hero of Sudan Peace," *The East African,* January 17–23, 2005.

Omer, El Haj Bilal. *The Danagla Traders of Northern Sudan: Rural Capitalism and Agricultural Development.* London: Ithaca Press, 1985.

O'Neill, Norman. "Class and Politics in the Modern History of the Sudan." In Norman O'Neil and Jay O'Brien (eds.), *Economy and Class in Sudan.* Brookfield, VT: Avebury.

Osman, Mohamed. "El-Bashir: Peace Initiative Does Not Mean Separating Religion from the State," Associated Press, July 22, 2001.

Pan-African News Agency. "Mahdi's Withdrawal Dents Opposition Alliance," March 24, 2000.

———. "Gadaffi Vows to Reconcile Sudanese Belligerents," June 20, 1999.

———. "USCR Criticizes U.S. Efforts in Sudan," March 23, 1999.

Pipes, Daniel. *Slave Soldiers and Islam: The Genesis of a Military System.* New Haven: Yale University Press, 1981.

Prendergast, John. "Senator Danforth's Sudan Challenge: Building a Bridge to Peace," *CSIS Africa Notes,* no. 5, January 2002.

Pronk, Jan. *Report of the UN Secretary General's Special Representative to Sudan,* February 2005. New York: United Nations Secretariat.

"Protocol on the Improvement of the Humanitarian Situation in Darfur," Abuja, November 9, 2004.

Prunier, Gérard. *Darfur: The Ambiguous Genocide.* London: Hurst, 2005.

Qatar News Agency. "Sudan/Darfur/Libya Declaration," May 17, 2005.

Rahhal, Suleiman Musa. *The Right to Be Nuba: The Story of a Sudanese People's Struggle for Survival.* Lawrenceville, NJ: Red Sea Press, 2001.

Ranger, Terence. "The Invention of Tradition." In Eric Hobsbawm and Terence Ranger (eds.), *The Invention of Tradition in Colonial Africa.* Cambridge: Cambridge University Press, 1983.

Raymond, Kelly C. *The Nuer Conquest: The Structure and Development of an Expansionist System.* Ann Arbor: University of Michigan Press, 1985.

Refugees International. *No Power to Protect.* The African Union Mission in Sudan. Washington, DC: Refugees International, November 2005.

Report of the Secretary-General Pursuant to Paragraph 6 and 13 to 16 of Security Council Resolution 1556, 2004.

Reuters. "Breakthrough in Sudan-U.S. Relations," March 6, 2000.

———. "Nigeria Seeks Compromise Formula in Sudan Peace Talks," May 1, 1993.

Rogier, Emeric. "No More Hills Ahead? The Sudan's Tortuous Ascent to the Heights of Peace," Clingendael Security Paper No. 1. The Hague: Netherlands Institute of International Relations Clingendael, August 2005.

Rolandsen, Oystein H. *Guerrilla Government: Political Changes in the Southern Sudan in the 1990s.* Sweden: Nordiska Afrikainstitutet, 2005.

Rubin, Barry. The Long War for Freedom: The Arab Struggle for Democracy in the Middle East. Hoboken, NJ: John Wiley and Sons, 2006.

Salih, A. Mohamed. "The Bible, the Qur'an and the Conflict in South Sudan." In Niels Kastfelt (ed.), *Scriptural Politics: The Bible and the Koran as Political Models in the Middle East and Africa.* Trenton, NJ: Africa World Press, 2004.

Sansone, Livio. *Blackness Without Ethnicity: Construction of Race in Brazil.* New York: Palgrave Macmillan, 2003.

———. "From Africa to Afro: Use and Abuse of Africa in Brazil." Amsterdam: South-South Exchange Programme for Research on the History of Development (SEPHIS); Dakar: Council for the Development of Social Science Research

(CODESRIA), 1999.

Scott, Don. "Disaster in Sudan: Why Is West Ignoring the Cries for Aid?" *Ottawa Citizen*, July 27, 1993.

Scott, James C. *Domination and the Art of Resistance*. New Haven, CT: Yale University Press, 1990.

Scroggins, Deborah. *Emma's War*. New York: Pantheon Books, 2002.

Segal, Roland. *Islam's Black Slaves: The History of Africa's Other Black Diaspora*. London: Atlantic Books, 2001.

Sei, Tabitha J. "The Intergovernmental Authority (IGAD) and the Sudanese Peace Process." In Korwa Adar et al. (eds.), *Sudan Peace Process: Challenges and Future Prospects*. Pretoria: Africa Institute, 2004.

Sharkey, Heather J. *Living with Colonialism: Nationalism and Culture in the Anglo-Egyptian Sudan*. Berkeley and Los Angeles: University of California Press, 2003.

Sikainga, A. Ahamad. *City of Steel and Fire: A Social History of Atbara, Sudan's Railway Town, 1906–1984*. Portsmouth, NH: Heinemann, 2002.

———. "Military Slavery and the Emergence of a Southern Sudanese Diaspora in the Northern Sudan, 1884–1954." In Jay Spaulding and Stephanie Beswick (eds.), *White Nile, Black Blood: War, Leadership, and Ethnicity from Khartoum to Kampala*. Asmara, Eritrea: Red Sea Press, 2000.

———. *Slaves into Workers: Emancipation and Labor in Colonial Sudan*. Austin: University of Texas Press, 1996.

Simone, T. Abdou Maliqalim. *In Whose Image: Political Islam and Urban Practices in Sudan*. Chicago: University of Chicago Press, 1994.

Slim, Hugo. "Dithering Over Darfur? A Preliminary Review of the International Response," *International Affairs* 80, no. 5 (2004).

Spaulding, Jay, and Lidwien Kapteijns (eds.). *An Islamic Alliance: 'Ali Dinar and the Sanusiyya, 1906–1916*. Evanston, IL: Northwestern University Press, 1994.

Speakers of Truth and Justice. *The Black Book: Imbalance of Power and Wealth in Sudan*. 2000. Khartoum.

"Speech by President Daniel arap Moi on the Occasion of Sudanese Peace Talks," September 6, 1994. Nairobi: IGAD Secretariat.

"Statement by Dr. Hussein Suleiman Abu Salih, Minister of Foreign Affairs," March 1994. Nairobi: IGAD Secretariat.

Steele, Jonathan. "Darfur Wasn't Genocide and Sudan Is Not a Terrorist State," *The Guardian*, October 7, 2005.

Sudan Democratic Gazette. "Promoting Reconciliation: Has Egypt Derailed IGAD Peace Process on Sudan?" February 2001.

———. "El Mahdi Returns to a Tumultuous Public Welcome in Khartoum," December 2000.

———. "As IGAD Unravels at the Helm, What Are the Prospects for Peace in Sudan?" December 2000.

———. "The IGAD Peace Process: Between a Rock and a Hard Place," September 2000.

———. "SPLA Leader Suspends Participation at IGAD to Placate Egypt and Libya," June 2000.

Sudan Liberation Movement and Sudan Liberation Army (SLM/SLA) Political Declaration. Khartoum, February 2003.

Sudan People's Liberation Army (SPLA). Act 1994, Secretariat of Legal Affairs, 1994.

"Sudan's Position on 'State and Religion' and 'Self-determination': Report on Government Position on the Fourth Round of IGADD Talks That Took Place in Nairobi, September 7, 1994," Embassy of Sudan, Nairobi, September 22, 1994.

Suliman, Mohamed. "Civil War in the Sudan: The Impacts of Ecological Degradation." In Girma Kebbede (ed.), *Sudan's Predicament: Civil War, Displacement and Ecological Degradation*. Aldershot, UK: Ashgate Publishing, 1999.

———. "Ethnicity from Perception to Cause of Violent Conflict: The Case of the Fur and Nuba Conflicts in Western Sudan." Paper presented at the CONTICI International Workshop, Bern, Switzerland, July 8–11, 1997.

Swiss Review of International Affairs. "Our Goal Is to Topple the Khartoum Regime: Interview with John Garang, Head of the SPLA," June 1997.

Talhami, H. Ghada. *Suakin and Massawa Under Egyptian Rule: 1865–1885.* Washington, DC: University Press of America, 1979.

Tvedt, Terje. *The River Nile in the Age of the British: Political Ecology and the Quest for Economic Power.* London: I. B. Taurus, 2004.

United Nations. *Report of the International Commission of Inquiry on Darfur to the United Nations Secretary-General.* Geneva: UN, January 25, 2005.

United Nations News Service. "Annan Welcomes Promising Developments Related to Sudan's Troubled Darfur Region," New York, June 10, 2005.

United Press International. "Sudan Said to Mobilize Against Uganda," November 9, 1995.

US Department of the Army, Foreign Areas Studies Division. *Area Handbook for the Republic of the Sudan.* Washington, DC: Government Printing Office, 1966.

US Department of State. "U.S. Offers Three Resolutions to Speed End of Crisis in Darfur," March 23, 2005.

US Department of State, Bureau of African Affairs. "Testimony by E. Brynn on U.S. Policy Toward Sudan," March 22, 1995.

US Department of State, Office of the Spokesman. "Press Availability of Secretary of State Madeleine K. Albright and Kenyan President Daniel arap Moi, State House Nairobi, Kenya," October 22, 1999.

Wade, Peter. *Race and Ethnicity in Latin America.* London: Pluto Press, 1997.

Wai, Dunstan. *The African-Arab Conflict in the Sudan.* New York: Africana, 1981.

Wakoson, Elias N. "The Dilemmas of South-North Conflict." In Francis Deng and P. Gifford, *The Search for Peace and Unity in the Sudan.* Washington: Woodrow Wilson Center Press, 1987.

Warburg, Gabriel. *Islam, Sectarianism, and Politics in Sudan Since the Mahdiyya.* Madison: University of Wisconsin Press, 2003.

Washington Declaration, October 22, 1993. Washington, DC: US Institute of Peace.

Washington Post. "Mr. Powell and Darfur," September 9, 2004.

———. "U.S. Review of Sudan Terrorist Link Gains Urgency," June 27, 1993.

West, John. "Sudan Government's Offensive May Alarm Neighbors," Reuters, August 12, 1993.

Wöndu, Steven, and Ann Lesch. *Battle for Peace in Sudan: An Analysis of the Abuja Conferences, 1992–1993.* Lanham, MD: University Press of America, 2000.

Woodward, Peter. "Somalia and Sudan: A Tale of Two Peace Processes." *The Round Table* 93, no. 375 (July 2004).

Works, John A. *Pilgrims in a Strange Land: Hausa Communities in Chad.* New York: Columbia University Press, 1976.

Wrong, Michela. "Peace Talks Postponed to April," Pan-African News Agency, November 11, 1997.

Wylde, B. Augustus. *'83 to '87 in the Soudan: With Account of Sir William Hewett's Mission to King John of Abyssinia,* vol. 1. New York: Negro University Press, 1969.

Xinhua News Agency. "Sudan Hopes for Initiative to End Civil War," August 7, 1999.

———. "Sudan Opposes Creation of 'Safe Areas' in Southern Sudan," June 5, 1993.

Index

Abboud, Ibrahim, 80–81
Abdallah Muhammad Ahmad, as self-
  proclaimed Mahdi, 140
Abyei: displacement and dispossession
  of, 58; peace agreement and, 170
Abuja peace talks, 94–95, 154–155,
  156–158; criticisms of, 158
Addis Ababa negotiations, 61, 84–88,
  124, 147, 153; and creation of semiautonomous southern state, 86; failure of, 90–91, 112; key elements of,
  87; mediators of, 85; Nimeiri's abrogation of, 88; and regional power
  imbalances, 85
Afewerki, Issaias, 104, 108, 113, 118
African conflict: institutionalized international tokenism in, 176; and international accountability, 149–150;
  norm of nonintervention in, 149
African identity: adoptions of, 31; as
  affirmation of blackness/negation of
  slave status, 29; Arabization and, 20,
  25; as colonial construct, 31
African peace processes, questions of
  ownership in, 124
African Union (AU): and Darfur crisis,
  152, 153, 154, 172, 176; limited
  external involvement of, 79; military
  engagement of, 150; peace process
  and, 168; and sanctions against
  Sudan, 149
African Union Mission in Sudan
  (AMIS), 156; expansion of, 155;
  mediation inadequacy of, 158–159;

size and mandate of, 154
Afro-Arab(s): adoption of Arabic ideology by, 48; genealogies, construction
  of, 47; hegemony and privileging of,
  20, 47, 68; heritage, Islamism and,
  137; indigenous displacement by, 47;
  official discourse of, 21; phenotype
  of, 50; as self-proclaimed *awlad al-
  balad*, 20
Albright, Madeleine, 106, 109, 115
Ali Dinar ibn Zakariya, Kayra sultanate
  of, 60, 135, 140–141
Alier, Abel, 86, 87, 88
All Africa Conference of Churches, conflict mediation of, 85
Amin, Idi, 84, 85
Ancestral lands, appropriation of,
  61–62, 63
Anglo-Egyptian rule: consolidation of,
  48; Fur sultanate incorporation into,
  32, 134; indigenous nomenclatures
  and, 31; Mahdist jihad against, 140;
  origins of Sudan conflict in, 27
Annan, Kofi, 155
Ansar Party, 28
Anyanya guerrilla forces, 90; and Addis
  Ababa talks/agreement, 84–86, 87;
  early activities and influence of, 81;
  Israeli support for, 84; mutinies and
  desertions of, 88–89
Anyanya National Organization, 82, 91
Anyidi Revolutionary Government, 82
Arab League, Khartoum's isolation by,
  102

211

south conflict, 85
September 11, 2001, terrorist attacks,
and Sudanese-US relations, 119, 121
Settlers: Arabized/Islamized, integration
of, 21; civilizing mission of, 67;
early trekkers and pilgrims as, 55;
privileging of, 67, 68; transformed
into citizens with hegemonic rights,
65
Slave descendants, stigmatization and
exclusion of, 57
Slave economy, in centralized state, 60
Slavery: Arabization as ideological justification for, 25; and ethnic rivalry,
65; of Mahdist period, 59–60
Solongdungo, Sulayman, 137
Soony (political organization), 143–144
South Sudan Defense Forces (SSDF),
175
South Sudan Liberation Movement
(SSLM), 84, 85
Southern Front, 81, 82
Southern Sudan: administrative authority and politics in, 86; annulment of
autonomous status of, 88;
Arabization and Islamization of,
80–81; discovery of oil and redrawn
borders in, 88; elite mobilization in,
86; famine in, 111; geography of, 53;
history of feuds and wars fought in,
49; humanitarian crisis of 1989 in,
92, 93; negotiations for demilitarized
zones in, 96; 1957 elections in, 82;
oil resources in, 112; political/mili-
tary movements in, 81–82, 84, 85;
reconstruction challenges in, 175;
redivisions of, 61, 88; regional and
international support for, 84–85;
secession/self-determination movement in, 61, 81, 91; and *sharia* law,
91; south-south dialogue in, 175; territorial conquest and pacification of,
48; and 2005 peace agreements, 61.
See also Anyanya guerrilla forces
Southern Sudan Independence
Movement (SSIM), 107, 108
Southern Sudan Provisional
Government (SSPG), 82
Southern Sudanese peoples: alliances
among, 65–66; dominant image of,
49; Garang's campaigns against, 170;

southern guerrilla atrocities against,
65
Sudan: accession to independence, 80,
142; Arab migration and settlement
in, 46, 49, 52; emergence as sovereign state, 45; European and Turk
invasions of, 59; foreign debt of,
103; ideological construct of "north"
and "south" in, 51; ideological division of believers/masters and unbe-
lievers/slaves in, 51; international
isolation and freezing of aid to,
102–103, 107–108; politics of exclusion in, 142–143; respect for dialogue in, 177; Turkish-Egyptian rule
in, 59. *See also* Bashir government;
Government of Sudan (GOS)
Sudan African National Union (SANU),
founding and objective of, 81
Sudan Defence Force, 81, 143
Sudan Liberation Movement/Army
(SLM/A), 66, 137; adopted
"African" identity of, 31; Abuja participation of, 159; and Darfur conflict, 151–153, 156; and Darfur
Peace Agreement, 159; ethnic split
in, 157; and New Sudan vision, 170;
in peace negotiations, 168; Political
Declaration of, 151; UN accusations
against, 157
Sudan Peace Act, US congressional passage of, 122
Sudan People's Liberation
Movement/Sudan People's
Liberation Army (SPLM/A), 89, 91,
92; Abuja negotiations and, 158,
159; alliances with militia forces,
175; and Egyptian-Libyan plan, 115,
120; ethnic fissures in, 93–94; formation of, 88; Garang's leadership
of, 169; government's declaration of
war on, 90; IGAD initiative and, 102,
104, 107, 112, 113; internal rupture
in, 102; and Koka Dam Declaration,
90; mobilization, NDA alliance with,
114; and north-south conflict, 119;
and peace initiatives, 92, 93, 94, 174;
and resumption of civil war, 89–90,
92; and vision of New Sudan, 56;
Western powers' backing of, 169
Sudanese Allied Forces, 107–108

About This Publication

Embroiled in civil war since independence, Sudan has also suffered from the failure of both regional and international actors to fully come to terms with the scope of the complex issues involved. *Sudan: The Elusive Quest for Peace* contributes to a fuller understanding of those issues, exploring the factors that have contributed to the conflict from the days following independence to the present.

Iyob and Khadiagala concisely examine the cultural, sociopolitical, economic, and geographical facets of the prolonged hostilities, then assess a sequence of mediation efforts. They also distill the web of grievances that fuel the current conflict in the Darfur region. They conclude with a thoughtful analysis that highlights the potential obstacles to sustainable peace in Sudan in the decades to come.

Ruth Iyob is associate professor of political science at the University of Missouri—St. Louis and senior policy adviser to the Africa Program at the International Peace Academy. Her publications include *The Eritrean Struggle for Independence: Domination, Resistance and Nationalism, 1941–1993*. **Gilbert M. Khadiagala** is associate professor of comparative politics and African studies at the Johns Hopkins School of Advanced International Studies. He is author of *Allies in Adversity: The Frontline States in Southern African Security, 1975–1993,* and coeditor of *African Foreign Policies: Power and Process.*

The International Peace Academy

The International Peace Academy (IPA) is an independent, international institution dedicated to promoting the prevention and settlement of armed conflicts between and within states through policy research and development.

Founded in 1970, the IPA has built an extensive portfolio of activities in fulfillment of its mission:

- Symposiums, workshops, and other forums that facilitate strategic thinking, policy development, and organizational innovation within international organizations.
- Policy research on multilateral efforts to prevent, mitigate, or rebuild after armed conflict.
- Research, consultations, and technical assistance to support capacities for peacemaking, peacekeeping, and peacebuilding in Africa.
- Professional-development seminars for political, development, military, humanitarian, and nongovernmental personnel involved in peacekeeping and conflict resolution.
- Facilitation in conflict situations where its experience, credibility, and independence can complement official peace efforts.
- Outreach to build public awareness on issues related to peace and security, multilateralism, and the United Nations.

The IPA works closely with the United Nations, regional and other international organizations, governments, and nongovernmental organizations, as well as with parties to conflicts in selected cases. Its efforts are enhanced by its ability to draw on a worldwide network of government and business leaders, scholars, diplomats, military officers, and leaders of civil society.

The IPA is a nonprofit organization governed by an international Board of Directors. The organization is funded by generous donations from governments, major philanthropic foundations, and corporate donors, as well as contributions from individuals and its Board members.

International Peace Academy Publications

Available from Lynne Rienner Publishers, 1800 30th Street, Boulder, Colorado 80301 (303-444-6684), www.rienner.com.

Sudan: The Elusive Quest for Peace, Ruth Iyob and Gilbert M. Khadiagala (2006)

Security Dynamics in Africa's Great Lakes Region, edited by Gilbert M. Khadiagala (2006)

Kashmir: New Voices, New Approaches, edited by Waheguru Pal Singh Sidhu, Bushra Asif, and Cyrus Samii (2006)

The Democratic Republic of Congo: Economic Dimensions of War and Peace, Michael Nest, with François Grignon and Emizet F. Kisangani (2006)

East Africa and the Horn: Confronting Challenges to Good Governance, edited by Dorina A. Bekoe (2005)

Western Sahara: Anatomy of a Stalemate, Erik Jensen (2005)

Exploring Subregional Conflict: Opportunities for Conflict Prevention, edited by Chandra Lekha Sriram and Zoe Nielsen (2004)

West Africa's Security Challenges: Building Peace in a Troubled Region, edited by Adekeye Adebajo and Ismail Rashid (2004)

War Economies in a Regional Context: Challenges of Transformation, Michael Pugh and Neil Cooper, with Jonathan Goodhand (2004)

The UN Security Council: From the Cold War to the Twenty-First Century, edited by David M. Malone (2004)

The United Nations and Regional Security: Europe and Beyond, edited by Michael Pugh and Waheguru Pal Singh Sidhu (2003)

The Political Economy of Armed Conflict: Beyond Greed and Grievance, edited by Karen Ballentine and Jake Sherman (2003)

From Promise to Practice: Strengthening UN Capacities for the Prevention of Violent Conflict, edited by Chandra Lekha Sriram and Karin Wermester (2003)

The Chittagong Hill Tracts, Bangladesh: On the Difficult Road to Peace, Amena Mohsin (2003)

Peacekeeping in East Timor: The Path to Independence, Michael G. Smith with Moreen Dee (2003)

From Cape to Congo: Southern Africa's Evolving Security Challenges, edited by Mwesiga Baregu and Christopher Landsberg (2003)

Ending Civil Wars: The Implementation of Peace Agreements, edited by Stephen John Stedman, Donald Rothchild, and Elizabeth M. Cousens (2002)

Sanctions and the Search for Security: Challenges to UN Action, David Cortright and George A. Lopez, with Linda Gerber (2002)

Ecuador vs. Peru: Peacemaking Amid Rivalry, Monica Herz and João Pontes Nogueira (2002)

Liberia's Civil War: Nigeria, ECOMOG, and Regional Security in West Africa, Adekeye Adebajo (2002)

Building Peace in West Africa: Liberia, Sierra Leone, and Guinea-Bissau, Adekeye Adebajo (2002)

Kosovo: An Unfinished Peace, William G. O'Neill (2002)

From Reaction to Conflict Prevention: Opportunities for the UN System, edited by Fen Osler Hampson and David M. Malone (2002)

Peacemaking in Rwanda: The Dynamics of Failure, Bruce D. Jones (2001)

Self-Determination in East Timor: The United Nations, the Ballot, and International Intervention, Ian Martin (2001)

Civilians in War, edited by Simon Chesterman (2001)

Toward Peace in Bosnia: Implementing the Dayton Accords, Elizabeth M. Cousens and Charles K. Cater (2001)

Sierra Leone: Diamonds and the Struggle for Democracy, John L. Hirsch (2001)

Peacebuilding as Politics: Cultivating Peace in Fragile Societies, edited by Elizabeth M. Cousens and Chetan Kumar (2001)

The Sanctions Decade: Assessing UN Strategies in the 1990s, David Cortright and George A. Lopez (2000)

Greed and Grievance: Economic Agendas in Civil War, edited by Mats Berdal and David M. Malone (2000)

Building Peace in Haiti, Chetan Kumar (1998)

Rights and Reconciliation: UN Strategies in El Salvador, Ian Johnstone (1995)